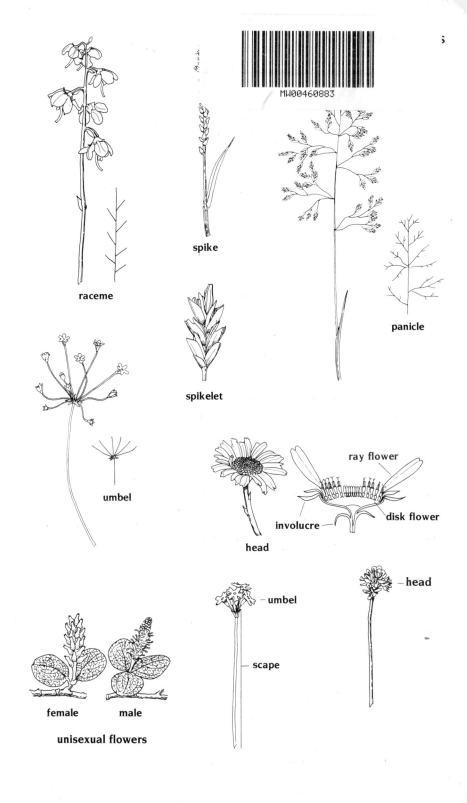

raceme

spike

spikelet

panicle

umbel

ray flower

disk flower

involucre

head

female   male

unisexual flowers

umbel

scape

head

*This book is dedicated to the people of Churchill
– true northern survivors!*

WILDFLOWERS OF CHURCHILL
and the Hudson Bay Region

Karen L. Johnson

Illustrated by Linda Fairfield
Photographs by Robert R. Taylor

MANITOBA MUSEUM OF MAN AND NATURE, WINNIPEG, 1987

ACKNOWLEDGEMENTS

Many individuals and organizations contributed to the preparation and publication of this book. I am grateful to the Canada Council for Explorations Grant #600-80-1014-9 which supported most of the direct field work, photography and art work in 1981 and to the Manitoba Museum of Man and Nature Foundation Fund which provided a grant to complete the field and art work in 1982. The Manitoba Heritage Federation Inc. contributed much of the printing and publication costs for the book, the Churchill Ladies Club provided funds for its promotion and The Canadian National Sportsmen's Show provided funding for a Museum field trip to Cape Tatnam in 1982.

I am especially grateful to Robert R. Taylor and Linda Fairfield whose photographs and artwork, respectively, illustrate most of the book. Their work, often under adverse environmental conditions, is the real basis of this book and allows it to be easily used by the general public. Several other people (listed in the photo credits) contributed photographs of plants we were unable to obtain ourselves.

Many other people, including staff and volunteers at the Museum and local people at Churchill, contributed time, information and effort to the book. I would like to thank them all although the following deserve special mention: Gloria Keleher and David White for checking specimens and nomenclature; Dr. Wm. Cody for thoroughly and helpfully reviewing the manuscript; Sid Kroker for providing information for, and reviewing, the Prehistory section; Drs. Robert Wrigley and Jennifer Shay who carefully reviewed and edited most of the manuscript; Lorraine Brandson who reviewed the Historical section; staff, researchers and visitors at the Churchill Northern Studies Centre for assistance and inspiration; and Diane Erickson of Churchill who provided much inspiration, gentle nagging and the Foreword.

Many thanks are also due the Design Department of the Museum for design and layout of the book, especially to Betsy Thorsteinson for the detail drawings in the explanations and to David Hopper, Eric Crone, Teri McIntyre and Kim Crossley whose work helped make the book so visually attractive.

Finally, last but certainly not least, sincere thanks go to Barbara Anderson, Louise Duhamel, Jennifer Warrington, and Barbara Glassey who typed, retyped, and word-processed the manuscript and to Linda Nelson who did the typesetting under trying circumstances. Also a special thanks to Valerie Hatten who carefully reviewed the manuscript so many times. They organized, reviewed and checked the whole project for consistency and accuracy and, without them, I really couldn't have done it!

I would like to sincerely thank two Friends of the Museum, the Minister and Special Conservation Fund of the Manitoba Department of Natural Resources and the Churchill Ladies Club for the funding necessary to complete the second printing of this book. New photographs were contributed by Janina Swietlik and myself and a new watercolour by Linda Fairfield. Table 1 was redone and other corrections made by Christine Clifford. David Hopper again nobly handled the necessary redesign and liaison with the printers.

WILDFLOWERS OF CHURCHILL AND THE HUDSON BAY REGION

CONTENTS

FOREWORD

The Churchill area has a diversity of plant habitats: fresh water, salt water, tundra, taiga, transition zones. While there are several books that describe and illustrate plants growing in subarctic, arctic, and more moderate climates, for the person without an extensive background in botany, or who has not invested much time and effort in plant identification, there has been no one book that would describe and illustrate the plants to be seen in the Churchill area. This book answers that long-standing need for anyone (tourist, visitor, local inhabitant) who has ever wondered what a particular plant is named, where it can be found, or what it looks like. The photographs by Robert Taylor and sketches and watercolours by Linda Fairfield illustrate a good portion of the plants found here. Many thanks to Bob Taylor, Linda Fairfield and most of all to Dr. Karen Johnson for conceiving the idea for this book, working so hard researching and putting it together and, most importantly, having it published.

Diane Erickson, a grateful Churchillian.

INTRODUCTION

I have been fascinated by the plants of Churchill and the west coast of Hudson Bay ever since first visiting that region in the early 1970's. Although small in size, these plants often grow in great numbers, carpeting large areas along the coast with their purple, pink, white, and yellow flowers during the short growing season. Many people have asked me about the plants of this region, especially the showy or unusual wildflowers. These questions came from biologists and other scientists working around Hudson and James bays as well as from travellers and naturalists who were simply visiting there. Unfortunately no non-technical guide book covering the great variety of wildflowers along the bays has been available and most people visiting the region are unable to use technical floras. This book attempts to provide a non-technical guide to the plants of the region. It will be most useful in the areas around Churchill and York Factory, as these are the most accessible parts of the bay, but should be helpful in all parts of the Hudson and James bays region.

The book uses a simple key system to identify the plants and is illustrated with colour photographs, watercolour paintings, and black and white drawings of some 200 common flowering plants, ferns, and fern allies found in the Hudson Bay region. Because little information on the natural and human history of this unusual region is readily available, a short background section is included at the beginning, and a list of references and complete list of the vascular plants of Churchill at the end of the book.

Please collect the wildflowers of this region only with a camera or artist's pen or brush. Although many occur locally in great abundance, they may be rare elsewhere in Manitoba or Canada. Some, including most orchids, Lewis' Wild Flax and several of the saxifrages, are uncommon to rare even at Churchill. Please be responsible in your enjoyment of these lovely plants and resist the temptation to pick them for each one that you take leaves one less for others to enjoy and to maintain its species' population.

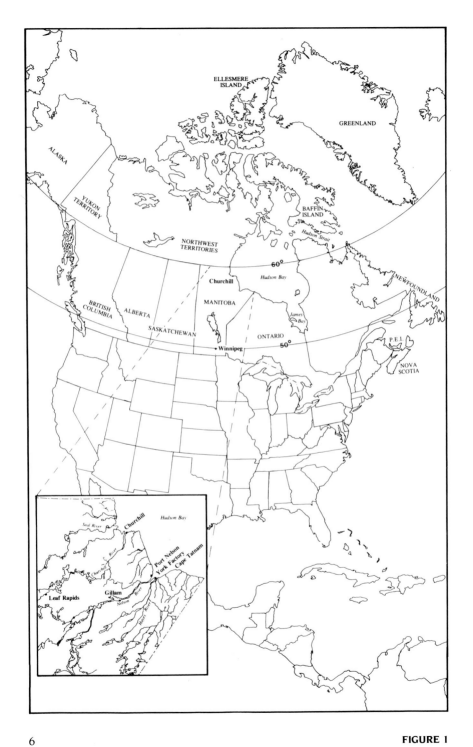

6

FIGURE 1

A BRIEF NATURAL AND HUMAN HISTORY
OF THE CHURCHILL REGION

NATURAL HISTORY – *Geography*

Churchill is located on the western shore of Hudson Bay, in the northeastern corner of the Province of Manitoba, Canada at a latitude of nearly 59°N (Fig. 1). At the junction of three major natural regions, the Arctic Tundra, Boreal Forest and Arctic Marine biomes, and easily accessible by rail or air, Churchill has long attracted travellers and scientists. Many different kinds of birds, mammals, and plants occur in the area because its transitional nature provides habitats for both northern and southern species as well as the maritime ones associated with the bays.

The climate, soils, and vegetation of the region are determined and dominated by Hudson Bay – a large mid-continental extension of the Arctic Ocean. The bay creates a gigantic 'cold warp' in central North America, causing arctic and subarctic conditions to extend much further south than in continental areas to the east and west. Much of the information in the following section is drawn from Beals (1968), MacIver (1982), and Scoggan (1959) for those who would like to learn more about the region.

Climate

Climatic records for Churchill indicate that this coastal region of Hudson Bay has long cold winters and short cool summers with short variable spring and fall seasons (Table 1). Average July temperature is 12°C (54°F), that of January -28°C (-18°F). The highest temperature ever recorded was nearly 33°C (91°F) in both July and August while the lowest was -45°C (-49°F) in both January and February. Frost and snow may occur in any month of the year but are unusual in July and August. Precipitation is 40 cm (16 in.) per year, slightly more than half (22 cm (9 in.)) falling as rain, the rest as nearly 1.8 m (6 ft.) of snow. July has the highest average rainfall while November averages nearly twice as much snow as any other month. Churchill records the fewest hours of sunshine per year in Manitoba, the result of short winter days and frequent fogs.

Wind direction and velocity have a major effect on climate and vegetation and combined with low temperatures explain the stunted growth of trees in the region. Predominately north winds, carrying snow and ice crystals in the winter and sand and salt in the summer, create the twisted one-sided 'krummholz' spruce trees which are such a distinctive feature along much of the coast. Wind-carried particles and the drying out of buds on the windward side of the trees cause the death of buds and branches on that side resulting in a lop-sided tree. As they say in Churchill, "It takes two trees to make a Christmas tree up here!" Blowing snow and ice crystals also cause a bare spot on the trunk of exposed trees by moving just above the sur-face of the snow and killing all buds and branches in the zone of movement. This results in trees with bushy bottom branches protected by the snow cover and a tiny 'flag' of branches on the leeward side at the top of the trunk. In exposed areas along the coast, snow, salt and ice 'pruning' restrict willows and other shrubs, as well as the spruce trees, to sheltered areas behind rocks and under snowdrifts.

In summer the effect of wind direction on local weather is dramatic. If the wind is from the east or northeast, off the bay with its central ice cover, the temperature will be near freezing with a heavy cloud or fog cover. If the wind changes to the west or south, which can happen very quickly, the skies clear, temperatures rise to as high as 30°C (86°F), and biting insects come out in hordes. It pays to be prepared for both very warm and damp cold weather if you are planning to visit the region during June, July, or August, as you can experience both within hours.

The Hudson Bay coastline is free of ice for between four and five months of the year. June 15 is the average date for the ice to go out of Churchill Harbour and freeze-up occurs between the end of October and the middle of November. In winter narrow leads along the coast kept open by tidal action are the only open water and 'sea smoke' or ice fog from these leads can cover large areas along the coast for long periods of time.

Another very important climatically controlled factor at Churchill is **permafrost** – frozen ground which persists throughout the summer. Churchill lies in the zone of continuous permafrost and ice has been found in bedrock cracks as deep as 44.5 m (146 ft). Permafrost is closest to the surface under areas of organic soils because of their insulating qualities. It prevents water from draining away thus causing the development of muskegs and bogs. It is deeper or absent under well drained areas such as beach ridges and along rivers and in tidal areas next to the bay where moving water occurs. Permafrost greatly influences the landscape and vegetation of the Hudson Bay Lowlands, especially inland from the coast, and creates some unusual problems for human settlers and activities in that region.

Because Churchill has higher summer temperatures and a longer growing season than places such as Chesterfield Inlet (63°N latitude), its climate is considered subarctic rather than arctic. However it is on the boundary between the true arctic and subarctic zones as indicated by the mixture of northern and southern plants and animals found there.

Geology

The ancient bedrock of the Precambrian Shield underlies the entire coastal region but is usually hidden in the Churchill area by younger Ordovician and Silurian limestones and dolomites. However the grey rocks found on the eastern side of the Churchill River, including Cape Merry and the coastal cliffs towards the Rocket Range, are outcrops of Precambrian Churchill quartzite. Here an ancient sandstone was turned into harder quartzite by compression from overlying beds of marine sediments and water. The younger limestones and dolomites are exposed along the western shore of the Churchill River and to the south and east of Churchill. Excellent examples of the contact between the quartzite and overlying sedimentary rocks can be seen at several places along the base of coastal cliffs just east of the town of Churchill at low tide. Reef corals fastened themselves to the quartzite ridges in Silurian times and fragments of these as well as other fossils can often be found along the shores of the Churchill River and Hudson Bay.

Most of the land around Hudson Bay is covered by glacial till of Pleistocene age or by marine deposits. The surface has only a gentle slope and this, along with permafrost, results in vast poorly drained plains of peat broken only by lakes and ponds, outcrop ridges, glacial features such as eskers and moraines, and marine-related features such as raised beach ridges.

Signs of recent glaciation are everywhere. Glacial striations, the grooves and scratches left by rocks embedded in glacial ice, are common on the outcrop ridges around Churchill as is evidence of the planing and polishing effect of the ice sheet itself. Hudson Bay was close to the centre of the Wisconsin Laurentide ice sheet which covered the region with more than 2 700 m (8,800 ft) of ice and depressed the land at least 300 m (1,000 ft) some 18,000 to 25,000 years ago. Melting of the ice sheet 8,000 to 9,000 years ago created the Tyrrell Sea which flooded the area to a depth

NORMALS

STATION: CHURCHILL A, MAN. LAT: 58°45'N LONG: 94°04'W ELEVATION: 29 METRES (ASL)

ELEMENT	UNIT	JAN.	FEB.	MAR.	APR.	MAY.	JUN.	JUL.	AUG.	SEP.	OCT.	NOV.	DEC.	ANNUAL
Mean maximum temperature	°C	-23.6	-21.7	-15.7	-5.4	2.2	10.8	16.8	15.3	8.5	1.3	-8.3	-18.2	-3.2
Mean minimum temperature	°C	-31.4	-30.0	-25.1	-14.8	-5.1	1.5	6.8	7.2	2.2	-4.4	-15.9	-26.1	-11.3
Mean from maximum/minimum	°C	-27.5	-25.9	-20.4	-10.1	-1.5	6.2	11.8	11.3	5.4	-1.5	-12.1	-22.2	-7.2
Extreme maximum temperature	°C	0.0	1.1	5.6	28.2	27.2	31.1	33.9	32.8	27.8	20.6	7.2	2.2	33.9
Extreme minimum temperature	°C	-45.0	-45.4	-43.9	-33.3	-21.7	-9.4	-2.2	2.2	-11.7	-24.4	-36.1	-40.0	-45.4
No. of days with frost	Days	31	28	31	30	29	13	1	*	9	25	30	31	258
Mean rainfall	mm	T	0.1	0.6	2.0	13.5	39.9	45.6	58.3	44.5	15.4	1.0	0.2	221.1
Mean snowfall	cm	20.1	15.4	19.6	22.9	18.8	4.2	0.0T	0.0T	6.2	29.2	39.8	23.8	200
Mean total precipitation	mm	15.3	13.1	18.1	22.9	31.9	43.5	45.6	58.3	50.9	43.0	38.8	20.9	402.3
Greatest rainfall in 24 hrs	mm	0.3	1.3	16.2	8.4	22.4	32.5	52.3	51.1	42.2	26.2	4.0	1.8	52.3
Greatest snowfall in 24 hrs	cm	16.0	12.7	22.6	25.4	47.6	15.7	T	T	17.5	36.1	35.1	21.8	47.6
Greatest precipitation in 24 hrs	mm	12.9	12.7	21.9	25.4	55.6	32.5	52.3	51.1	42.2	35.8	35.1	21.8	55.6
No. of days with measurable rainfall	Days	*	0	*	1	5	9	11	13	12	6	1	*	58
No. of days with measurable snowfall	Days	11	10	10	10	7	2	0	0	4	14	18	14	100
No. of days with measurable precipitation	Days	11	10	10	10	11	10	11	13	14	17	18	13	148
Bright sunshine	Hours	80.4	131.7	188.6	203.7	195.3	233.7	285.1	232.1	110.8	61.7	49.5	55.3	1827.9
Possible # hours of sunshine	Hours	220	259	367	435	525	551	548	478	385	317	233	196	4514
Average wind speed	km/h	24.2	24.1	22.2	22.6	22.2	20.7	19.3	20.5	23.7	24.9	25.6	22.7	22.7
Prevailing wind direction		W	WNW	WNW	NW	NNW	N	N	NNW	NNW	NW	WNW	W	WNW
Station pressure	kPa	101.31	101.34	101.63	101.40	101.33	100.88	100.66	100.73	100.73	100.78	101.02	101.22	101.09

TABLE 1

of 150 m (500 ft) above the present coast. Removal of the weight of the ice caused the depressed land to rise, a process called **isostatic rebound** or **isostacy.** The land rose rapidly at first, up to 5 m (16 ft) per 100 years, but has now slowed to about 1 m (3-4 ft) per 100 years. Evidence for isostacy is found in the fossil inland beach ridges, the 'high and dry' ship's anchor rings on the western side of the Churchill River, and in areas such as Sloop's Cove where ships once anchored and which are now far too shallow to serve as harbours.

The rebounding land continually creates new coastal habitats that are themselves uplifted and 'moved' inland. These evolve towards a landscape of shallow inland peatlands separated by the 'fossil' beach ridges, sandbars, sandspits, and storm ridges which once occured along the edge of the Bay. You can see this repeated pattern of ridge and bog clearly from the air and less clearly from the train when travelling toward the bay. In the south, the older and better drained ridges have light coloured ground lichens and spruce trees while the wet intervening bogs and fens are lush flat green areas. As many as six fossil beach ridges per kilometer (ten per mile) occur in places around Hudson Bay, all paralleling the present coastline.

Water – Tides and Other Effects

Water – both fresh and salt – is another important factor in the environment of the Hudson Bay Lowlands. The salt water of the two bays not only influences the climate of adjacent land areas, it turns Manitoba and Ontario into maritime provinces complete with tides, seaweeds, whales and polar bears, scallops and shrimps, seabirds and sea anemones, and marine fish such as capelin and sculpins.

Tides are one of the most distinctive features of a maritime region and one which few people expect to see in Manitoba – a 'prairie province.' Tides are giant waves produced by the gravitational pull of moon and sun. Two high tides occur every day on Hudson Bay, 12 hours and 25 minutes apart and shifting 50 minutes later each day. The highest points on each tide occur when the moon is directly over the bay or in a straight line with it on the other side of the earth. Lowest tidal points occur when the moon is halfway between the high points. These twice-daily changes in water level expose intertidal zones of pools, rocks, and beaches which range in width from a few meters along the estuary of the Churchill River to a couple of kilometers along the coast.

When moon and sun line up with the earth their combined pull is greatest and results in the highest tides, up to 4.3 m (14 ft) at Churchill. These **spring tides** occur every two weeks during the new and full moon. The lesser **neap tides** of some 3.4 m (11 ft) occur between the spring tides, when moon and sun are furthest out of line and tend to cancel each other out.

If you are planning to visit the western side of the Churchill River, take a boat trip out into the bay, or just beachcomb along the coast, it is wise to check the tide tables published monthly by Transport Canada. They can usually be found posted in such strategic locations as the airport, post office, town centre, motels, and Parks Canada Office in Churchill. Otherwise you are likely to find yourself at high tide when you want to beachcomb, or low tide when you want to cross the Churchill River, a nearly impossible feat.

The coastal region also contains thousands of freshwater pools, ponds, and lakes as well as parts of the watersheds of numerous rivers. The Nelson, Hayes, Churchill, and Seal rivers are the four largest in this area and their estuaries provide important shelter and food for wildlife, especially waterfowl and white whales, as well as access to the Port of Churchill for large ships. The mixing of fresh and salt water in these estuaries produces a wide range of habitats for plants as well as animals including some extensive salt marshes.

Up to 90 percent of the flow of the Churchill River has been diverted through Southern Indian Lake to the Nelson River for hydroelectric power generation. The long term effects of this diversion are still being studied but the town of Churchill has had to move the pumping plant which provides its fresh water several kilometers further up the Churchill River because of increased salinity and decreased water levels in the lower stretches of the river.

Plants of the Region

About 400 different native vascular plants are known to occur in the Churchill region. These include the horsetails, clubmosses, ferns, conifers, and flowering plants but not the abundant lichens, fungi, mosses, and algae. Unfortunately, few studies on the lower plants of this area have been done, and they are difficult to identify without high-powered microscopes and special chemical tests. This is especially true of the marine algae or 'seaweeds' that you see on rocks and in tidal pools along the coast. This guidebook therefore covers only the commonest and most interesting flowering plants and a few of the more important non-flowering ones in the region. I have also included some of the most abundant and easily recognizable grasses, sedges, and rushes. Though these plants and their flowers tend to be small and inconspicuous, they make up more than one-third of the flora of the region and are ecologically very important. All orchids, heaths, louseworts, and other showy or unusual plants have been included, since these are the most noticeable. A complete list of the vascular plants known for the Churchill region and reference to several technical floras are included at the end of the book for those who would like to try to identify the more difficult plants.

Origins and Distribution

After the glaciers melted and the Tyrrell Sea retreated, plants had only bare rock and gravel to colonize. Sketchy evidence indicates that the first groups to reinvade the region, some 2,500 to 3,000 years ago, were hardy grass-like sedges followed by heaths (blueberries and their relatives), willow and birch shrubs and, finally, spruce trees. They probably came from the south, east, and west from refugia (unglaciated areas) where they had survived during the glacial period. Almost all are hardy and widespread plants; more than 88 percent occur across North America and 52 percent range across the Northern Hemisphere in their respective latitudinal zones. The majority of native plants found at Churchill are subarctic-boreal rather than true arctic in distribution, although many true arctic species reach their southern limit here.

The largest group of Churchill plants (38 percent) are of high subarctic distribution. These include the Moon Fern (Botrychium lunaria), Round-Leaved Orchid (Orchis rotundifolia), Yellow Anemone (Anemone richardsonii), and Small Grass-of-Parnassus (Parnassia kotzebuei). Low subarctic or boreal plants (26 percent) include most of the cotton-grasses (Eriophorum spp.), the Northern Lady's-Slipper (Cypripedium passerinum), Water-Hemlocks (Cicuta spp.), and Canada Buffaloberry (Shepherdia canadensis). The arctic element is divided into low arctic (20 percent) and high arctic (16 percent) species. Low arctic plants include the Bog Asphodel (Tofieldia pusilla), Snow Willow (Salix reticulata) and Seaside Lungwort (Mertensia maritima) while high arctic ones include the Alpine Bluebell (Campanula uniflora), Purple Rattle (Pedicularis sudetica) and Broad-Leaved Fireweed (Epilobium latifolium).

Some of the most interesting plants at Churchill are those that have come in with grain shipments on the railroad, as ballast from foreign ships, and on the shoes,

11

clothing, and baggage of travellers from all over the world. Hardy and widespread plants such as the Common Dandelion (*Taraxacum officinale*), Stickseed (*Lappula echinata*), White Clover (*Trifolium repens*), Wormseed Mustard (*Erysimum cheiranthoides*), Shepherd's-Purse (*Capsella bursa-pastoris*), Stinkweed (*Thlaspi arvense*) and Chickweed (*Stellaria media*) occur on disturbed areas and waste places in the townsite, Port, and Rocket Range. Many are completely hardy at Churchill and have become naturalized members of the flora. As long as disturbance continues in the region – and there is always natural disturbance of some type – some of these plants will persist. In just this way, with seeds carried first by wind, water, birds, and other animals, plants originally colonized the region. New species from the south and some of the hardy weeds will doubtless eventually take their place as full-fledged members of the flora. Because many common weeds are well covered in other publications, none of them are described in this book. If you find a common flowering plant, especially on disturbed areas, that you can't find in this guidebook, it is probably a weed. One excellent reference is **Common Weeds of Canada** (Mulligan, 1987).

Habitats and Communities

Plants usually grow together in groups of different species called **plant communities** and in specific kinds of places called **habitats.** Community composition is determined by factors such as soil texture, drainage, exposure (north/south, protected/unprotected) and amount of salt found in a given area. Communities are usually named after their most obvious plants, landforms, or soil types, examples being the Hummocky Bog, Lichen-Heath, Ice Ridge, or Ledge and Crevice communities. Some plants, such as Bog-Rosemary (*Andromeda polifolia*), Red Bearberry (*Arctostaphylos rubra*), Purple Paintbrush (*Castilleja raupii*), and Scrub Birch (*Betula glandulosa*), are tolerant of a wide variety of habitat conditions and occur in several different communities. Others, such as the Sea-Beach Sandwort (*Honckenya peploides*) and Lewis' Wild Flax (*Linum lewisii*), require specific environmental conditions and occur in only one community.

Figure 2 illustrates some of the common plant communities found in the Churchill area and the landforms and exposures with which they are associated. Brief descriptions and a short list of the common plants of these communities are given below. As you become familiar with the region, you will come to expect and look for certain species or combinations of species in particular habitats. You will also be able to use the community lists and species accounts to look for a particular plant by checking the community type(s) in which it grows and then learning to identify the landforms which support those communities. You should be able to find almost any plant shown in the guidebook in bloom if you visit the right habitat at the right time of year.

The communities described below closely follow those shown in Figure 2 and generally run inland from the coast in sequence.

* ( ) and scientific name indicates plant not covered in species' accounts

I. COMMUNITIES ON SAND AND CLAY

a. Foreshore Area: Strand and Salt Marsh Communities

These communities occur from low tide to just above the high tide levels. Sandy beach areas develop a **strand** community of halophytes (salt-loving plants) and hardy colonizers of unstable soils. Flat sand or clay areas which are regularly flooded by tides develop a **salt marsh** community dominated by halophytic sedges and grasses.

Strand Plants	Both Communities	Salt Marsh Plants
Sea-Beach Sandwort	Egede's Cinquefoil	Salt Sedge* (*Carex subspathacea*)
Seaside Sedge	Four-Leaved Mare's-Tail	Seaside Buttercup

Strand Plants	Both Communities	Salt Marsh Plants
Smooth Orache	Sea-Shore Chamomile	Hairgrass-Like Reed Grass*
Scurvy-Grass	Seaside Plantain	(*Calamagrostis deschampsoides*)
Seaside Lungwort	Arctic Chrysanthemum	Fisher's Dupontia*
	Western Dock	(*Dupontia fisheri*)
		Seaside Arrow-Grass

b. Open Dune Communities

Inland from the foreshore area occur unstable sand dunes supporting a typical community of scattered colonizing plants with extensive root systems which help them to hold the shifting sands. Common plants include:

Sea-Lime Grass	Alpine Fescue	Branched and
Purple Paintbrush	Pygmyflower	Beautiful Cinquefoils
Yarrow	Sea-Shore Chamomile	Sand-Dwelling Rock-Cress
Spike Trisetum	Red Bearberry	

c. Stable Dunes

Above and behind the unstable dunes are stable dunes with a continuous cover of plants. Common plants are:

Red Bearberry	White Mountain-Avens	Fireweed
Glacier Sedge	Purple Paintbrush	Canada Buffaloberry
Sweet Vetch	Snow Willow	Broad-Leaved Fireweed
Yarrow		

d. Damp Dune Hollows

Occasionally there are wet areas of sand in sheltered hollows that have a high water table or temporary pools of saline water caught during high tides. If saline, the damp area has a salt marsh community (see Foreshore Salt-Marsh for plants); if freshwater, it usually has the following plants:

Yarrow	Alpine Bistort	Large Grass-of-Parnassus
Purple Paintbrush	Sheathed Sedge	Greenland and Erect Primroses
Stemless Raspberry	Arctic Chrysanthemum	

e. Sandy Pools

Shallow pools occur both on the dunes where the water table is high and on rock outcrops where sand is blown into depressions. Common plants include:

Common Mare's Tail	Sago-Pondweed*	Arctic Rush
Dwarf Scouring-Rush	(*Potamogeton pectinatus*)	

II. COMMUNITIES ON OUTCROP RIDGES

White Spruce trees and large shrubs of Dwarf Birch often occur at the junction of sand and rock.

a. Lichen-Heath Community

This community occurs on peaty soils in exposed areas where no trees can survive. It is dominated by heath-like shrubs – relatives of Blueberry and Labrador Tea. Lichens are abundant and form much of the ground cover. Common plants include:

+Red Bearberry	+Alpine Bilberry	+Dry-Ground Cranberry
+Alpine Azalea	Black Crowberry	+Lapland Rose-Bay
Alpine Milk-Vetch	White Mountain-Avens	
Snow Willow	Lapland Lousewort	(+ = Heath Family)

b. Ledge and Crevice Communities

Sheltered areas in the rocks provide protection from wind and frost and have scattered trees of White Spruce as well as a variety of ferns and less hardy plants including:

Moon Fern	Fragile Fern	Large-Flowered Pyrola
Hoary Whitlow-Grass*	Common Juniper	One-Sided Wintergreen
(*Draba incana*)	Early Sandwort	Tufted and Three-Toothed
Alpine Bluebell	Northern Black Currant	Saxifrages
Snow and other dwarf willows		

13

c. White Spruce Scrub Community

The trees are stunted, seldom over 4 m (13 ft) tall and are found in slight depressions where soil accumulation and protection from the wind is greatest. In shaded and moister areas the ground layer includes the following plants:

Velvet Bells	Northern Comandra	Small Northern Bog Orchid
Stemless Raspberry	Round-Leaved Orchid	Three-Leaved Solomon's-Seal
Cloudberry	Bog Asphodel	One-Flowered Wintergreen
Early Coralroot	Lesser Wintergreen	Large and Small
Yellowrattle	Lapland Lousewort	Grass-of-Parnassus

d. Pools and Freshwater Lakes

The plants found in these aquatic habitats vary greatly but some of the common ones are listed below:

Submerged or Floating Plants	Marginal or Partly Submerged Plants
Mare's-Tails	Water-Hemlock
Spiked Water-Milfoil	Creeping Spike-Rush
Northern Water-Starwort*	Cotton-Grasses (Tall & Beautiful)
(*Callitriche hermaphroditica*)	Baltic Rush
Slender-Leaved Pondweed	Marsh Ragwort
Narrow-Leaved Bur-Reed	Northern Bur-Reed

III. PLANT COMMUNITIES OF THE PLAIN

Most of the large flat areas ('plains') around Churchill are covered by a layer of peat. This along with the underlying permafrost layer results in the presence of many pools and lakes as well as bogs, fens, and marshes. Three main plant communities exist, but they intergrade and many intermediate types exist – all wet! A fourth freshwater meadow-marsh community exists near streams and rivers where there is water movement through the soil.

a. Ice Ridge Communities

A low raised ridge is present around the edges of most of the lakes and ponds on the 'plains'. This is caused by the expansion of surface ice in winter which pushes the peat at the edges up into mounds. These ridges are better drained than the surrounding areas and a distinctive community occurs on them dominated by:

Yellow Anemone	Water Sedge	One-Spike Cotton-Grass*
Swamp Horsetail	Sweet Gale	(*Eriophorum scheuchzeri*)
Buck-Bean	Myrtle-Leaved and	
Dwarf Birch	Lime Willows	

b. Hummocky Bog and Muskeg Communities

These wet peaty areas are also called peat bogs, low wet tundra, and sedge meadows. Lack of trees creates a bog in one area while scattered Black Spruce or Tamarack trees turn another into muskeg. Many species are present but the following are typical:

Bog Rosemary	Labrador Teas	Northern Bog and Scant Sedges
Sweet Gale	Swamp Cranberry	Yellow Marsh Saxifrage
Purple Rattle	Cloudberry	Marsh & Seaside Arrow-Grasses
Northern Stitchwort	Tufted Bulrush	Flame-Coloured Lousewort
Meadow Bitter Cress	Bog Laurel	

c. Black Spruce-Larch Forest Community

Several kilometers inland from the coast, out of range of salt spray from the bay and on slightly better drained areas including the raised permafrost features called 'palsas', occur nearly closed Black Spruce forests with some Tamarack. Common ground cover plants include lichens and:

Labrador Tea	Cloudberry	Early Coralroot
Bog Laurel	Stiff Club-Moss*	Green-Flowered Bog Orchid
Alpine Bilberry	(*Lycopodium annotinum*)	

d. Freshwater Meadow-Marsh Communities

Along the Churchill River and many of the smaller streams are extensive areas of marsh dominated by various grasses and sedges. They differ from bogs by having water moving slowly through them at least part of the year. Plants include:

Water Sedge	Common Mare's-Tail	Duckweed* (*Lemna* spp.)
(and many others)	Buck-Bean	Marsh Cinquefoil

IV. PLANT COMMUNITIES OF THE GRAVEL RIDGES

These occur on the fossil beach ridges and glacial deposits such as eskers and kames.

a. Lichen-Heath Communities

On the dry and exposed summits of the gravel ridges occur Lichen-Heath communities with the following typical plants:

Purple Saxifrage	Canada Buffaloberry	White Mountain-Avens
Alpine Bistort	Alpine Arnica	Red and Alpine Bearberries
Yarrow	Cut-Leaved Anemone	Hoary Draba* (*Draba incana*)
Lacerate Dandelion		

b. Sedge Meadow Community

Sedge Meadows can occur along the edges of gravel ridges where drainage is poor. Plants include:

Greenland Primrose	Arrow-Leaved Colt's-Foot	Scant and Northern Bog Sedges
Seaside Arrow-Grass	Yellow Marsh Saxifrage	Flame-Coloured Lousewort
Lapland Buttercup	Swamp Cranberry	Arctic Blue Grass* (*Poa arctica*)

c. Willow-Bog Birch Thicket Community

Along the edges of gravel ridges and streams, on the ice ridges around the shores of lakes and ponds, and on slightly better drained areas in the bog and muskeg communities are found extensive shrub thickets. These are usually made up of several species of willows and Dwarf Birch but in more protected areas can include Green Alder and other shrubs. Plants include:

Dwarf Birch	Marsh Reed Grass	Green Alder* (*Alnus crispa*)
Baltic Rush	Short-Capsuled, Hoary,	
Sweet Gale	and Flat-Leaved Willows	

d. White Spruce Forest Community

This community is found on moist gravel ridges and is similar in composition to the White Spruce Scrub Community found on the Outcrop Ridge.

FIGURE 2
Common plant communities of the Churchill region
and their relationship to landforms.

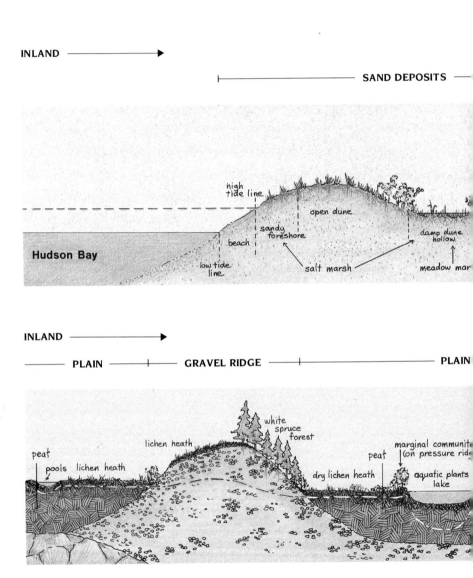

INLAND ⟶

SAND DEPOSITS ⟶

high tide line

open dune

sandy foreshore

beach

damp dune hollow

Hudson Bay

low tide line

salt marsh

meadow mar

INLAND ⟶

PLAIN ⟶ GRAVEL RIDGE ⟶ PLAIN

white spruce forest

lichen heath

peat

pools lichen heath

peat

marginal communit (on pressure rid

dry lichen heath

aquatic plants lake

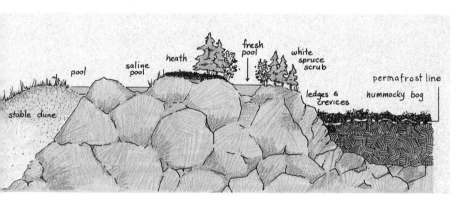

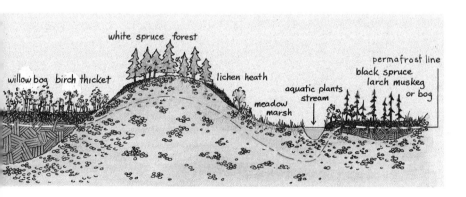

HUMAN HISTORY – Notes on the Prehistory and History of the Hudson Bay Region and Churchill

PREHISTORY:

Not much is known of the pre-European-contact inhabitants of the Hudson Bay region, mainly because of the difficult access to, and working conditions in, much of the area. This brief discussion is drawn mainly from McGhee (1978), Manitoba Department of Cultural Affairs and Historical Resources (1983), Gordon (1975), and Meyer (1977). These books contain more information and additional references on this topic.

1700-800 B.C.: Pre-Dorset: The Pre-Dorset were Palaeo-Eskimos, members of the general culture called the Arctic Small Tool tradition (ASTt) and part of the first migration of Asiatic-type peoples across the arctic. They came from Siberia via Alaska and the western arctic and were the first to successfully adapt to living in the harsh arctic environment. They made and used distinctive small flint and other stone tools, bone and ivory harpoon heads, and circular soapstone lamps and relied mostly on caribou and the smaller sea mammals such as seals and walrus for food. They did not use snow houses (igloos) or large sleds and dog teams and thus had to winter on shores or inland areas. Several of their house sites have been found at or near Churchill on ridges or hills about 32-35 m (105-115 ft) above sea level. These sites would have been islands in Hudson Bay at the time of their occupation and have since been uplifted to their present level by isostatic rebound.

800 B.C. to A.D. 1000: Dorset: The Dorset peoples were also members of the ASTt culture and are believed to have developed from Pre-Dorset groups of the central and eastern arctic, just north of Hudson Bay. They may be the semi-legendary 'Tunit' of historic Inuit legends and were also of an Asiatic rather than North American Indian racial stock. Their small tools, knives and harpoon points were of different styles than those of the Pre-Dorset and they used oval or rectangular soapstone lamps. The presence of snow knives, ivory shoes for sled runners and snow creepers for boots suggest that they probably made snow houses and had the technology to live on the sea ice during the winter while hunting seals. They lived mainly off caribou, walrus, and seals, apparently more successfully than the Pre-Dorset from the larger size of their settlements and middens (refuse-heaps). The two known Dorset sites in the Churchill area, one dated to 130 B.C., occur 19.5-23 m (66-76 ft) above sea level.

A.D. 1000 to 1600: Thule (Inuit): The Thule culture arose from a second great migration of Asiatic-stock peoples from northern Alaska eastward to Greenland and represents a totally different culture from the preceeding ASTt. These people were the ancestors of the modern Inuit, apparently displacing the earlier Dorset culture although they may have intermarried with, and taken some technology from, that group. A warmer climate from about A.D. 900 to 1200 allowed the large whales on which they relied to live throughout the high arctic and probably prompted their migration into the region. The invention of the float-harpoon allowed them to successfully hunt whales which provided them with a relatively secure source of large amounts of meat and blubber. Large and small skin boats, specialized harpoon and other whale hunting equipment, more developed sleds and bows, barbed arrowheads, and copper tools were characteristic of their culture. They lived in comfortable permanent winter houses along the coast although they probably also used temporary snow houses during winter hunts on the sea ice. As the climate cooled after A.D. 1200, the large whales could no longer live in the high arctic and most of the Thule either moved south along the coasts or permanently inland. The rest adapted their technology for inland summer living and winter hunting on the sea ice to survive in northern areas. There are no known Thule sites at Churchill, only the occasional possible tool or other artifact to indicate that they might have ventured this far south.

The Thule were the first Inuit to make contact with Europeans, initially early Norse explorers and settlers in the Greenland area and then other European whalers, fishermen, and explorers in the fifteenth century.

At the same time, from about A.D. 1200 to 1400, a group called the Thaltheilei were moving into the inland subarctic areas of present-day northern Saskatchewan and Manitoba and the southern Northwest Territories. These were Indians of the Athapaskan language group and are the ancestors of the present-day Chipewyans. They lived off the barren-ground caribou herds in this region and may have occasionally reached the coast of Hudson Bay to fish and hunt sea mammals. The only artifact indicating an early Indian presence at Churchill is one projectile point tentatively dated at about A.D. 1000.

A.D. 1600-: Historic Inuit: Modern Inuit are directly descended from the Thule and have almost always lived north and west of Churchill. The inland Caribou Inuit lived on the barren-grounds north of the Thaltheilei and present-day Chipewyan territories with the coastal Inuit much further north along Hudson Bay where the sea ice was more stable and winter hunting more secure. They did come down into the Churchill area from about A.D. 1600 onwards, probably in response to the cooler climate of the 'Little Ice Age' which occured around then. Most sites in the Churchill area are along the coast, 7 m (23 ft) to 18 m (60 ft) above sea level, and were probably made by Caribou Inuit during occasional visits to fish and hunt sea mammals. The sites include round or dumbbell-shaped tent rings, caches, kayak rests, graves and fox traps and contain caribou spears, bows, snow knives and goggles, and rolls of birch bark. Later sites contain a mixture of European trade goods and traditional tools.

HISTORY: (POST-EUROPEAN CONTACT)

Many histories and biographies deal with the events and people of the post-contact era on Hudson Bay. Morton (1957) gives an overview of the Manitoba portion of that history while MacIver (1982) is a more detailed account of the history of Churchill. Both books contain references to many other sources of information on this topic.

1610: Henry Hudson, in search of the North-West Passage to the Orient, discovered the strait and bay that bear his name. After wintering with his sick and demoralized crew near the mouth of Rupert River at the southwestern end of James Bay, he was cast adrift in an open boat and never heard of again.

1612: Thomas Button, continuing the quest and hoping to find traces of Hudson, wintered at the mouth of the Nelson River, taking possession of the adjacent land for England.

1619: Jens Munck, son of a Danish nobleman, discovered the mouth of the Churchill River and wintered there rather than attempt the hazardous return voyage during the stormy autumn season. Scurvy and exposure killed all but Munck and two others who managed to return to Denmark. Native people, coming across the strangely garbed bodies a few months after Munck left, named the river, "River-of-the-Strangers".

1631: By this date, seventeen expeditions (sixteen English and one Danish) had approached the boreal forest belt from the Arctic Ocean while in the south the French had come within easy reach of it from the St. Lawrence River.

1650: Defeat of the Huron Indians by the Five Nations shattered the machinery of the French fur trade.

1661: Medard Chouart des Groseilliers (the "Mr. Gooseberry" of the old Hudson's Bay Company documents) and Pierre Esprit de Radisson penetrated the beaver country of the boreal forest, tapping the stream of furs at its source. The subsequent rejection by the French Court of Groseilliers' plans for new ventures to Hudson Bay gave the English an entry to the great fur belt and proved decisive in the history of the Canadian Northwest.

1668: Groseilliers, with an English expedition under the command of Captain Zachary Gillam, reached Rupert River on James Bay. There the building of Fort Charles provided the first direct link of the Northwest with Europe.

1670: King Charles II of England granted a charter to the "Governor and Company of Adventurers of England trading into Hudson's Bay" and their successors, constituting them "the true and absolute lords and proprietors" of that vast practically unknown territory draining into Hudson Bay, with sole trade and commerce rights to a region larger than half of Europe. In rapid succession trading posts were established at the mouths of the Albany, Moose, Rupert, Nelson, Severn, and Churchill rivers and the whole territory received the name Rupert's Land, after the chief promoter and first governor, Prince Rupert.

1684: York Factory was established near the mouth of the Hayes River following the destruction of Fort Nelson by the French in the preceding year. This post was the oldest permanent settlement in Manitoba until its abandonment in 1957. It long served as the main supply centre of the Hudson's Bay Company, with goods from England for the interior, and furs collected there for the return voyages, passing through it.

1686: John Abraham explored the Churchill River, naming it after Lord Churchill, the newly appointed governor of the Company.

1689: A party including the explorer Henry Kelsey built the first Fort Churchill on the west bank of the river estuary and it was destroyed by fire the same year.

1690: Henry Kelsey traveled from York Factory up the Hayes, Nelson and Minago rivers, reaching the Saskatchewan River near the present town of The Pas the following year. He was the first European to see the native people and buffalo of the plains.

1717: James Knight, the first Governor-in-Chief on the Bay, rebuilt the timber Fort Churchill on its original location. It was later renamed "Prince of Wales Fort" in honour of George, Prince of Wales, later George II.

1731: The threat of French domination of the Bay induced the Hudson's Bay Company to commission the Governor of Churchill to build a new stone Fort Prince of Wales on Eskimo Point. A battery of guns was also set up at Cape Merry, on the opposite shore, to face the fort and protect the mouth of the Churchill River. The Fort, designed by British military engineers, was completed in 1771 during the governorship of Samuel Hearne. Its dimensions were 94.5 m (310 feet) east and west and 96.6 m (317 feet) north and south. Masonry walls were nearly 5 m (17 feet) high and angular bastions guarded each corner. The ramparts, originally 7.6 m (25 feet) thick, were later brought up to 12.8 m (42 feet) in thickness.

1743-51: The earliest important work referring to the natural history of the Hudson Bay region, **A Natural History of Uncommon Birds and of Some Other Rare and Undescribed Animals,** by George Edwards was published.

1770: Samuel Hearne set out from Fort Prince of Wales on a famous overland journey during which he discovered the Coppermine River and Great Slave Lake. In 1768, "northern Indians" (Chipewyans) brought pieces of copper to the Churchill post saying that they had gotten them on the banks of a "Far Away Metal River" which flowed into a northern ocean to the northwest. After almost unbelievable hardship and misfortune, Hearne reached the mouth of the Coppermine in 1771 and returned to Churchill the following year after an absence of almost eighteen months. He was appointed chief or governor at Churchill in 1776. Unaware that England and France were at war, Hearne, with a garrison of only 39 men, was obliged to surrender Fort Prince of Wales to Admiral de la Perouse and a force of 300 French soldiers in 1782. Hearne was reinstated as governor at Churchill when peace was reestablished the following year.

1774: Establishment by Hearne of Cumberland House in present-day Saskatchewan marked the beginning of a policy of penetration into the interior by the Hudson's Bay Company in answer to rival fur traders.

1794: David Thompson surveyed a new route between Cumberland House and York Factory via Goose, Reed, and Burntwood lakes to the Nelson River.

1811: Conveyance to Lord Selkirk, for the settlement of a group of Scottish colonists, of an area of about 300,000 sq. kilometers (116,000 sq. miles) in present-day Manitoba, Saskatchewan, North Dakota, and Minnesota. Miles Macdonell was chosen Governor of Assiniboia, as the region was then named and set out with an advance party to prepare for the settlers the following year. The group was forced to winter at the mouth of the Nelson River and the following spring traveled up the Hayes River, down Lake Winnipeg, and up the Red River to establish the Red River Colony near what is now Winnipeg. This was the beginning of the present vast agricultural settlements on the western prairies.

1819-22: Sir John Franklin's first overland expedition was made from York Factory to the mouth of the Coppermine River via the Hayes and Saskatchewan rivers and Great Slave Lake. He was accompanied by John Richardson, navy surgeon and naturalist.

1821: Union of the rival Hudson's Bay and North West Companies. The disappearance of competition for the interior trade meant that native people now had to travel much greater distances to the main trading posts. The lower part of the Churchill River, with its treacherous currents, was completely abandoned as a trading route.

1870: The Red River Settlement was organized as the Province of Manitoba.

1885: Canadian Pacific Railway spanned the continent.

1911: The contract for the first 298 kilometers (185 miles) of grading on the Hudson Bay Railway between The Pas and Churchill was let.

1912: The boundaries of Manitoba were extended to the sixtieth parallel and to the shores of Hudson Bay, including about half the former area of the District of Keewatin.

1929: Completion of the Hudson Bay Railway. It was originally planned to end at Port Nelson at the mouth of the Nelson River and by 1918 the right-of-way was cleared and graded to this point. Construction work then stopped because of a shortage of ships and material following the First World War. Work was resumed in 1927 and the track completed to Mile 356 at which point a swing was made north to the Churchill River. Its mouth provided a natural haven in the roughest seas and was not subject to heavy silting like the Nelson. It was feared that the foundation of the 120 kilometer (75 mile) stretch over frozen muskeg south of Churchill would soften under the summer sun and absorb the roadbed but trials showed that a substantial gravel fill on top of the muskeg acted as an efficient insulator, preventing the foundation from giving way. The grain elevator and Port of Churchill were also completed in 1931. They are operated by Ports Canada, a Federal Crown Corporation. The Port is open to shipping about four months of the year with grain the primary export. The grain elevator has a capacity of 140,000 tonnes (5 million bushels). Completed before the advent of modern aviation, the Churchill railway provided the easiest means of access to the Canadian arctic. Churchill became the supply and medical base for remote northern settlements – reached first by ship and then by plane. Scientists, naturalists, and travellers still find it an excellent way to see much of northern Manitoba and the most inexpensive access to the arctic.

1942-44: Some 2,000 United States Army troops were stationed at Churchill during the Second World War. The airport and Fort Churchill were constructed 8 kilometers (5 miles) east of the town of Churchill to serve as a link in the northern air ferry system to Europe.

1944-64: The Canadian Government took over Fort Churchill, using it as a base for arctic exercises and equipment trials by the Canadian and United States armies. A defense laboratory was built by the Canadian Army to look into military problems arising from working and living in the north, and the United States Army Corps of Engineers established the first Arctic Test Detachment there.

1957: The Churchill Research (Rocket) Range was established to support the International Geophysical Year, allowing instrumented rockets to be fired from a far northern site.

1959-65: The Research Range was revived, now run by the United States Army and Air Force for rocket and missile testing and research.

1966-86: The Research Range was taken over by the National Research Council of Canada for studies on the earth's upper atmosphere. Most functions were moved to Gimli, Manitoba in 1980, but several large rocket launches still took place at the Research Range each winter until 1985.

1958-75: Churchill served as regional headquarters for the Keewatin Region of the Northwest Territories. A vocational school for Inuit was established at Fort Churchill during the sixties and as a result of these two institutions a small community of Inuit grew up at Akudlik, about half-way between Fort Churchill and the town of Churchill. Most Inuit left Churchill when the regional headquarters offices moved north to Rankin Inlet in 1975 and the vocational school was closed.

1964: The Canada Department of Public Works took over responsibility for Fort Churchill and the military presence diminished. A small detachment of Canadian Forces personnel was again present from 1970 to 1980 and then withdrawn.

1971-74: The Churchill Redevelopment Plan took place, with the construction of new townhouses and apartments in the centre of town and of the Churchill Town Centre along the edge of the bay. The Town Centre complex provided a unified and beautiful environment for the new hospital, two schools, a library, municipal office, swimming pool, curling and hockey rinks, and many other facilities.

1976: The Churchill Northern Studies Centre was established in the old Northwest Territories Headquarters and other buildings at Akudlik. This organization provides logistical support and quarters for scientists and educators studying the many fascinating natural and human features found in the Churchill region. It moved out to the former Rocket Research Range in 1986.

1980-81: Most of the buildings of Fort Churchill were torn down leaving only the airport and a couple of other buildings occupied by the Provincial Government and Federal agencies on that site.

A NOTE ON NAMES

Common or colloquial names are given as the main listing for each plant because of the non-technical nature of this guidebook. Such names can be very useful, especially if they are accurate descriptions of the wildflower, e.g., 'Velvet Bells', but have several problems. They vary greatly from region to region and over time and there is no universally accepted 'right' common name for a particular plant. The plant called Dry-Ground Cranberry, for example, is also known as Mossberry, Rock or Mountain Cranberry, Cowberry, Lingonberry, and Pomme-de-Terre. Alternate names are given in the species account for each plant and listed in the index. Entirely unrelated plants are also called by misleading similar names, e.g. Cotton-Grass, Grass-of-Parnassus, Scurvey-Grass, and Whitlow-Grass – none related to the true grasses. Many plants also have no common name because they are small and inconspicuous or of no use to human beings. In this case the common name used is a direct English translation of the scientific one, e.g. the Glacier Sedge (*Carex glacialis* Mack.).

For the above reasons, I have included the scientific names of all plants covered in this guidebook as they are constant anywhere in the world and are an exact means of identification and reference. Such names are used by botanists and serious amateurs everywhere and are the only ones used in the technical floras given as references for confirmation of identity or further information on a particular plant.

Scientific names are in Latin and written in Latinized form. They are always italicized and follow a binomial ("two-name") system. The Dry-Ground Cranberry, for example, is *Vaccinium vitis-idaea* L. *Vaccinium*, the **genus** or generic name, is always capitalized and represents a distinct group of one to many **species** – the basic 'kinds' of plants. The genus *Vaccinium* also includes the true blueberries such as the Alpine Bilberry or Blueberry (*Vaccinium uliginosum* L.). The **species** name, in this case *vitis-idaea* (Greek for "always living" or "evergreen") or *uliginosum* (Latin for "full of moisture"), comes second and is never capitalized. The "L." after the species names stands for the authority, or person who named that particular species – in this case Linnaeus, the Swedish botanist who established and codified the binomial system. Scientific names do have meaning and tend to be descriptive of the plant, to refer to a geographical area or particular habitat in which it grows, or to honor persons who have been connected in some way with botany or that particular plant. Information on the meaning of the scientific names is given in some Comments sections of the species accounts.

Groups of related genera (plural of genus) having a typical flower structure and other similar features are further classified into **families.** Some common and easily recognizable families are the Pea Family (Leguminosae), Sunflower Family (Compositae), Parsley Family (Umbelliferae), and Rose Family (Rosaceae). The Rose Family contains in addition to the roses (genus *Rosa*), the cinquefoils (*Potentilla* spp.), raspberries (*Rubus* spp.) and Mountain-Avens (*Dryas* spp.). The abbreviations 'sp.' and 'spp.' are used for 'species', singular and plural, e.g., when a particular species is unknown or unimportant (sp.) or when more than one species is included (spp.).

Common names in this guidebook are taken from **Budd's Flora of the Canadian Prairie Provinces** except for more widely used regional names or where none is given. Scientific names are from Porsild and Cody, **Vascular Plants of the Continental Northwest Territories, Canada,** or, if not covered there, from Scoggan, **Flora of Canada.**

25

EXPLANATION OF BASIC TERMS

Some technical botanical terms are necessary in any book on plants, if only to reduce the descriptions and keys to a reasonable length. I have tried to keep them to a minimum and to clearly illustrate and/or define them. The terms needed to answer the five questions are explained in detail in the following paragraphs. Others which you will come across in the keys, subkeys and text are listed and defined in the Glossary or illustrated on the endpapers or in the subkey headings for that particular group.

FLOWERS: REGULAR, IRREGULAR, INDISTINGUISHABLE

Regular flowers are radially symmetrical, which means that their petals or petal-like parts (rays in flowers like Daisies) are arranged around the centre of the flower like the spokes of a wheel. Each petal or similar part is nearly identical in size, shape and colour to all the others. If the petals or parts are united (as in flowers like those of the Blueberry or Alpine Bluebell), the lobes of the flower are likewise similar in size, shape and colour. The great majority of flowers are regular in shape including such common and well known ones as buttercups, blueberries, Fireweed, and cinquefoils.

> **CAUTION:** Some flowers grow close together in a spike or head; clover is a good example. In checking the flower parts to determine if they are regular and how many there are, you need to pull off a single flower and examine that, not use the characteristics of the whole head. Odd-numbered (i.e., 5- and 7- parted) flowers can still be regular and even-numbered ones (6-parted orchids) irregular.

Irregular flowers are not radially symmetrical, that is, their petals or similar parts are not identical in size, shape and colour. These flowers often have different upper and lower parts called **lips** as in the Snapdragon – a common cultivated

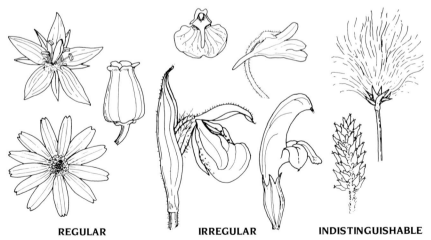

REGULAR   IRREGULAR   INDISTINGUISHABLE

irregular flower. Other familiar irregular flowers include orchids and members of the Pea or Bean Family.

Indistinguishable flowers have either no visible petal-like parts or the parts are so small that it is difficult to make out their number and arrangement.

CAUTION: A flower may be very small and still have parts that are quite easy to recognize and count. If you can't find your wildflower after trying the Indistinguishable section, reexamine it, preferably with a 5- or 10- power magnifying glass to make sure that it is, in fact, impossible to count the parts. Plants that have no true flowers and reproduce by spores or cones, such as the ferns and conifers (spruce trees, etc.), are also found in this section.

WILDFLOWERS, SHRUBS, and TREES

For the purposes of this guide, a **wildflower** is any plant that grows in a natural state and is not a tree or shrub as defined below.

Tree: A woody perennial, usually with a single main stem or trunk which is over 3 m (10 ft) in height at maturity.

Shrub: A woody perennial with a stem usually less than 3 m (10 ft) high at maturity and often much branched. Some wildflowers are also bushy and much branched, so the real distinguishing feature is the toughness or woodiness of the shrubs' main stems.

Many arctic plants, especially members of the Willow and Heath Families, are what are called Dwarf Shrubs, only a few cm (in) tall. It is sometimes difficult to recognize them as shrubs but they all have persistent woody stems although these may creep along the ground rather than stand erect. These plants are usually listed in the Shrub section of the Locator Keys so you should check your plant carefully to see if it has a woody stem.

ARRANGEMENT OF THE LEAVES: BASAL, ALTERNATE, OPPOSITE, and WHORLED

Leaves growing from the base of the plant are, logically enough, **basal leaves;** those growing above the base are **stem leaves.** Many plants have both but some have only basal leaves. When the stem leaves grow directly across from each other in pairs (2 at each node), they are **opposite;** when they occur singly on the stem (1 at each node), they are **alternate.** If they grow in circles of 3, 4, 5, etc. (3, 4,

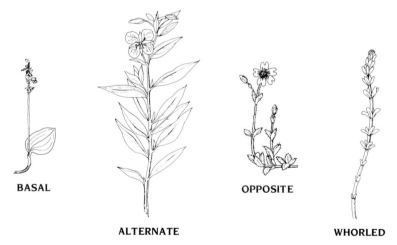

BASAL　　　　　　　　　　　　　　　　**OPPOSITE**

ALTERNATE　　　　　　　　　　　　　　**WHORLED**

5, etc. at each node), they are termed **whorled.** A **node** is simply any point on a stem where a leaf occurs. When determining the leaf arrangement on a plant, avoid if possible the tips of the stems. Leaves are crowded there and it may be difficult to see their arrangement. Select a part of the main stem where the leaves are widely spaced and distinct. If there is only one stem leaf, it is considered alternate.

TYPES OF LEAVES: ENTIRE, TOOTHED, LOBED and DIVIDED

If the margin of the leaf is even and unbroken, the leaf is **entire.** If the margin has more or less regular shallow indentations, the leaf is **toothed.** Included here are leaves with wavy and scalloped edges as well as those with pointed teeth.

If the leaves have deeper indentations that separate the leaf blade into several sections but do not reach the mid-rib, they are **lobed.** Familiar examples of lobed leaves are those of maple and oak trees.

> **EXCEPTION:** Leaves that are lobed only at the base, such as heart-shaped and arrow-shaped leaves, are considered entire or toothed depending on their margins.

Often a leaf is actually **divided** all the way to the mid-rib into separate parts which are known as **leaflets.** Most ferns, buttercups, anemones, and Yarrow are good examples of plants with divided leaves. In this guide, if some of the leaf indentations go **almost** to the mid-rib, the leaf is considered to be divided, even though the divisions are not strictly leaflets. In borderline cases, the plant will appear in the key under both lobed and divided.

A divided leaf may sometimes be mistaken for a branch and the leaflets for individual leaves. Leaflets may be distinguished from leaves in several ways including the fact that leaflets of a divided leaf all lie in the same plane, the whole leaf forming a flat surface, and the fact that all leaflets look alike in shape and are nearly the same size. Branches, however, have leaves that vary greatly in size and appearance and that normally face in different directions, not in the same plane. Branches also bear flower and leaf **buds** which divided leaves do not.

Always select the largest or best-developed leaves, usually the lower ones, when determining the leaf type. If two kinds of leaves are present (usually basal and stem leaves) those with the deepest indentations determine the category in which it should be placed. For example, if some of the leaves are lobed and some divided, the plant should be classified as having divided leaves. The various leaf shapes are illustrated and identified on the back endpapers of the book.

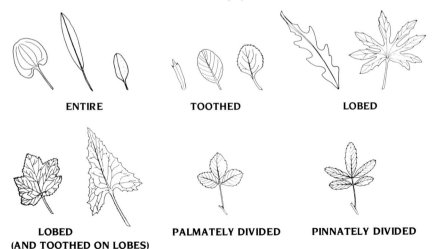

ENTIRE   TOOTHED   LOBED

LOBED   PALMATELY DIVIDED   PINNATELY DIVIDED
(AND TOOTHED ON LOBES)

FLOWERS AND THEIR STRUCTURE

Plants with flowers are technically known as angiosperms ("hidden seed") and are the dominant group of vascular plants on earth today. They possess true flowers, which are more advanced and complex than the reproductive structures of the ferns or gymnosperms ("naked seeds") from which they almost certainly evolved. Even their common name of 'flowering plants' gives an idea of the great significance of the flower in this group.

Structurally the true flower is a shortened and highly modified spore-bearing shoot, possibly derived from something similar to a gymnosperm cone. Both cones and flowers have the same function, which is to produce seed by sexual reproduction, although they use different means to achieve that goal.

The basic **flower** consists of four series of parts arranged in whorls or circles around a central axis. These are:

1. an outer series of modified leaves or bracts called **sepals**, which are usually, although not always, green in colour and help protect the inner parts. They are collectively called the **calyx**;
2. an inner series of modified leaves or bracts called **petals**, which are often coloured and attract pollinators. They are collectively called the **corolla**;
3. one or more series of functional male structures, the **stamens**, made up of a thread-like **filament** and a pollen-producing sac-like **anther**; and
4. an inner series of female structures (often only one) called the **pistil(s)** or **carpel(s)** which have a basal **ovary** containing **ovules** which mature into **seeds** when fertilized by the pollen.

If petals and sepals are attached **below** the base of the ovary, the ovary is **superior** (to the petals and sepals). If the petals and sepals are attached above or part way up the ovary, the ovary is considered **inferior** (to the petals and sepals). In angiosperms, the seeds are enclosed ("hidden") within the ovary which is topped by a **style** and **stigma**, the latter receiving pollen grains during pollination.

Most plants have **perfect flowers** with both male and female structures but some have flowers with only one series of sexual parts **(unisexual flowers)**, either stamens **(staminate flowers)** or pistils **(pistillate flowers)**. Plants with unisexual flowers can have both sexes in different places on the same plant, as in Dwarf Birch and Sweet Gale, or each sex on a different plant as in the willows and poplars.

Flowers occur in different arrangements in different species and these are important characteristics for identification. Only a few of the technical terms for these arrangements have been used in this book (e.g., spike, head, umbel) and these are illustrated on the front endpapers.

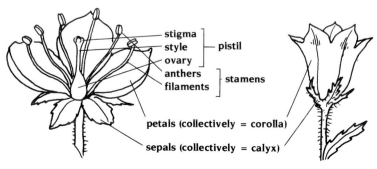

stigma ⎤
style ⎦ — pistil
ovary
anthers ⎤
filaments ⎦ stamens

petals (collectively = corolla)

sepals (collectively = calyx)

GLOSSARY

A page number or the abbreviation FE (front endpaper) or BE (back endpaper) following a definition refers to the place where an illustration of, or further information on, the term may be found.

achene: a small, dry, single-seeded fruit which does not split open.
alpine: regions above treeline on mountains and the plants and animals living there.
alternate: borne singly along a stem, 1 at a node; not opposite. (27)
Amphi-Atlantic: occuring on both sides of the Atlantic Ocean but lacking on the Pacific side of the world.
angiosperms: plants possessing true flowers and which have their seeds enclosed within a fruit-forming ovary.
annual: a plant which completes its life cycle from germination to death within 1 year.
anther: the pollen-bearing part of a stamen. (29)
aquatic: a plant growing completely in water.
arctic: the region north of treeline and south of the pole in the Northern Hemisphere and the plants and animals living there.
awn: a long hair- or bristle-like extension from a bract or flower part; common in grass flowers. (318)
axil: the upper angle between a leaf and the stem. (28)
axillary: borne in the axil of a leaf.

basal: borne at or near the base of the stem. (27)
beak: a firm, prominent, elongated tip.
berry: a pulpy fruit with several seeds and no stony layer, e.g., a blueberry.
biennial: a plant that completes its life cycle in 2 years and then dies, usually flowering in the second year.
bisexual (of flowers): 2 sexes; containing both male (stamens) and female (pistils) reproductive organs in a single flower = perfect. (29)
blade: the broad flat part of a leaf. (28)
bloom: a whitish waxy or powdery coating, easily rubbed off.
boreal: northern forested areas and the plants and animals living there.
brackish: somewhat salty; a mix of fresh and sea water.
bract: a very small or modified leaf, usually growing at the base of a flower or flower cluster. (29) (FE)
bristle: a stiff hair on the surface of a leaf or stem.
bulblet or bulbil: a small bulb, especially one growing in a flower cluster.

calcareous: containing a high proportion of lime or calcium.
calyx: the outer circle or series of flower parts, made up of sepals; usually green but sometimes brightly coloured. (29)
capitate: in a dense cluster or head.
capsule: a dry fruit that splits open into 2 or more sections at maturity.
carpel: = pistil. (29)
catkin: a pendulous spike of simple, usually unisexual flowers such as those of the willows and birches. (29, 240) (FE)
ciliate (of a leaf, petal, etc.): fringed with small hairs along the edges.
circumpolar: occuring throughout the arctic regions of the Northern Hemisphere.
clasping (of leaves): partially surrounding the stem. (BE)

cleft: deeply cut.

cordate (of leaves): heart-shaped. (BE)

corolla: the second circle or series of flower parts, made up of petals and usually brightly coloured. (29)

deciduous: having leaves that fall off at the end of the growing season; not evergreen.

deflexed: sharply bent or turned downward.

disk: in composite flowers like the Alpine Arnica, the central part of the flowering head; also the tiny tubular flowers making up the disk, i.e., *disk flower*. (FE)

divided (leaf): cleft to, or almost to, the base or the midrib into several smaller 'blades' or leaflets. A 2- to 3- times-divided leaf has each of its segments divided again and sometimes yet again into leaflets.

dorsal (of a leaf, petal, etc.): the upper side.

drupe: a pulpy or fleshy fruit containing a single seed enclosed in a hard shell or stone, e.g., plum, cherry, peach.

elliptical: broadest in the middle and tapering equally toward both rounded ends. (BE)

emergent: a plant growing in water but with its main stem and leaves extending out of, and above, the water level.

entire: with an edge unbroken by teeth, lobes or divisions of any kind. (28) (BE)

evergreen: remaining green throughout the dormant season (winter).

exserted: projecting or protruding out of or beyond a container, as stamens from a corolla.

family: a group of related plants. Families are divided into genera, which are further divided into species. (25)

ferns: a group of non-woody, flowerless, and seedless plants which reproduce by spores but which have roots, stems and leaflike fronds.

fertilization: fusion of male and female gametes (reproductive cells) in the ovary of a flower after pollination.

filament: the anther-bearing stalk of a stamen. (29)

floret: 'tiny flower' – a small flower, usually part of a dense head or spike. (FE)

flower: the structure concerned with sexual reproduction in higher plants. It consists of 4 series of parts: sepals, petals, stamens, pistils. (29)

free (of sepals, petals, etc.): not joined to each other or to any other part of the flower.

fruit: the seed-bearing product or part of a plant.

genus (plural: genera): a group of closely related species. The genus is designated by the first word in the Latin scientific name of a species and is always capitalized. (25)

glabrous: smooth, without hairs or projections.

gland: a structure which secretes liquids including sticky, oily, watery and resinous substances.

glandular: possessing glands; having a secretory hair or other structure that produces nectar or some other liquid.

glaucous: with a waxy grayish-blue surface covering.

globular: round, like a globe or ball.

glumes: the 2 bracts or scales found at the base of a spikelet in the grasses. (318)

grain: a single-seeded, small, hard fruit (usually of a grass).

gymnosperm: a woody plant which has no true flowers and bears its seeds 'naked' on the surface of scales in structures called 'cones', e.g., spruce and larch.

habitat: the kind of place in which a plant usually grows; e.g., bogs, seashores, forests, etc.

halophyte: a plant that tolerates salty conditions.

head: a group of flowers joined together in a short, dense, terminal cluster as in the clovers and all members of the Sunflower or Composite Family. (FE)

heath: a member of the Heath or Heather Family such as the bearberries, blueberries and Labrador teas which usually prefer acid, peaty soils.

herb: a non-woody plant.

herbaceous: not woody.

indistinguishable: said of flowers with no visible petal-like parts or with parts so small that it is difficult to make out their number or arrangement. (26)

inferior: an ovary with the sepals, petals and stamens attached to its tip or top. Opposite of *superior*. (29)

inflorescence: any arrangement of more than 1 flower. (FE)

involucre: a circle of bracts below a flower or flower cluster; a single part is an '*involucral bract*'. (FE)

irregular: said of flowers in which the parts are dissimilar in size, shape or arrangement; not radially symmetrical. (26)

joint: (1.) point on a stem where 2 sections are visibly joined together, usually resulting in a slight swelling; e.g., grasses and members of the Buckwheat Family; (2.) section of a fruit pod separated from others by a constriction; e.g., Northern Hedysarum.

lanceolate (of a leaf): lance-shaped; broader toward one end and tapering to the other like a lance; usually 3 or more times longer than wide. (BE)

lateral: arising from, or attached to, the side (of a stem, trunk, leaf, etc.).

leaf: a broad, flattened photosynthetic structure found in most plants; composed of a stalk (*petiole*) and flat *blade*. (BE)

leaflet: each separate part of the blade of a divided leaf. (28) (BE)

lemma: the outer scale-like bract enclosing the individual reduced flowers of the grasses. (318)

lentical: a small, usually light-coloured, corky spot, dot, or line on the young bark of shrubs or trees.

linear (of a leaf): long and narrow with parallel edges. (BE)

lip: the distinctive upper and/or lower part of many irregular flowers. (26)

littoral: a coastal region, especially the shore zone between the high and low tide marks.

lobe: 1 of the segments of a leaf or flower, usually rounded and extending less than 1/2 way to the base or midrib. (26, 28)

maritime: relating to the sea or ocean.

mealy: covered with small dust-like particles resembling cornmeal.

membranous: thin, dry and semi-transparent; resembling a membrane.

midrib: the central or largest vein of a leaf or leaflet.

montane: the cool, moist zone found below treeline on mountains and dominated by evergreen trees; the plants and animals which live there.

node: any point on a stem where a leaf occurs. (27) (BE)

oblanceolate (of leaves): much longer than wide, broadest near the tip, and tapering toward the base. (BE) obovate (of leaves): shaped like an inverted egg with the narrow end below the middle. (BE)

ochrea/ocrea: a cup-shaped structure formed by the joining of stipules or leaf bases around a stem. (BE)

opposite: arranged in pairs on the stem; (of leaves) 2 at each node. (27)

oval: broadly elliptical. (BE)

ovary: the enlarged base of the pistil that produces the seeds. (29)

ovate (of leaves): shaped like an egg with the narrow end above the middle. (BE)

ovule: immature seed prior to fertilization and development.

palea: the inner scale-like bract enclosing the individual reduced flowers of the grasses. (318)

palmate (of leaves): with the lobes or leaflets radiating from a central point like the fingers of a hand. (28) (BE)

panicle: an elongated branched flower cluster. (318) (FE)

pappus: bristles, hairs, etc. on top of the fruit (achene) of members of the Sunflower or Composite Family.

parasite: a plant that gets its food from another living plant.

peat: dead, fibrous but undecomposed plant material with a high water content. Formed in wet sites such as bogs and marshes where lack of oxygen and low temperatures in the north prevent decay. Thick layers can build up, especially in bogs, from remains of the peat mosses (*Sphagnum* spp.).

pedicel: the stalk of a single flower. (FE)

pendulous: hanging or drooping down, used of flowers or fruits.

perennial: a plant that normally lives more than 2 years.

perfect flower: flowers containing both functioning male (stamens) and female (pistils) structures = bisexual.

perianth: sepals and petals or calyx and corolla together; the non-reproductive parts of the flower. (29)

perigynium (plural: perigynia): the papery sheath (bract) that encloses the fruit (achene) in sedges. (300)

persistent: remaining attached rather than falling off.

petal: one of the second series of parts in a flower; usually brightly coloured and collectively called the *corolla*, especially when fused together. (29)

petaloid: petal-like; coloured and resembling a petal.

petiole: the stalk of a leaf connecting the blade with the stem. (27, 28)

pinnate (of leaves): divided in such a way that the leaflets are arranged on both sides of a common stalk, like the pinnae of a feather. In once-pinnate leaves, the stalk is unbranched; in 2-3-times-pinnate leaves, the stalk is branched once or twice, with each of the branches having leaflets. (28) (BE)

pistil: the central female reproductive part of a flower; composed of stigma, style and ovary. Also called *carpel*. (29)

pistillate flower: a unisexual flower having pistils but no stamens.

pod: a dry fruit, the legume of the Pea Family

pollen: the tiny male spores produced by the anther.

pollination: the transfer of pollen grains from stamen to stigma. *Cross-pollination* occurs between flowers of different plants of the same species; *self-pollination* occurs between flowers of the same plant or within a single flower.

prostrate: lying flat on the ground.

pubescent: covered with soft, short hairs.

punctate: shallowly pitted or dotted, often with glands.

raceme: an elongated unbranched flower cluster with stalked flowers arranged along a central stem. (FE)

ray: in composite flowers like the Alpine Arnica, the outer strap-like or petal-like flowers encircling the disk flowers in the flower head, i.e., *ray flower*. (FE)

reflexed: abruptly turned downward or backward.

regular: having all parts alike in size and shape; radially symmetrical. (26)

resins: substances produced by plants from glands or wounds which harden into solids.

rhizome: = rootstalk.

rib: a prominent vein of a leaf.

root: the lower, usually underground, part of a plant. It anchors the plant and absorbs water and minerals.

rootstalk: = rhizome; a horizontal, underground stem usually involved in spreading the plant by vegetative reproduction.

rosette: a circular cluster of leaves, usually at the base of a plant. (BE)

runner: a slender, prostrate branch usually involved in spreading the plant by vegetative reproduction.

saline: containing a high proportion of salts.

saprophyte: a plant that gets its food from dead organic matter; usually non-green in colour.

scale: a tiny colourless leaf found on some plant stems or flowers.

scape: a leafless flower stalk. (FE)

scarious: thin, dry, membranous; not green.

scurfy: covered with tiny scale-like particles.

seed: a fertilized and ripened ovule, consisting of the embryo (undeveloped plant) and its coats of food supply and protective layers.

semi-aquatic: plants which can live either in water or on very wet soils.

sepal: one of the first (outer) series of parts in a flower; usually green and collectively called the *calyx*, especially when fused together. (29)

sessile: without a stalk or petiole.

sheath: a thin membrane surrounding the stem. See *ochrea*. (BE)

shrub: a woody perennial, smaller than a tree (under 10 m tall), usually with several stems.

species: each distinct kind of plant. A species has a 2-word Latin scientific name, the first word of which (always capitalized) designates the genus and the second the species, e.g., the scientific name of the Alpine Azalea is *Loiseleuria procumbens*. (25)

spike: an elongated flower cluster with stalkless flowers arranged along a central stem. (300, 318) (FE)

spikelet: 'little spike'; a tiny cluster of stalkless flowers common in grasses and sedges. (300, 318)

spur: hollow, tubular projection of a flower, usually containing nectar.

stamen: the male organ of a flower consisting of a slender stalk (filament) and a knob-like, pollen-bearing tip (anther). (29)

staminate flower: a unisexual flower having stamens but no pistils.

stem: the main supporting axis of a plant which bears leaves with buds in their axils.

stigma: the pollen-receiving tip of the pistil. (29)

stipule: a small leaf-like growth at the base of a petiole. (BE)

style: the part of the pistil between the stigma and ovary. (29)

subtend: to occur immediately below, as a bract *subtending* a flower.

succulent (of leaves or stems): juicy, fleshy; soft and thickened in texture.

superior: an ovary with the sepals, petals and stamens attached at or below its base. Opposite of *inferior*. (29)

taproot: a single major root, often fleshy, which continues downward in the same direction as the stem grows upward.

tepal: sepals and petals nearly identical in shape, form and colour; often found in the Lily and Rush Families.

terminal: at the end or tip of a stem or branch.

terrestrial: a plant growing on land, in soil.

toothed (of leaves): having several to many small indentations along the edge of the blade. (28) (BE)

trailing: running along the ground but not rooting.

tree: a woody perennial plant with a single branched trunk and few or no branches arising from the base; usually over 3 m at maturity.

tube (of flowers): the part of the calyx or corolla made up of fused or united sepals or petals; usually bell- or trumpet-shaped.

tuber: a short thickened underground branch bearing buds; stores food.

tundra: areas without trees in high mountains or northern latitudes.

umbel: a flower cluster in which all the flower stalks radiate from the same point like the ribs of an umbrella, e.g., dill, onions, etc. (FE)

unisexual (of flowers): having stamens or pistils but not both.

vascular: having veins or vessels; able to conduct water and nutrients from roots through stems to leaves and branches.

vein: one of the network of tiny channels or vessels in a leaf through which water and nutrients flow.

ventral: the lower side (of a leaf, petal, etc.).

whorled: arranged in a circle around a central point; commonly used to refer to three or more leaves coming from the same node. (27, 28)

wildflower: here used to mean any native vascular plant (not including algae, mosses, fungi, etc.). Usually herbs but also shrubs and trees.

wing: (1.) a flat, narrow membranous or leathery expansion extending along a stem, stalk or other part; (2.) the 2 side petals in a Pea or Bean Family flower.

xerophyte: a plant adapted to living in extremely dry conditions.

HOW THE KEY SYSTEM WORKS

Identification of a wildflower or other plant begins by answering five basic questions about it. The answers determine the group to which it belongs and you then refer to this group in the **Locator Keys.** These in turn are keyed to a page or section in the text where the plant and others similar to it are described and illustrated. Complete the identification by matching your plant to descriptions and illustrations in that section or, in the case of large or difficult groups, by referring to a subkey to that group and through that to the specific page.

It is of course possible to simply look through the book for a picture which matches the plant. However this can be misleading because of the natural variation which occurs in plants, the different stages of growth of your plant and the illustrated one, and the fact that some plants are only described in Notes and not illustrated. I hope, therefore, that readers will find the Locator Key system convenient to use as well as a more dependable and logical means of identification than merely looking through the book.

THE FIVE QUESTIONS

Flower Type
1. Is the flower regular (radially symmetrical) or irregular, or are the flower parts indistinguishable or nonexistent?
2. If regular, how many petals or similar coloured parts does it have?

Plant Type
3. Is the plant a wildflower, shrub, or tree?
4. If a wildflower, is it without leaves, or if it has leaves, are they all at the base of the plant, or are they arranged singly on the stem (alternate) or opposite one another in pairs or whorls?

Leaf Type
5. Are the leaves entire (with even and unbroken edges) or are they toothed, lobed or divided?

If you need an explanation or more information on the terms used above and in the keys, turn to the next sections, the Glossary or the endpapers of the book where all of the terms used are explained and/or illustrated.

DETERMINING THE PLANT GROUP
AND GROUP NUMBER

Each plant is classified in three ways using the headings in the FIVE QUESTIONS, i.e., **Flower Type**, **Plant Type**, and **Leaf Type**. The combination of these three classifications determines the **plant group** (indicated by a **group number**) to which the wildflower belongs.

The three classifications are:

Flower Type

1. Irregular Flowers
   (No local plants have Flowers with 2 Regular Parts)
3. Flowers with 3 Regular Parts
4. Flowers with 4 Regular Parts
5. Flowers with 5 Regular Parts
6. Flowers with 6 Regular Parts
7. Flowers with 7 or more Regular Parts
8. Flower Parts Indistinguishable or Nonexistent

Plant Type

1. Wildflowers with No Apparent Leaves
2. Wildflowers with Opposite or Whorled Leaves
3. Wildflowers with Basal Leaves Only
4. Wildflowers with Alternate Leaves
5. Shrubs
6. Trees

Leaf Type

1. No Apparent Leaves
2. Leaves Entire
3. Leaves Toothed or Lobed
4. Leaves Divided

The answers to the first two of the Five Questions allow you to assign the plant to one of the sections under **Flower Type**; the answers to the third and fourth questions will send you to the appropriate section under **Plant Type** and the answer to the fifth question will refer you to the proper section under **Leaf Type**.

Now combine the three section numbers as a 3-digit **group number**. For example, if the plant has an irregular flower (section 1 under **Flower Type**), is a wildflower with basal leaves (section 3 under **Plant Type**), and has entire leaves (section 2 under **Leaf Type**), its group number is 132. Another example: willows will be found in plant group 852 or 853 because they have indistinguishable flower parts (8–), are shrubs (85-), and have either entire (852) or toothed (853) leaves.

USING THE LOCATOR KEYS

Once you have the **group number**, find it in the left hand margin of the Locator Keys which begin on page 4l. The numbers are arranged in ascending order from the first to the last pages of the Keys. The wildflower should be among those on the pages mentioned on the right hand side of the Locator Key section under the group number. You can use the subsections of the Locator Key under the group number to come closer to your actual plant. The final step is to check the plant with the description and illustration on the page(s) given in the key.

To show how the system works on a wildflower which occurs in the Churchill region, here is an illustration of the Marsh Cinquefoil, and how you would use the key system to identify it.

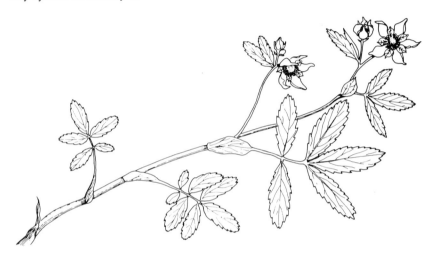

Step 1. **Answer the Five Questions.** The answers are:
  1. The flower is regular (radially symmetrical).
  2. It has 5 regular parts
  3. The plant is a wildflower
  4. The leaves are alternate on the stem
  5. The leaves are divided

Step 2. **Determine the group number** by matching your answer to the classifications on page 37. They are also given on the inside of the front cover:
  Regular flower with 5 parts: 5
  Wildflower with alternate leaves: 4
  Leaves divided: 4
  The group number for Marsh Cinquefoil is 544.

Step 3. **Find group number 544 in the Locator Keys.** Here is how the Locator Keys treat group number 544 (Page 47):

Leaves once palmately divided

  Leaflets 3; all terrestrial plants

    Flowers pink .... STEMLESS RASPBERRY   206
                          (*Rubus acaulis*)

    Flowers yellow .... CINQUEFOILS   208
                          (*Potentilla* spp.)   218-20

  Leaflets more than 3

    Flowers white; terrestrial

      plant...................................... SMALL WOOD ANEMONE   152
                          (*Anemone parviflora*)

    Flowers yellow; aquatic

      plant..................... SMALL YELLOW WATERCROWFOOT   202
                          (*Ranunculus purshii*)

Leaves one or more times pinnately divided

  Flowers white

    Flowers from same point (umbel); plants smooth;
    leaves twice divided into narrow,
    toothed segments .... WATER HEMLOCK   210
                          (*Cicuta mackenzieana*)

    Flowers from different points; leaves many times very
    finely divided

    Plant terrestrial; flowers with 5 (4-6) rays or 'petals'
    in compound heads; leaves lance-shaped
    in outline... YARROW/MILFOIL   212
                          (*Achillea nigrescens*)

    Plant aquatic; flower not in compound heads; leaves
    round or heart-shaped
    in outline............ LARGE-LEAVED WATERCROWFOOT   154
                          (*Ranunculus aquatilis*)

  Flowers yellow, red or purple .... CINQUEFOILS   208
                          (*Potentilla* spp.)   214-18

      The **first choice** in this subsection of the Key is to decide whether the leaves on the plant are palmately or pinnately divided. In this case they are pinnately divided which takes you to the second part of the Key. The **second choice** is then on the colour of the flowers, white versus other, which, the plant having purple/red flowers, takes you to the last part of the Key, the Cinquefoils. Each paired choice, and you should always check both choices for each step, is indicated by having the left hand margins aligned. The Marsh Cinquefoil will be found on one of the pages given in the right hand margin, along with its pinnately- divided-leaved, yellow-flowered relatives.

Step 4: **Turn to pages 214 through 218** where you will find the 4 members of this group described, 3 fully illustrated and one mentioned in a Note. As all except the Marsh Cinquefoil have yellow flowers, the final choice is clear.

      If the plant is not shown in the illustrations, read the COMMENTS and NOTE sections for each species in the group. These refer to similar plants on other pages and to closely related ones which could not be shown for lack of space.

If none of the descriptions fit the plant, you may have made an error somewhere along the way. Go back and redo every step in the key, paying special attention to any choices where you were uncertain. If you **were** uncertain at a particular step, try making the other choice (or another choice) which also seems to fit and see where you end up in the Key. You may have to do this several times, although I have tried to make the Key choices as clear and distinct as possible.

If you still cannot find the plant, it may be a rare or uncommon species which is not covered in the book, or it may be different from the normal pattern in some way (too small or too lush because of environmental patterns; an extra petal or two), or it might be a hybrid that even a trained botanist would find difficult to pin down. Such cases are unusual and the great majority of plants found in the Hudson Bay region should be readily identified using this book.

A complete list of all the vascular plant species known from Churchill is provided in the Appendix. There are, of course, many more arctic species in northern Hudson Bay and southern species around James Bay but again, the majority of species you are likely to encounter will be shown in the book or listed on the Technical Species List. If the plant keys to a genus or group, but doesn't match any of the descriptions provided, it is probably an uncommon member of that genus in the Churchill region.

If you would like to track it down further, consult one of the technical floras (Hulten, or Porsild and Cody) mentioned in the References. The keys in these books are more complicated, but work in basically the same way as those in this book, and illustrations are provided for most species.

As you gain experience in using this Key system, you will find that you can ignore the three-digit **group number** and use the Locator Key directly. This Key system is adapted from one used in **Newcomb's Wildflower Guide**, an excellent guidebook for wildflowers of the eastern United States and Canada.

A NOTE ABOUT SUBKEYS

Several large groups of plants that occur in this region have members which are very similar in appearance and separated on somewhat technical and difficult-to-see characters. These groups, the RUSHES, GRASSES, SEDGES, and WILLOWS, are provided with SUBKEYS at the beginning of their sections to aid you in identifying the common species. If you recognize the plant as a member of one of these groups, you can turn directly to that subkey or section to check on the species.

LOCATOR KEYS

IRREGULAR FLOWERS

FLOWERS WITH THREE REGULAR PARTS
(Only 1 plant in this section)

FLOWERS WITH FOUR REGULAR PARTS

* Phyllodace coerulea — Mtn heather — Cape Merry
Parnassia Kotzebuei — Goose Crk bog
* Linum lewisii u — Miss Piggy
* Betula occidentalis — NOT
  (neoalaskiana) HERE
* Campanula uniflora — Cape Merry
                      — Sloop's Cove
Draba alpina — rocks across from eNSC + other areas
     aurea — Road sides along Launch Rd
* Epilobium latifolium — N + S side of Ramsay R
Honkenya peploides — Bird Cove ↳ E. side
Ranunculus lapponicus — Landing Lake Rd bog ↳ also R Lake Rd beach ridge
Don't have? ⟨ parviflora
              richardsonii
Saxifraga aizoides — Ramsay Rd side
          — Launch Road side
          caespitosa — Rocks at Bird Cove back ouse
          cernua — Bird cove in its gravel area
          hirculus — Goose Crk bog
          — Akudlik marsh
          oppositifolia — lots of places in open tundra
* Kalmia microphylla — this variety not here only polifolia
Carex microglochin ⟨
              ↳ Bird Cove back ridge west side (common)

Josh — orchid Group
Room # 17

Diane Erickson
675 - 8866

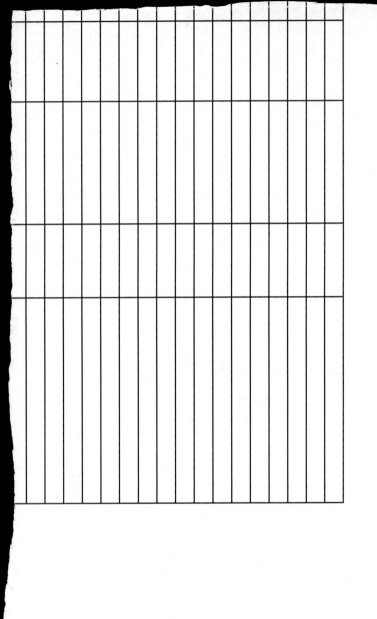

43

44

47

SHRUBS

FLOWERS WITH SEVEN OR MORE REGULAR PARTS

(Look under 5 regular parts if you can't find the flower here
e.g., ANEMONES, BUTTERCUPS, etc.)

WILDFLOWERS

FLOWERS WITH SEVEN OR MORE
REGULAR PARTS

WILDFLOWERS

*scale-like leaves present on flowering stem

FLOWERS WITH SEVEN OR MORE REGULAR PARTS

FLOWERS PARTS INDISTINGUISHABLE OR NONEXISTENT

FLOWER PARTS INDISTINGUISHABLE
OR NONEXISTENT

FLOWER PARTS INDISTINGUISHABLE OR NONEXISTENT

WILDFLOWERS

SHRUBS

(Following page)
Sandy beach showing typical dark ridge of
decomposing marine algae, Foreshore
Strand and Open Dune communities.
Foreshore community dominated by clumps
of Sea-Beach Sandwort and Open Dune
community by the tall Sea Lime Grass.

WILDFLOWER DESCRIPTIVE SPECIES ACCOUNTS

Text

All Species Accounts follow the format described below with the exception of the much condensed accounts on grasses and sedges.

Bold face headings at the top of the text page give the three classifications of the wildflower based on its flower type, plant type, and leaf type (see inside front cover and "How the Key System Works" section).

The group number and most acceptable common name of the Wildflower is then given on the upper left hand side, e.g. 123 YELLOWRATTLE followed by the scientific name in parentheses (*Rhinanthus borealis* Chab.). Across from this, on the upper right hand side, is given the common family name, e.g. FIGWORT FAMILY, and under this the scientific family name, e.g. Scrophulariaceae. The other categories contain the following information on this plant:

OTHER NAMES: Other common or regional names used for the plant. All are listed in the index.

DESCRIPTION: Physical features of the wildflower including height, types of leaves, flower colour and size, inflorescence, type of fruit, etc. which are useful in identification. Measurements are given in metric units, i.e. mm (millimeter), cm (centimeter), m (meter) and a metric ruler is given on the inside of the front cover. Tiny means under 5 cm tall; small means 5 to 15 cm tall.

HABITAT: The kind of places where this particular plant grows. The broad geographical range of habitats is given first and then habitats or plant communities in which it is found in the Churchill and Hudson Bay regions.

FLOWERING: The range of dates during which the wildflower can be expected to be found in bloom in the Churchill region.

COMMENTS: Anything of particular help in locating or identifying this wildflower or in distinguishing it from similar plants described elsewhere in the species accounts. Also interesting facts about its names, uses, or other features.

NOTE: A description and distinguishing features of one or more related plants **not illustrated** in the guidebook. Species covered in this way are given in bold face, e.g. ARCTIC LOCOWEED, when first introduced and then in lower case, e.g. Late Yellow Locoweed, as are species covered elsewhere in the guidebook.

RANGE: The geographical distribution of the plant. The world range is given first and then its distribution in the Hudson Bay region.

Illustrations

A combination of colour photographs, watercolour paintings, and pen and ink drawings has been used on the facing page to illustrate the plants as each medium has different strengths and weaknesses. Photographs have more vivid colours and show more of the surroundings of a particular plant but water colours usually have more accurate colour and can show all aspects – i.e. flowers and fruits – and all sides of a plant. Black and white drawings actually show more detail than watercolours for plants such as grasses and sedges which do not have brightly coloured leaves and flowers.

The flower colour shown is the most common for that species but all possible colours are given in the Description section.

IRREGULAR FLOWERS

Wildflowers With No Apparent Leaves; saprophytic orchids
with no green pigment....

III **Early Coralroot**

(Corallorhiza trifida (L.) Chat.)

ORCHID FAMILY
Orchidaceae

OTHER NAMES: Northern Coralroot

DESCRIPTION: Slender yellowish green **orchid**, 10-20 cm high, with **long brown leaf sheaths surrounding the lower stem.** The underground stem is coral-like (source of the common and scientific names), pale, and brittle. The 2-10 small 4-8 mm long **yellow green flowers** have narrow 1-nerved sepals and petals and a **lip** which is often **purple-spotted.** Flowers erect; capsules reflexed, spindle-shaped, and 0.5-1 cm long.

HABITAT: Moist to dry peat: found in White Spruce, Heath, and Lichen-Heath communities on the outcrop and gravel ridges (often associated with *Dryas* mats) and in Black Spruce Muskeg and Bog communities inland.

FLOWERING: Late June to mid-July

COMMENTS: Coralroots are saprophytic orchids without the green pigment chlorophyll and therefore unable to manufacture their own food. They live on decaying wood and dead plants, using these tissues as their source of food. Their leaves have been reduced to bladeless brown sheaths around the stem but they can easily be recognized as orchids from their distinctive flower. This is like a miniature commercial orchid with inferior ovary topped by 3 sepals, 2 petals, and a distinctive lobed lip. Not uncommon, the Early Coralroot can usually be found during its flowering period if you are willing to look closely at the ground in the proper habitats. Good places near Churchill include dry heaths along the coast road towards the airport, and bogs and muskegs along the Goose Creek road.

RANGE: Circumpolar wide ranging low arctic-subarctic-boreal species: occurs all around Hudson and James bays south of latitude 63°.

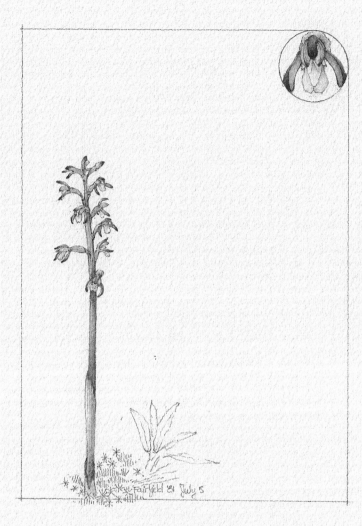

Coralloriza maculata

Fairfield '81 July 5

IRREGULAR FLOWERS

Wildflowers with Opposite Entire Leaves....

122 *Heart-Leaved Twayblade*

(*Listera cordata* (L.) R. Br.)

ORCHID FAMILY
Orchidaceae

OTHER NAMES: Lesser Twayblade; Twayblade Orchid

DESCRIPTION: A delicate perennial **orchid, 5-25 cm high**, its single **stem bearing a pair of opposite sessile** entire **triangular to heart-shaped leaves near the middle.** A good distinctive feature is that the distance between the lowest flowers and the leaves is greater than the length of the leaves. The **tiny**, 1-3 mm long, **greenish red to brownish purple flowers** have a **deeply divided lip** which is about twice the length of the petals. Fruit a small inflated ribbed capsule with the withered flowers at its tip.

HABITAT: Mossy areas under White Spruce in our region: White Spruce and Spruce/Larch Bog communities on outcrop and gravel ridges on both sides of the Churchill River.

FLOWERING: July

COMMENTS: This small orchid is seldom found even in southern regions. It is extremely rare at Churchill although this may be more the result of small size and dull coloration than actual numbers. The only Heart-Leaved Twayblades I've ever seen at Churchill were in a bog under White Spruce along the Goose Creek Road in mid-July. I was crawling along on the moss looking for an Early Coralroot which I had seen in bloom there the previous summer. The first Twayblade was 5 cm (2.5 inches) tall with 5-10 tiny, 1 mm long, flowers. Once I had seen the first plant, I quickly spotted 5 others, all on the same mossy hummock, but found none elsewhere in the area. It is an exquisite little plant and well worth 'bogging' to see.

RANGE: Circumpolar boreal-subarctic-montane species with large gaps: occurs around Hudson and James bays south of the latitude of Churchill (about 59° N).

NOTE: The NORTHERN TWAYBLADE (*Listera borealis* Morong.) is even less common than the Heart-Leaved but grows in similar habitats along the southern part of Hudson and James bays. It differs from the Heart-Leaved in having **oblong rather than triangular leaves** which are longer than the distance between the lowest flowers and leaves and a **slightly notched** rather than deeply divided **flower lip.**

60

x 6

IRREGULAR FLOWERS

Wildflowers with Opposite Toothed Leaves; flowers dark purple,
over 1 cm long....

123 **Velvet Bells**

(Bartsia alpina L.)

FIGWORT FAMILY
Scrophulariaceae

OTHER NAMES: Alpine Bartsia

DESCRIPTION: Erect, 5-15 cm high, tufted, glandular-hairy, **dark coloured perennials** with a somewhat woody rootstalk. Leaves opposite, oval, coarsely toothed, sessile and clasping, the lowermost scaly, the upper 1-2 cm long, dark purple, drying black. Flowers to 2 cm long, **corolla long-tubed, dark purple, snapdragon-like**, solitary in the upper leaf axils and forming a dense cluster at the tip of the stem. Calyx 4-lobed, stamens 4 in two pairs under the upper lip of the flower. Fruit a 1 cm long capsule which produces winged seeds.

HABITAT: Moist to dry open peaty, mossy, and gravelly areas: Heath communities on the outcrop and gravel ridges and Hummocky Bog, Lichen-Heath and Pressure Ridge communities inland. Often found at the edge of, or just under, willows and White Spruce in the Churchill area and sometimes on disturbed moist gravel. Occurs in grass-dominated arctic meadows further north.

FLOWERING: July to early August: peak usually mid-July

COMMENTS: This extremely attractive small relative of the Snapdragon is found throughout the Churchill area except immediately along the coast. It is certainly not rare and can easily be found in the proper habitats during July. The black colour of the dried plant results from chemicals produced by its semi-parasitic life style as Velvet Bells gets some of its food from the roots of other plants. Most members of the Figwort or Snapdragon Family are semi-parasites and they, as well as most true parasites and saprophytes, also blacken on drying.

RANGE: Amphi-Atlantic subarctic-arctic-montane species. Near the northern and western limits of its range at Churchill, it occurs from the Manitoba/Northwest Territory border around most of the southern and eastern sides of Hudson Bay although it appears to be missing between Churchill and the Ontario border.

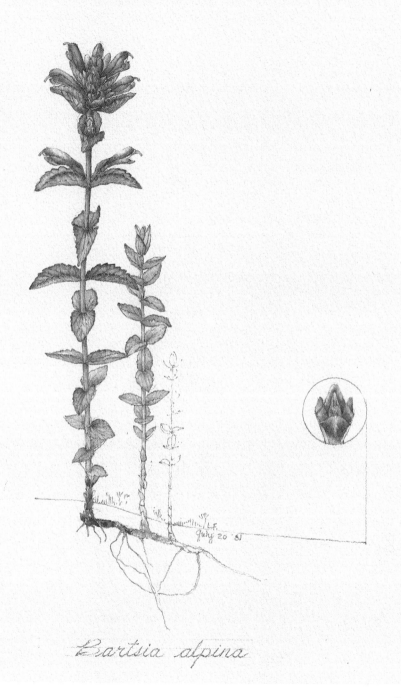

Bartsia alpina

IRREGULAR FLOWERS

Wildflowers with Opposite Toothed Leaves; flowers yellow, 1 cm or under....

123 ***Yellowrattle***

(*Rhinanthus borealis* Chab.)

FIGWORT FAMILY
Scrophulariaceae

OTHER NAMES: Yellow Rattlebox; Rattleseed; Boreal or Northern Yellow Rattle

DESCRIPTION: A somewhat branching annual plant, 30-50 cm tall, with **opposite sessile coarsely toothed** lanceolate, **3-5 cm long leaves. Flowers chrome yellow, snapdragon-like**, 6-10 mm long, and borne in the axils of upper leaves. **Calyx** hairy, 4-toothed, greenish yellow, thin, flattened sideways and **greatly inflating** at maturity. It contains the fruiting capsule which produces round winged 4 mm wide seeds.

HABITAT: Dry open sand or gravel areas, preferably calcareous, often pioneering on disturbed soils: Sandy Foreshore and Stable Dune communities, disturbed gravel along roadsides.

FLOWERING: Late July through August: peak usually in early August

COMMENTS: Yellowrattle is one of those annuals which seem to spring from nowhere in the late summer and fall. It occurs only occasionally but is relatively easy to find along the coast and on disturbed roadsides. The common name comes from the rattling of the large seeds within the dried capsule. It is another of the semi-parasitic members of the Figwort Family which blacken upon drying (see Velvet Bells pg. 62).

RANGE: Primarily a North American (Greenland/Iceland) subarctic to boreal-montane species: occurs in our region from the southern Northwest Territories around James Bay to about half-way up the eastern side of Hudson Bay.

IRREGULAR FLOWERS

Wildflowers with Opposite Toothed Leaves; flowers white and purple, under 1 cm long; calyx not inflated....

123 Northern Eyebright

FIGWORT FAMILY
Scrophulariaceae

(*Euphrasia arctica* Lange)

OTHER NAMES: Arctic Eyebright

DESCRIPTION: **Slender annuals,** 2-25 cm high, with 3-10 pairs of small oval **coarsely toothed sessile leaves.** The 3-8 mm long **snapdragon-like flowers** occur in a rather dense leafy spike and are **white with lavender or pale blue veins,** the upper lip bluish tinged, the lobes of the flaring lower lip notched in the centre. Mature capsules much larger than the long-toothed calyx, about as long as the petals.

HABITAT: Open, often disturbed areas, usually sand or gravel: Stable Dune, outcrop and gravel ridge communities; roadsides and other disturbed sites around Churchill.

FLOWERING: Late July through August: annual and therefore late in the growing season

COMMENTS: These small annuals occur in dense masses on disturbed gravel areas such as roadsides in the late summer and fall. The small flowers are very attractive and well worth a good look through a hand lens. *Euphrasia* is the Greek word for "cheerfulness" and the common names are an allusion to the ancient belief in the plant's value in clarifying eyesight and curing other ills of the eye.

RANGE: Primarily North American arctic-subarctic, boreal-montane species; found in similar habitats in a few places in Eurasia: occurs all around Hudson Bay except the far northwestern quarter.

IRREGULAR FLOWERS

Wildflowers with Basal Entire Solitary Leaf; flowers greenish white with spur....

Small Northern Bog Orchid

(*Habenaria obtusata* (Pursh) Richards.)

ORCHID FAMILY
Orchidaceae

OTHER NAMES: Blunt-Leaved Orchis; Blunt-Leaf Orchid

DESCRIPTION: Slender perennial orchid, 10-25 cm high, with a smooth stem and **one** sessile basal oval to lanceolate **blunt-tipped leaf.** The small **greenish white orchid-type flowers** are about 1 cm long in a few-flowered cluster at the tip of the stem. The **lip** of the flower is **narrow and deflexed;** the **spur slender** and about as long as the lip. The fruit is a stalked capsule.

HABITAT: Moist mossy or peaty sheltered areas, usually under shrubs (willows or Dwarf Birch) or spruce trees: White Spruce communities on outcrop and gravel ridges; under larger shrubs and muskeg trees everywhere except immediately along the coast.

FLOWERING: Late June to end of July: peak usually in mid-July

COMMENTS: This small orchid is common-to-abundant in moss mats throughout the Churchill area. It and the Round-Leaved are the two commonest orchids in the region but the Small Northern Bog Orchid is much smaller, inconspicuous in colour, and therefore more likely to be overlooked. Its flowers are regularly cross-pollinated by mosquitoes and the insects can often be seen flying near the plants with 'horns' of yellow pollen masses on their heads. You can see the pollination mechanism in action by poking a pencil, pen, or small twig under the hood of the flower. The sticky pollen masses will spring forward and attach themselves to the intruder.

RANGE: Widespread boreal to subarctic species, primarily North American but found in a few scattered localities in northern Eurasia: occurs all around Hudson and James bays except on the far northern coast.

Churchill
July 3 1981

L.F.

Habenaria obtusata

IRREGULAR FLOWERS
Wildflowers with Basal Entire Solitary Leaf; flowers white with purple spots....

Round-Leaved Orchid

(*Orchis rotundifolia* Banks)

ORCHID FAMILY
Orchidaceae

OTHER NAMES: Rhizome Orchis; Small Round-Leaved Orchid; Fly-Specked Orchid

DESCRIPTION: A perennial **orchid**, 4-25 cm high, with a smooth scape from a short rhizome with fleshy fibrous roots. The **single**, oval to almost round, **leaf** is **basal** or nearly so and 2-8 cm long, often with 1-2 sheathing scales below it. **Flowers** few (to 10) and showy, 1-1.5 cm long, **white or rose with** a **short slender spur**, the 3-lobed **lip white with purple spots**. Fruit an elliptical capsule.

HABITAT: Moist peaty and mossy areas; restricted to sphagnum bogs in the south: White Spruce communities on outcrop and gravel ridges; Hummocky Bog communities usually under or near willows, and disturbed moist peaty areas.

FLOWERING: July

COMMENTS: This very attractive small orchid was first described from specimens seen or collected from Hudson Bay by Sir Joseph Banks, a botanical collector and patron of the sciences, who accompanied Captain Cook on his first voyage. It is common to locally abundant at Churchill, usually occurring in large patches and easily spotted by its distinctive flowers. Especially good places to look for it are the peatlands behind Bird Cove and Camp Nanook and moist disturbed peaty areas near Akudlik.

RANGE: North American (Greenland) boreal species: occurs around southern Hudson Bay from Churchill to the eastern side of James Bay.

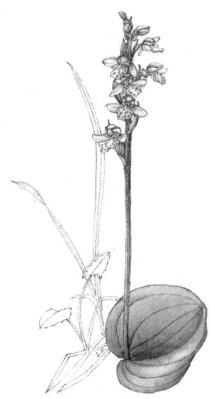

Churchill
July 5, 1981

Orchis rotundifolia Banks
ROUND-LEAVED ORCHID

71

Wildflowers with Basal Entire Leaves in a rosette of
several succulent leaves....

132 *Common Butterwort*

(*Pinguicula vulgaris* L.)

BLADDERWORT FAMILY
Lentibulariaceae

OTHER NAMES: Bog-Violet

DESCRIPTION: Dwarf perennial herb, usually under 10 cm in our region, with a **basal rosette of yellow green entire succulent sticky** or 'greasy' 1-3 cm long **leaves with inrolled edges.** Scape slender, solitary, essentially smooth, bearing a single light to dark purple **violet-like flower,** 1-2 cm long, with a flower tube with white hairs in the throat and a long straight spur. Fruit a ball-shaped capsule.

HABITAT: Open moist peat; damp calcareous sand, gravel, and clay: Heath communities on outcrop and gravel ridges; Hummocky Bog community and gravel and clay shores of streams, ponds, and lakes.

FLOWERING: July to early August: peak usually early to mid-July

COMMENTS: The basal rosettes of this little carnivorous plant are completely distinctive – nothing else resembles them. Their sticky and greasy leaf surfaces trap and digest small insects and I have seen close to 500 black flies stuck on one large Butterwort at Churchill. The digestive enzyme present in the leaves is used to curdle milk in some Scandinavian and Eastern European countries.

The Common Butterwort is abundant at Churchill in most moist open areas fairly close to the coast. The young leaf rosettes can be seen expanding in late June with the flowers appearing soon after.

RANGE: Circumpolar alpine-subarctic to boreal species: occurs south of latitude 61° all around Hudson and James bays.

NOTE: The SMALL or HAIRY BUTTERWORT, (*Pinguicula villosa* L.), is also found at Churchill and scattered locations elsewhere along Hudson Bay. It can be distinguished from the Common by its **smaller size** (flowers always less than and leaves usually only 1 cm long), by its **hairy lower scape,** and by its habitat. It grows only on hummocks of S*phagnum* or other **acid-loving mosses** in inland bogs such as those along the Goose Creek and Landing Lake roads. This tiny plant requires close inspection (usually from your knees) to find its rosettes and flowers and blooms in early to mid-July.

Pinguicula vulgaris

LF
82 JULY 10

73

IRREGULAR FLOWERS

Wildflowers with Alternate Entire Leaves; flowers more than 3,
whitish, without spur....

132
142

Hooded Lady's-Tresses

(*Spiranthes romanzoffiana* Cham. and Schlect.)

ORCHID FAMILY
Orchidaceae

DESCRIPTION: A perennial **orchid**, 15-40 cm high, from fleshy roots which sometimes resemble tubers. Lower half of stem leafy with narrow to lanceolate alternate entire leaves which are reduced to bracts on the upper half. **Flowers** usually **numerous** and **in 3 spirals**, 1-1.5 cm long, **white and fragrant**, the sepals and 2 petals forming an upper hood, the lower lip fiddle-shaped. Bracts longer than the flowers. Fruit a small elliptical capsule.

HABITAT: Bogs, wet meadows and edges of streams, usually calcareous: Meadow-Marsh, Hummocky Bog and Willow Thicket communities; moist gravel along roadsides; edges of streams, pools, and lakes. Often associated with willows or other shrubs.

FLOWERING: Late July to mid-August

COMMENTS: This very attractive late-blooming orchid is the only one in our area with white flowers in a spiral. It tends to grow in clumps of 3-12 and is reasonably common around Churchill. Good places to look for it are the meadow-marshes along the Goose Creek Road and disturbed gravel areas near Akudlik. The flowers are sweetly fragrant, reminding some people of vanilla, also an orchid. The plant was named after Nicholas Romanzoff, an eighteenth century Russian minister of state and patron of the sciences.

RANGE: Boreal North American species with relict populations in Ireland and Scotland: occurs in our region from Churchill south around Hudson Bay to the eastern side of James Bay.

SPIRAL PLAN

AUG 15 1977

CHURCHILL

Spiranthes romanzoffiana

133
134
143
144

Purple Rattle
(*Pedicularis sudetica* Willd.)

FIGWORT FAMILY
Scrophulariaceae

OTHER NAMES: Swedish Lousewort; Sudetan Lousewort; Fernweed

DESCRIPTION: Low perennial herb (usually under 30 cm) with a cluster of **basal long petioled deeply lobed leaves**, the narrow lobes again toothed or lobed. One to several **smooth dark purple stems** from a stout branched rhizome, stem sometimes bearing 1 to 3 small lobed leaves. The terminal flower cluster at first dense but elongating in fruit, bearing a **white-woolly cluster** of **deep pink** to **dark reddish purple flowers. Flowers** 1.3 to 2.5 cm long, 2-lipped **like a snapdragon**, the upper lip helmet-shaped with 2 distinct teeth near the tip, the lower 3-lobed. Fruit an oblong capsule with a short beak and containing a few large seeds.

HABITAT: Moist to wet calcareous tundra and lake shores: Wet Meadow and moist to wet Heath communities near the coast and along the edges of ponds and streams.

FLOWERING: Early July to early August: peak usually mid-July

COMMENTS: This is the showiest of the 6 species of lousewort found at Churchill because of the size and colour of its flowers and its tendency to grow in large groups. It can be easily found in mid-July on the gravel beaches around ponds along the Launch and Landing Lake roads, east of Akudlik, and inland from Bird Cove. All the louseworts are believed to be semi-parasitic and darken drastically on drying. Their generic name comes from the Latin word for ''louse'', the result of a belief that cattle feeding where some species were common became infested with lice. All species of *Pedicularis* can be eaten raw or used as a pot-herb, the roots or young flowering stems being used in this fashion by both Siberian and North American native peoples.

RANGE: Circumpolar (absent in Greenland) wide ranging arctic-alpine and montane species: occurs around the northern and western but not up the eastern coast of Hudson Bay and all around James Bay.

July 18. '81

Pedicularis sudetica

IRREGULAR FLOWERS
Wildflowers with Basal Divided Leaves....

134 *Late Yellow Locoweed*

PEA FAMILY

(*Oxytropis campestris* (L.) DC. var. *johannensis* Fern.)

Leguminosae

OTHER NAMES: Northern Yellow Oxytrope; Field Oxytrope

DESCRIPTION: Perennial plant from a stout many-headed taproot with **basal, pinnately-divided,** 5-15 cm long **leaves** with an odd number of opposite 1-2 cm leaflets which are oval to lanceolate in shape and covered with silky hairs. Scape 10-30 cm tall, with a dense cluster of 6-25 flowers which elongates in fruit. Calyx with sharp awl-like teeth and a mixture of black and white hairs. **Flowers yellow, creamy white, or blue purple, pea- or bean-shaped,** 1.2-2.0 cm long with a fine point on the lower recurved beak. Fruit a 1-2 cm long pod (legume) which is erect, sessile and covered with black and white hairs.

HABITAT: Sandy, gravelly, and rocky areas; also dry heath: Stable Dune community; Heath and Lichen-Heath communities on the outcrop and gravel ridges and disturbed dry to moist gravel.

FLOWERING: July to early August

COMMENTS: Our particular locoweed is easily identifiable except for the variation in flower colour. The yellow-flowered form is fairly common in dry areas near the coast although never present in large patches. The blue/purple-flowered form has only rarely been seen, usually on dry heath on the outcrop ridge. Both can easily be told from the closely related milk-vetches (*Astragalus* spp.) by their leafless scapes. Milk-vetches, by contrast, have true stems with pinnate leaves. Almost all locoweeds produce chemicals which can be **poisonous** to man and animals. Their common name comes from the 'loco' way horses and other animals act after eating the plants. This is not a good group to nibble!

RANGE: This complex species (or complex of species) is of circumpolar arctic, subarctic, and boreal distribution, with large gaps in North America. One botanist goes so far as to call this group an especially wide rubbish-heap of species and it may include many unrelated plants. The yellow-flowered form occurs from near the Manitoba/Northwest Territories border south along Hudson Bay to the western coast of James Bay. The blue-flowered form is known only from Churchill on the western side of the Bay and near the northeastern tip on the eastern side.

NOTE: Another species of locoweed, BELL'S or the ARCTIC LOCOWEED (*Oxytropis bellii* (Britt.) Palibine) has also been reported from gravel areas at Churchill and the northern end of Hudson Bay. It differs from the Late Yellow in having **fewer larger dark purple flowers** and **leaflets** usually **in whorls of 3-4** rather than opposite pairs.

The only other locoweed you are likely to see on Hudson Bay is, appropriately enough, the HUDSONIAN LOCOWEED or OXYTROPE (*Oxytropis hudsonica* (Greene) Fern.). It occurs on gravel beaches and ridges along the southern and northwestern coast of Hudson Bay but is not known along the Manitoba coast from the Northwest Territories to York Factory. It has **fragrant light purple flowers**, is **densely black haired** on the flowering head, and has obvious glands all over the plant which are best seen with a good hand lens. Neither of the other species has glands.

IRREGULAR FLOWERS

Wildflowers with Alternate Entire Leaves; 1 to 3 flowers with white pouched lip....

142 ## Northern Lady's-Slipper

ORCHID FAMILY
Orchidaceae

(Cypripedium passerinum Richards.)

OTHER NAMES: Franklin's Lady's-Slipper; Sparrow's-Egg Lady's Slipper

DESCRIPTION: Perennial **orchid** with 15-25 cm tall leafy stems from a thick creeping fibrous rootstalk. Stem **leaves** 3-4, **large and sticky-hairy** on both sides. **Flowers** 1-3, usually one, **fragrant** and subtended by a leafy bract. Sepals green and distinctly veined, about 1.5 cm long, the upper hood-shaped and nearly covering the opening of the '**pouched' lip petal**, the lower more linear and longer than the side petals. **Petals pale green to pure white, the sac-like lip translucent and inflated,** 1-2 cm long, and purple-spotted inside. Fruit a 2-3 cm long erect oblong capsule.

HABITAT: Moist basic or calcareous sandy or gravelly areas, usually associated with spruce trees or tall shrubs: White Spruce and Willow communities on outcrop and gravel ridges and moist disturbed gravel areas such as roadsides.

FLOWERING: July: peak usually mid-month

COMMENTS: This is the largest and showiest of the native orchids and the only lady's-slipper found on Hudson Bay, reaching its northern limit at Churchill. The 'pouch' of the flower lip is absolutely distinctive and characteristic of the lady's-slippers. It often occurs in clumps of several dozen plants but these tend to be widely separated. A good place to look for it is among willows on the southern edge of the road just west of Akudlik. It also occurs just east of the airport road across from Akudlik as well as near White Spruce by the crashed Lambair plane on the outcrop ridge. In life, with the purple spots showing through, the flower's lip reminded botanists of a bird's egg. This resulted in both the specific and one of the common names as *passerinum* means "of sparrows".

RANGE: Boreal to barely subarctic North American species; mostly western North American with disjunct populations on the northeastern shore of Lake Superior and the Mingan Islands in the St. Lawrence River: found from Churchill south to the eastern shore of James Bay but completely missing from the eastern and northern coasts of Hudson Bay.

seed capsule

Cypripeduim passerinum
NORTHERN LADY'S SLIPPER

Churchill
July 13, '81

L.F.

81

Wildflowers with Alternate Entire Leaves; flowers greenish with a spur....

142 ## *Green-Flowered Bog Orchid*

ORCHID FAMILY
Orchidaceae

(*Habenaria hyperborea* (L.) R.Br.)

OTHER NAMES:	Northern Green Orchis or Orchid; Northern Bog Orchid; Northern Green Leafy Orchid
DESCRIPTION:	Fairly stout leafy stemmed perennial, 7-40 cm high, with oblong lanceolate to lanceolate leaves. **Lower** flower **bracts as long as,** or longer than, the **small greenish or greenish yellow orchid-type flowers.** Flowers few to numerous, about 1 cm long, in a dense slender spike. Flower **lip entire, lanceolate,** tapering to a **blunt tip, spur slightly longer than lip.** Fruit a plump 1-1.5 cm long capsule.
HABITAT:	Wet places, especially river banks, lake shores, mossy spruce woods, and muskegs: Damp Dune Hollow, Stable Dune, Wet Meadow, Hummocky Bog (under willows) and White Spruce communities.
FLOWERING:	July to early August: peak usually mid-July
COMMENTS:	A common and widespread orchid, more widespread than, but not as abundant as, the Small Northern Bog Orchid in the Churchill area. Especially common around the ponds and lakes along the Landing Lake Road and behind Akudlik.
RANGE:	Wide ranging boreal North American (Greenland/Iceland) species: found from Churchill south around Hudson Bay to about half way up the eastern coast.

Churchill
July 28, 1981

Habenaria hyperborea

Wildflowers with Alternate Entire leaves; more than 3 rose to purple flowers....

142 *Purple Paintbrush*

FIGWORT FAMILY
Scrophulariaceae

(*Castilleja raupii* Pennell)

OTHER NAMES: Raup's Painted-Cup; Indian Paintbrush

DESCRIPTION: Tufted perennial, 15-30 cm high, from a short branching taproot. Stems bear alternate **sessile narrow** 4-5 cm long **leaves,** usually entire but sometimes having 1 or 2 very narrow lobes or appendages. Inflorescence dense and compact, the **inconspicuous** two-lipped **snapdragon-like flowers hidden behind** much larger and **showier pale pink to dark purple floral bracts.** The flowers are green with purple margins, the upper lip helmet-shaped, the lower 3-lobed. Fruit is a short, plump capsule.

HABITAT: Well-drained open areas, mossy stream and lake shores: Sandy Foreshore, Open and Stable Dune communities; Heath and Lichen-Heath communities on outcrop and gravel ridges; wet meadows and disturbed moist gravel on roadsides and ridges.

FLOWERING: Late June to mid-August: peak usually mid-July

COMMENTS: The Purple Paintbrush, like many in its family, is a semi-parasitic plant which gets part of its food from the roots of grass-like plants (see Velvet Bells). It is widespread and common to abundant in the Churchill region especially on sandy beach and dune areas along the coast and on gravel ridges. It takes its name from the cluster of brightly coloured floral bracts which make the plant look as if it had been dipped in paint.

RANGE: Subarctic western North American species reaching its eastern limit at James Bay: occurs south along the western coast of Hudson Bay from latitude 62°N extending around to the eastern side of James Bay.

NOTE: Other species of paintbrushes have yellow and red flower bracts but the only one known to occur on Hudson Bay is the PALE or LABRADOR PAINTBRUSH (*Castilleja elegans* (Ostenf.) Malte) which has been found along the northwestern coast. It has **yellow or yellow green bracts.**

Castilleja raupii

JULY 24 '8? LF

CHURCHILL

85

IRREGULAR FLOWERS

Wildflowers with Alternate Deeply Lobed Leaves; yellow flowers with dark blunt tips....

143
144

Flame-Coloured Lousewort

(*Pedicularis flammea* L.)

FIGWORT FAMILY
Scrophulariaceae

OTHER NAMES: Flame-Tipped or Upright Lousewort

DESCRIPTION: Low perennial, 2-20 cm high with nearly hairless, often reddish, **simple unbranched stems** from widely branching fleshy yellow roots. **Leaves** mostly basal but 1-3 alternate stem leaves present, all blades **deeply pinnately-lobed,** the oval **lobes toothed.** Inflorescence usually few-flowered, of scentless narrow 6-10 mm long **snapdragon-like flowers,** the **beakless helmet deep yellow with a distinct blackish red to purple tip,** the lower lip bright yellow. Fruit a long stalked 1-1.5 cm long dark pointed capsule.

HABITAT:

Moist calcareous meadows and marshes; drier peat or gravel: Meadow-Marsh, Heath, and Hummocky Bog communities.

FLOWERING:

COMMENTS: Late June to early July

This smallest of the louseworts is inconspicuous but not uncommon at Churchill. It is really a beautiful little plant, seldom reaching over 10 cm in our area and growing most typically as scattered individuals on moist to dry heath along or fairly close to the coast. Cape Merry, Bird Cove, the coast road, and near Launch are good places to look for it. You must get down on your knees and look closely to find it, but once seen, the dark-tipped yellow flowers are unmistakeable and unforgettable. See the comments on Purple Rattle (pg. 76) for other information on louseworts.

RANGE:

Primarily North American arctic-alpine species with a few sites in northern Europe: occurs around most of Hudson and northern James bays with apparent gaps on the east central side of Hudson Bay and between Churchill and the Ontario border.

NOTE:

The PURPLE LOUSEWORT (Pedicularis parviflora J. E. Sm) has been reported from York Factory and a few other sites on the western side of Hudson Bay. It has **rose purple flowers** and many alternate pinnately-lobed stem leaves.

Churchill
July '81

Pedicularis flamea

IRREGULAR FLOWERS

Wildflowers with Alternate Deeply Lobed Leaves; yellow flowers....

Lapland Lousewort
(*Pedicularis lapponica* L.)

FIGWORT FAMILY
Scrophulariaceae

OTHER NAMES: Lapland Rattle

DESCRIPTION: A low, 10-20 cm high perennial from a slender branching rootstalk. One to several **unbranched purplish brown stems** bear alternate, **lanceolate, pinnately-lobed leaves** which have a broad central part and small oval toothed lobes. Basal long-petioled leaves are gradually reduced in size upwards along the stem. Terminal inflorescence short, few-flowered, with horizontal **fragrant light yellow snapdragon-like** 10-15 mm long **flowers**. Upper **helmet-shaped flower lip arched, with** a short but **obvious beak** at right angles to the lip; lower lip 3-lobed and about as long as the upper. Fruiting capsule dark, 1-1.5 cm long, oblong to lanceolate in shape and sharply pointed.

HABITAT: Dry to moist open peaty areas: Heath and Lichen-Heath communities especially associated with White Spruce on the outcrop ridge.

FLOWERING: Late June to mid-July

COMMENTS: This small lousewort is relatively common on heath areas at Churchill, especially those near the coast. It can be found on Cape Merry, along the Launch Road, near Akudlik, and at Bird Cove.

RANGE: Circumpolar subarctic-arctic-alpine species: occurs all around Hudson Bay.

NOTE: The only other common yellow lousewort at Churchill is the LABRADOR LOUSEWORT or EYEBRIGHT PEDICULARIS (*Pedicularis labradorica* Wirsing). This species is usually taller than the Lapland, **much-branched** and has **no beak but 2 small teeth** on the often red or purple spotted flower helmet. It blooms during July and is found in similar habitats but usually further inland than the Lapland. It is a circumpolar arctic-alpine-boreal species and is found at most places around Hudson Bay. For more information on the louseworts see the comments section of Purple Rattle (pg. 76).

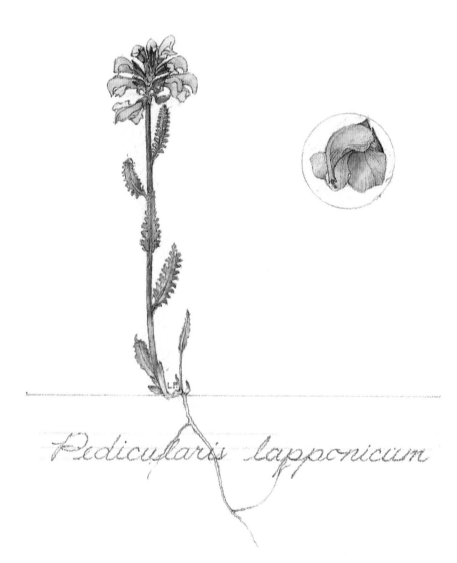

Pedicularis lapponicum

IRREGULAR FLOWERS
Wildflowers with Alternate Deeply Lobed Leaves; purple flowers....

143
144
Elephant's-Head
(*Pedicularis groenlandica* Retz.)

FIGWORT FAMILY
Scrophulariaceae

OTHER NAMES: Greenland Lousewort; Little Elephants; Little Red Elephants

DESCRIPTION: A nearly smooth perennial plant with stout erect **dark reddish purple stems**, 30-60 cm tall from a taproot. **Leaves long-petioled** and often clustered at the base, gradually reduced in size and becoming sessile on the upper stem, **pinnately-lobed**, the lobes strongly toothed or again deeply lobed. 1-1.5 cm long **pink to dark purple flowers** are borne in an elongated spike, 5-15 cm long. They **look like little pink elephant heads** (ears, trunk and all) and are absolutely distinctive. Nothing else in the North looks anything like them and you needn't even have been drinking to see them. The 'trunk' is the upper lip of the flower which curves forward and upwards well beyond the lower lip, 3 lobes of which form the 'ears' and lower part of the 'elephant's head'. Fruit is a blackish oval sharp-tipped capsule.

HABITAT: Damp humus areas and banks of streams and gullies, usually on calcareous soil: Meadow-Marsh communities and disturbed moist gravel near water.

FLOWERING: Mid-July to early August

COMMENTS: Unfortunately, this striking plant is not common at Churchill. There are 2 fair-sized colonies along streams just behind and to the west of Akudlik and it has also been reported from wet meadows near Launch and "wet open glades in the woods just south of town". It is very common further south on the beach ridges between York Factory and the Ontario border. The beautiful little flowers are designed to prevent hybridization with other species of louseworts, the position of the stigma and style within the long 'trunk' ensuring that only pollen from the same species gets to the stigma. See comments on Purple Rattle (pg. 76) for other information on louseworts. Purple Rattle sometimes keys to this section. It has mostly basal deeply lobed leaves and a detailed description may be found under that species on page 76.

RANGE: North American (Greenland) subarctic-alpine species: occurs in our region from the latitude of Churchill south around Hudson and James bays.

90

Pedicularis groenlandica

IRREGULAR FLOWERS

Wildflowers with Alternate Divided Leaves with More Than 3 Leaflets;
round pods which split open along one side....

144 *Alpine Milk-Vetch*

(*Astragalus alpinus* L.)

PEA FAMILY
Leguminosae

DESCRIPTION: Low, matted perennial plant with **weak, creeping, freely branched stems** which are seldom over 20 cm tall in our region. **Leaves** alternate, **pinnately-divided** into 11-29 oval to elliptical 1-2 cm long leaflets. Axillary flower stalks bear a short loose cluster of 9-15 mm long **whitish to blue purple pea-type flowers** which are usually darker at the tips. Fruiting pods (legumes) 8-12 mm long, plump, usually reflexed, and black hairy, with a distinct groove on top and a sharp point.

HABITAT: Moist to dry calcareous sandy to gravelly areas: Stable Dune community; heath and open gravel areas on outcrop and gravel ridges; disturbed gravel areas such as roadsides.

FLOWERING: Late June to mid-August: peak usually early to mid-July

COMMENTS: One of the commonest wildflowers on the exposed summits of the outcrop and gravel ridges at Churchill. This small relative of the pea is locally abundant and produces attractive large mats of bluish flowers in season. Especially good places to look for it are the beaches below the town centre and near Fort Prince of Wales.

RANGE: Circumpolar widespread arctic-subarctic-alpine species: found all around Hudson and James bays.

NOTE: The only other milk-vetch found in our region is the far less common ELEGANT or PRETTY MILK-VETCH, (*Astragalus eucosmus* Robins.), which is occasionally found from Churchill south around Hudson and James bays. It grows in the same habitats and blooms at about the same time as the Alpine Milk-Vetch. It can be distinguished by its **taller, non matted form;** smaller, well separated, completely **dark blue purple flowers;** its fewer and narrower leaflets, and its shorter and ungrooved pods.

92

IRREGULAR FLOWERS

Wildflowers with Alternate, Divided Leaves; more than 3 leaflets and flat
pods which split into sections....

144 **Northern Hedysarum**

PEA FAMILY

(Hedysarum mackenzii Richards.)

Leguminosae

OTHER NAMES: Mackenzie's Hedysarum; Wild Sweet Pea; Sweet Vetch (local)

DESCRIPTION: Perennial with numerous 15-35 cm high stems from a woody base and thick fibrous taproot. Alternate **leaves pinnately-divided** into 7-17 linear lanceolate, 1-1.5 cm long **leaflets**, smooth and green above, **silvery hairy below. Flowers** 5-25, **red purple or rarely pure white, pea-or bean-like, fragrant,** 2.5-3 cm long and in a very showy elongating inflorescence. **Fruiting pods** (legumes) **flat and jointed** breaking into 3-6 oval, one-seeded, conspicuously veined segments at maturity.

HABITAT: Rocky slopes; calcareous clays, sands and gravels, often along river and lake shores: Sandy Foreshore, Open and Stable Dune communities along the coast; disturbed gravel and sandy areas on gravel ridges and roadsides.

FLOWERING: End of June to end of July

COMMENTS: This abundant showy and sweet scented plant annually forms masses of reddish purple on the beaches and gravel ridges around Churchill, usually in early July. Locally called 'Sweet Vetch', it often grows with Dryas and they give fantastic floral displays of purple and white. There are conflicting reports on its edibility and, as the family has some very poisonous members (see locoweeds), it is probably just as well not to nibble on it. Especially good places to look for it at Churchill are the cobble beaches along the northern side of Cape Merry and around Fort Prince of Wales and the gravel ridges near the 'radar' domes. It differs from the closely related locoweeds in having leaves along the stem and from the milk-vetches in having flat segmented pods rather than round unjointed bean-type ones.

RANGE: North American arctic-subarctic-alpine species: occurs from the northwestern corner of Hudson Bay to the northern parts of James Bay; apparently missing on the eastern side of Hudson Bay.

NOTE: The ALPINE or AMERICAN HEDYSARUM (Hedysarum alpinum L. var. americanum Michx.) has been found in a few places along the western side of Hudson Bay. It differs from the Northern in having **more leaflets, fewer pod segments, unequal calyx teeth shorter than the calyx tube** and two-toned **light pink to pale purple unscented flowers.**

Churchill

Hedysarum mackenzii

FLOWERS WITH THREE REGULAR PARTS
Wildflowers or Shrubs with Alternate, Entire Leaves

352
852

Black Crowberry
(*Empetrum nigrum* L.)

CROWBERRY FAMILY
Empetraceae

OTHER NAMES: Curlewberry

DESCRIPTION: **Dwarf matted shrub,** under 10 cm in height, with short (5 mm) thick **evergreen needle-like leaves resembling heather** or a tiny trailing spruce tree. Its tiny pink to purple flowers are so inconspicuous and of such short duration that they are seldom noticed. More characteristic is the developing **hard green berry** which turns a **deep purple black in the fall.** Crowberry forms extensive mats, often covering large areas of ground.

HABITAT: Acid moist peat and gravel everywhere around Churchill: Stable Dune, Hummocky Bog, and White Spruce Forest communities; outcrop and gravel ridges.

FLOWERING: June: usually very early just after snow melt.

COMMENTS: One of the most abundant of the dwarf shrubs at Churchill, its juicy edible black berries are relished by birds, mammals, and people. Although not the best of the local berries, having an insipid or mildly medicinal taste, they improve somewhat upon freezing and are a favourite of the Inuit.

RANGE: Circumpolar Northern Hemisphere mostly arctic-alpine species which comes south into the boreal forest in a few locations: occurs all around Hudson Bay.

Wildflowers with Opposite Entire Leaves; pink/purple flowers with petals indented or fringed....

422 ## Marsh Willowherb

(Epilobium palustre L.)

EVENING PRIMROSE FAMILY
Onagraceae

DESCRIPTION: An **erect branched** perennial **plant, 10-40 cm high, with long slender runners from the base that end in tiny scaly winter buds.** **Leaves** are opposite, sometimes alternate above, **sessile entire and narrowly lanceolate,** 2-5 cm long and smooth or covered with very fine curled hairs. **Flowers few, pink or whitish,** about 6 mm across, the **four petals shallowly notched** and borne above the **long inferior ovary. Fruit** a **narrow** 3-7 cm long **pod** containing numerous small seeds with whitish tufts of hairs.

HABITAT: Poorly drained peaty and sandy areas: Damp Dune Hollow, Salt-Marsh and Meadow-Marsh communities; damp ledges and crevices on the outcrop ridges and along the edges of ponds and streams.

FLOWERING: Late-July through August

COMMENTS: One of the most widespread small plants in wet places in our area, but never abundant at any one site. Two other tiny willowherbs have been recorded for the southern part of Hudson and James bays (see species list), but both are uncommon to rare at Churchill. The long narrow inferior ovary/pod with the tiny pink four-petaled flower at the tip is completely distinctive.

RANGE: Widespread circumpolar boreal-montane species: found all around Hudson Bay except on the eastern and northeastern sides.

FLOWERS WITH FOUR REGULAR PARTS

Wildflowers with Opposite Entire Leaves; petals entire, not lobed or fringed....

Arctic Gentian

GENTIAN FAMILY
Gentianaceae

(Gentiana propinqua Richards.)

OTHER NAMES: Felwort; Four-parted Gentian

DESCRIPTION: Erect smooth dwarf annual or biennial from a **small basal rosette of oblong sessile leaves.** Upper pairs of stem leaves widely spaced, lanceolate and sessile. Stems rarely over 20 cm tall, usually with many shorter slender flower-bearing branches from their bases. **Flowers** 4-parted, **solitary at the ends of branches,** grouped in clusters of 1-3 in the leaf axils. **Corolla lobes entire, deep blue to purple (rarely white)** and 1-2 cm long with bristle-tipped lobes. Sepal lobes unequal, the outer two 5-7 mm long and oval, the inner three 3-5 mm long and linear. Fruit a 1-2 cm long capsule.

HABITAT: Dry sunny slopes and open herbmats: Stable Dune and Sandy Foreshore communities; gravel ridges and disturbed gravel roadsides.

FLOWERING: Mid-July to the end of August: usually peak from the end of July to early August

COMMENTS: This is one of several common annual plants that an early summer visitor to Churchill would miss completely. Only the dead tattered remains of last year's plants are visible until late July or early August and then the roadsides, ridges, and beaches seem to be suddenly full of this attractive plant. Although small, it can have several dozen flowers on a single plant.

RANGE: Mostly North American low arctic-alpine species; also known from northeastern Asia. There are large gaps in its distribution and it occurs in our region only from Churchill south around Hudson and James bays to the southeastern corner of Hudson Bay.

Gentiana propinqua

432 *Alpine Whitlow-Grass*

(*Draba alpina* L.)

MUSTARD FAMILY
Cruciferae

OTHER NAMES: Alpine Draba

DESCRIPTION: Plants with a dense 1-3 cm **basal rosette of entire**, elliptical **somewhat fleshy leaves** with scattered rather long, stiff hairs. Flower scape stiffly erect and up to 15 cm high, sparsely covered with simple or branched hairs. **Flowers** 3 to 10, petals **yellow**, about twice as long as the 1.5-2.5 mm long hairy sepals. **Fruit pods smooth, broadest below the middle** and about 10 mm long.

HABITAT: Dry open places on peat, sand, or gravel: outcrop ridge and dry gravel ridges.

FLOWERING: Mid-June (or earlier) to mid-July: earliest on drier open areas and often blooming near edges of melting snowbanks.

COMMENTS: Common, especially on Cape Merry and near Fort Churchill; one of the earliest plants to bloom on the outcrop and gravel ridges after the Purple Saxifrage.

All mustard relatives have the easily recognized pattern of 4 petals, 6 stamens and a superior ovary which forms a round or elongated pod. Their scientific family name comes from the Latin word *crucifer* which means "cross", a reference to the cross-like arrangement of the petals.

RANGE: Circumpolar high arctic-alpine species: known in Manitoba only from Churchill; occurs intermittently all around Hudson Bay but not along James Bay.

June '81

Draba alpina

FLOWERS WITH FOUR REGULAR PARTS

Wildflowers with Basal or Alternate Entire Leaves; flowers yellow....

432
442

Northern Bladderpod

MUSTARD FAMILY
Cruciferae

(*Lesquerella arctica* (Wormsk.) S. Wats.)

OTHER NAMES: Arctic Bladderpod

DESCRIPTION: A low tufted perennial plant **densely covered with silvery starry hairs** and with a stout taproot. The cluster of spatulate basal **leaves**, really a **rosette**, is 2-6 cm wide while the 5-20 cm high flowering stems have only a few reduced leaves. The 2-14 **pale yellow flowers** have 5-7 mm long petals and are carried on long pedicels. The **fruiting pods look like tiny inflated balls**, 3-6 mm in diameter.

HABITAT: Dry sand and gravel areas: Sandy Beach, Foreshore and Dune communities; open areas on outcrop and gravel ridges and disturbed gravel roadsides.

FLOWERING: Early June to mid-July; mature fruiting pods by mid-July

COMMENTS: This interesting little mustard relative is occasionally found on dry dunes and disturbed gravel areas. Roadsides in the vicinity of Akudlik and Launch, and beaches near the wrecked Lambair plane and Fort Prince of Wales are good places to look for it. Its yellow flowers, ball-shaped fruits, and silvery starry hairs (easily visible with a hand lens) make it easy to recognize.

RANGE: Circumpolar but mostly North American arctic species: known in the Hudson Bay area only from Churchill and Southampton Island at the northern end of the Bay.

NOTE: GOLDEN WHITLOW-GRASS (*Draba aurea* Vahl) is an uncommon plant resembling the Northern Bladderpod found in similar habitats at about the same time. It occurs around the southern part of Hudson Bay and all of James Bay. It can be told from the Bladderpod by its **greater height**, **larger and more numerous stem leaves** and **much longer, often twisted fruiting pods**.

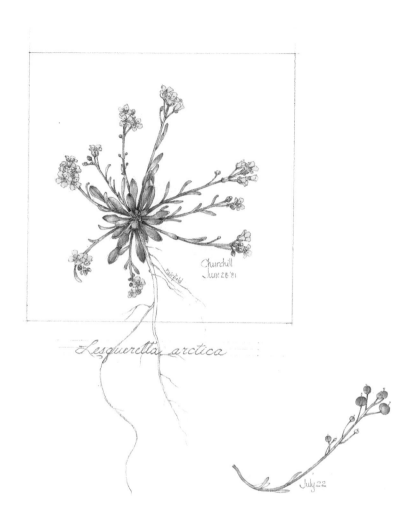

Churchill
June 28 '81

Fairfield

Lesquerella arctica

July 22

FLOWERS WITH FOUR REGULAR PARTS

Shrubs with Alternate, Entire, Evergreen Leaves and/or Wildflowers with
Alternate, Entire, Evergreen Leaves and Bell-shaped Flowers....

442
452
Dry-Ground Cranberry

HEATH FAMILY
(*Vaccinium vitis-idaea* L.)   Ericaceae

OTHER NAMES: Mossberry; Mountain, Rock or Lowbush Cranberry;
Cowberry; Red Whortleberry; Lingonberry; Partridge-
berry; Pomme de Terre.

DESCRIPTION: Low 10-20 cm high **woody plant** with **erect branches from
a trailing stem. Leaves evergreen**, 0.5-2 cm long, **with rolled
edges** and **usually a notched tip, dark green and shiny
above**, paler with black dots beneath. **Bell-shaped pink or
white** 5-8 mm long **flowers** are borne in small terminal
clusters. The **fruit** is an **edible juicy acid dark red berry**
about 6 mm wide.

HABITAT: Dry to moist peat, usually with mosses and/or lichens:
common in Heath communities on the outcrop and gravel
ridges and in Hummocky Bog and Lichen-Heath communities.

FLOWERING: July: usually early to mid-month. Berries do not fully ripen
until after the first hard frosts, usually in late August or
early September.

COMMENTS: This is the famous "lingonberry" or "lingberry" of Scandi-
navia, served with Swedish pancakes at restaurants and
imported at great expense by those unlucky enough not to
live where it grows. It is my personal favourite for jam or
sauce, the ripe berries having a tart distinctive flavour, far
superior to the true cranberry, and a beautiful deep red
colour. According to one authority, the North American
berries are smaller but superior in flavour to the commer-
cially harvested ones of Europe. The berries greatly improve
in flavour after a hard frost and are usually gathered then
and kept frozen until cooked. They are edible throughout
the winter and spring and the old berries provide a nice trail
snack when hiking on the outcrop cliffs or among the spruce
forests. Good crops of lingonberries are rare in the south
and it remains one of the benefits of living or travelling in
the North.

RANGE: Circumpolar subarctic-arctic, boreal-montane species: found
all around Hudson Bay.

FLOWERS WITH FOUR REGULAR PARTS

Wildflowers with Alternate Entire Evergreen Leaves; flowers with
4 recurved pink petals....

and/or Shrubs with Alternate Entire Evergreen Leaves; flowers with
4 recurved pink petals....

442
452

Swamp Cranberry

HEATH FAMILY
Ericaceae

(*Oxycoccus microcarpus* Turcz.)

OTHER NAMES: Cranberry; Small, Dwarf, Smallfruited and Bog Cranberry

DESCRIPTION: A **tiny delicate creeping plant** with slender trailing and rooting stems, 10-40 cm long. It bears **evergreen oval 3-6 mm long scattered leaves** which are entire, leathery dark green above and whitish below with inwardly rolled edges and somewhat pointed tips. The one-to-several, 3-8 mm long, **pale pink flowers** are **nodding** and long stalked **with 4 recurved petals.** The stamens form a cone protruding from the centre of the flower, causing it to look like a miniature shooting star flower. The fruit is a sour juicy red berry about 5-10 mm wide with brown or purple spots when young.

HABITAT: Acid peat bogs and muskegs, almost always with peat moss (*Sphagnum* spp.): found at Churchill in the Hummocky Bog and Spruce/Larch Muskeg communities, usually on sphagnum hummocks, and occasionally on moss hummocks around pools on the outcrop ridge.

FLOWERING: July: usually early to mid-month. Berries not usually ripe until late August or September

COMMENTS: A close relative of the 'true' cranberry of commerce, this tiny plant with the huge berries is relatively uncommon in the Churchill area and seldom found in quantities worth picking. It dislikes calcareous areas and so is found inland on acid peat bogs such as those along the Landing Lake Road. The berry is large and juicy but more insipid than that of the Dry-Ground Cranberry and far less common in this region. It can be used in the same way as you would use regular cranberries for sauce, jam, jelly, and in baking.

RANGE: Circumpolar boreal-subarctic-montane species: found from a latitude of 60° south all around Hudson and James bays.

FLOWERS WITH FOUR REGULAR PARTS
Wildflowers with Alternate Entire Leaves; flowers white....

442
443 **Scurvy-Grass**

(*Cochlearia officinalis* L.)

MUSTARD FAMILY
Cruciferae

DESCRIPTION:	A tiny, somewhat **fleshy, salt-tolerant** annual or biennial **plant**, usually under 8 cm in height. During the first year it is almost impossible to identify, being only a **rosette** of **triangular or oval entire leaves** on slender petioles. The **white** 3-7 mm long **flowers** appear early in the second season and are at first hidden among the leaves. The fruiting stems soon elongate and become arched or drooping, bearing a few scattered shallowly toothed leaves. The **smooth nearly round fruit pods** are 3-8 mm long.
HABITAT:	Moist saline and brackish areas: Sandy Foreshore, Beach, Dune, Damp Dune Hollows and Salt-Marsh communities.
FLOWERING:	Early to mid-July
COMMENTS:	Scurvy-Grass is strongly nitrogen-loving and therefore tends to be most common on sites rich in the manure of nesting sea-birds. The succulent leaves are edible both raw and cooked and are rich in vitamin C. It is not known whether northern native people made use of the plant, but it was collected and used in large quantities by seamen in the early 1800's who were continually threatened by scurvy – hence the common name of the plant. Bird Cove and Sloop's Cove are good areas around Churchill to look for it.
RANGE:	Circumpolar arctic species: found all around Hudson Bay except apparently from south of Churchill to James Bay. Also missing from the southern half of James Bay but present on both northern coasts.

III

442 ## *Fireweed*

(*Epilobium angustifolium* L.)

EVENING PRIMROSE FAMILY
Onagraceae

OTHER NAMES: Great Willowherb

DESCRIPTION: A stout erect perennial plant, 60-100+ cm high, densely leafy, from an underground woody rootstock. **Leaves** alternate, **entire or minutely toothed, willow-shaped, almost sessile,** 5-15 cm in length, paler and more distinctly veined beneath. **Flowers large** (to 3 cm across) and in long narrow clusters with the oldest flowers at the base and youngest at the growing tip. **Sepals 4**, narrower and **darker purple/red than** the **4 broad lilac coloured** (occasionally white) **petals. Fruit** a **reddish purple long narrow** somewhat 4-angled **pod**, 5-8 cm long, which splits to release the numerous small **hairy-tufted seeds.**

HABITAT: Disturbed soil and burnt over areas: Dry Stable Dunes; ledges and crevices of the outcrop ridge; disturbed areas on gravel ridges and roadsides.

FLOWERING: Mid-July through August: peak blooming period usually the latter part of July or early August

COMMENTS: The territorial flower of the Yukon, Fireweed is a pioneer plant which provides a vivid purple cover over recently burned or disturbed areas. Very common in the Churchill region, it covers large areas in the late summer and early fall with carpets of its reddish purple flowers.

All parts of the plant are edible. The leaves are used as a substitute for tea in Russia and the root is eaten raw by the Siberian Inuit. The pith is eaten fresh, cooked as soup, or dried and used in breadmaking. Young shoots can be cooked like asparagus and the flower stalks and leaves eaten in salads. It was introduced into parts of southern Europe to serve as a vegetable and is still popular in some countries.

RANGE: Circumpolar boreal-alpine species; wide ranging beyond the limit of trees but not truly arctic. One of the most widespread of all plants in the northern hemisphere. Found generally around Hudson Bay but apparently lacking along much of the Northwest Territories coastline north of Churchill.

442 *Broad-Leaved Fireweed/Willowherb*

(*Epilobium latifolium* L.)

EVENING PRIMROSE FAMILY
Onagraceae

OTHER NAMES: River Beauty; Broad-leaved Willowherb; Alpine or Dwarf Fireweed

DESCRIPTION: A low and sometimes bushy perennial plant usually with numerous short-hairy 15-50 cm tall stems arising from a woody rootstock. **Leaves** alternate (a few opposite), entire, **oval to oval-lanceolate** in shape, 2-5 cm long, **pale greyish or bluish green and somewhat fleshy. Flowers** few but **large and showy**, 2-5 cm across, in short leafy clusters. **Sepals 4, purple to reddish purple**, narrower than the **4 broad purple to rose-coloured (rarely white) petals.** Fruit a pod similar to that of Fireweed but only 2-6 cm long.

HABITAT: Moist, shady and gravelly soils: moist stable dunes and Dune Hollow communities; ledges on outcrop ridge; moist disturbed areas on gravel ridges, and along river and stream banks.

FLOWERING: Mid-July through August: peak usually the end of July

COMMENTS: Not as common as the taller Fireweed, this elegant relative is most often found on stable sandy shores around Churchill where it grows in nearly pure patches. Good places to look for it include the sandy areas below the wrecked Lambair plane and underneath the large antennas on the southern side of Launch Road. It also occurs on dry sheltered ledges on Cape Merry and moist gravel at Akudlik.

RANGE: Circumpolar (incompletely) arctic-montane species: found all around Hudson and James bays except along the south-western part of James Bay.

FLOWERS WITH FOUR REGULAR PARTS

Wildflowers with Alternate Lobed or Divided Leaves; flowers yellow....

443
444 *Marsh Yellow Cress*

(*Rorippa islandica* (Oeder) Borbas)

MUSTARD FAMILY
Cruciferae

OTHER NAMES: Iceland Yellow Cress

DESCRIPTION: A smooth annual or biennial, very variable plant from a weak tap root. 20-100 cm tall stem may be simple or branched, erect or prostrate. **Leaves** mainly along the stem, **oblanceolate in outline** and **pinnately toothed, lobed (most common), or divided**, the **large terminal lobe always toothed or lobed. Small pale yellow flowers** borne in elongating clusters at the tips of branches, sepals slightly longer than the petals; flowers **2-5 mm wide.** Flowers and **fruiting pods** usually present at the same time, pods **plump, 2-10 mm long** and **not over 4 times longer than wide.**

HABITAT: Freshwater wet disturbed places: Meadow-Marsh community; disturbed moist gravel areas such as roadsides, banks of rivers and lakes.

FLOWERING: Mid-July through August

COMMENTS: This Water Cress relative is common on moist disturbed sites at Churchill. Good places to find it are the banks of streams near Akudlik and where Goose Creek crosses the road. Like other cresses, the young leaves of both this plant and the American Winter Cress (see Note below) are edible and eaten raw or boiled as greens by native peoples.

RANGE: Circumpolar, wide ranging, non-arctic species: occurs from the latitude of Churchill south around both sides of Hudson and James bays.

NOTE: AMERICAN WINTER CRESS (*Barbarea orthoceras* Ledeb.) is a very similar plant, common at Churchill and along the southeastern coast of Hudson Bay. It also occurs in moist disturbed places including Stable Dune and Meadow-Marsh communities, stream banks, and disturbed moist areas on the gravel ridges. Flowering from late June to August, it can be distinguished from Marsh Yellow Cress by its **larger flowers (1-1.5 cm wide); narrow, 4-sided, 2-3 cm** long **fruiting pods,** and the **entire terminal lobe of its leaf.**
WORMSEED MUSTARD or WALLFLOWER (*Erysimum cheiranthoides* L.) is another weedy yellow-flowered mustard relative sometimes found on moist disturbed gravel in the Churchill area, southwestern part of Hudson Bay, and western James Bay. It can be distinguished from Winter Cress and Marsh Yellow Cress by its **nearly entire or only shallowly lobed or toothed leaves** and tiny **2-3 forked hairs on the leaves and pods.**

FLOWERS WITH FOUR REGULAR PARTS

Wildflowers with Alternate Toothed Leaves; flowers white to pale pink;
pods 1-3 times longer than broad....

443 *Smoothing Whitlow-Grass*

MUSTARD FAMILY
Cruciferae

(*Draba glabella* Pursh)

DESCRIPTION: A tufted or matted perennial plant with a loose 1.5-9 cm wide **basal rosette of** spatulate to **oblong, entire to few-toothed fresh green leaves covered with** soft, starry, forked or simple **hairs.** The 1-7 oval, toothed stem leaves are somewhat smaller. Flowering stems are simple to branching, 10-25 cm high, and have starry hairs on the lower parts. The flower clusters bear 5-15 **white flowers** with 3-5 mm long petals and are first dense heads but soon elongate. **Fruiting pods are hairless,** 6-15 mm long and **often somewhat twisted.**

HABITAT: Dry to moist rocky, gravelly, or grassy areas, usually calcareous; strongly nitrogen-loving, it tends to grow on or near animal dung: sheltered crevices and ledges on the outcrop ridge; open areas on gravel ridges; roadsides and other disturbed gravel areas.

FLOWERING: Late June to mid-July: pods and flowers usually found on the same plant and open pods present until at least late August.

COMMENTS: One of the commonest species in this group of difficult small mustard relatives found at Churchill, Smoothing Whitlow-Grass is found mostly on patches of damp soil in sheltered sites along the flanks of the outcrop ridge. Cape Merry, Fort Prince of Wales, and disturbed gravel areas around Akudlik are good places to look for it. It can be distinguished from the similar Sand-Dwelling Rock Cress by its shorter (0.5-1.5 cm vs. 1-3 cm) and wider pods and by the starry hairs on its stem.

RANGE: Wide ranging circumpolar arctic-alpine species: apparently missing from the York Factory to western Ontario section of the coast, but present elsewhere all around Hudson and James bays.

Draba glabella

Wildflowers with Alternate Toothed Leaves; fruiting pods more than 5 times longer than broad....

443 **Sand-Dwelling Rock Cress**

(*Arabis arenicola* (Richards.) Gelert)

MUSTARD FAMILY
Cruciferae

OTHER NAMES: Arctic Rock Cress

DESCRIPTION: Perennial 10-20 cm high plant with a **basal rosette** of **spatulate** sparsely-toothed **dark green** 2-4 cm long **leaves on slender petioles. Flower stems bear 3-4 sessile entire leaves and an elongating cluster of 5-20 white to pale pink or purple flowers.** The 4 reddish to green sepals are about 1.5-2.5 mm long and have a distinct transparent margin while the narrow petals are 3-5 mm in length. The **smooth greenish purple fruiting pods** are 1-3 cm long and about 2 mm wide.

HABITAT: Calcareous sand and gravel, often by lakeshores or riverbanks: sandy beach areas and open disturbed sites on the gravel ridges at Churchill.

FLOWERING: Late June to early August

COMMENTS: Occasional to common in the Churchill area, often found growing with Arctic Bladderpod on open dry sand. Good places to look for it at Churchill are Cape Merry and the beaches below the wrecked Lambair plane. It can be distinguished from the similar Smoothing Whitlow-Grass by its longer (1-3 cm vs. 0.5-1.5 cm) and narrower pods and by the lack of starry hairs on its stem.

RANGE: Arctic-subarctic species of eastern North America from Labrador to Great Slave Lake: found all around Hudson and James bays.

444 *Northern Flixweed*

(*Descurania sophioides* (Fisch.) Schulz)

MUSTARD FAMILY
Cruciferae

OTHER NAMES: Northern Tansy Mustard

DESCRIPTION: A 15-100 cm high biennial plant with simple or branching leafy stems from a **basal rosette of 2- to 3-times divided leaves** which remain green throughout the first winter and usually wither at the time of flowering. Stems and leaves bright green and glandular hairy with capitate glands, **not starry hairs.** Terminal flower clusters bearing many **tiny yellow flowers** are dense at first but elongate greatly as the pods develop. **Fruiting pods** 1-3 cm long, about **1 mm wide, somewhat curved** and on long very slender spreading pedicels.

HABITAT: Damp to dry gravel beds and disturbed soils: mostly disturbed roadsides and gravel areas in the Churchill region.

FLOWERING: Late July through August

COMMENTS: A native but weedy species, often spread by people and frequently growing on garbage heaps near human dwellings. Occasional to common on disturbed gravel in areas such as the Churchill townsite, Akudlik, and Launch. A close southern relative is known to cause **poisoning** in cattle when eaten in large quantities.

RANGE: Arctic-subarctic species of western North America and eastern Asia: known only from the Churchill to York Factory region on Hudson Bay.

NOTE: A very similar boreal plant, GRAY TANSY MUSTARD (*Descurania richardsonii* (Sweet) Schulz) occurs at Churchill in similar habitats and blooms at about the same time. It can be told from the Northern Flixweed by its **gray colour, starry hairs**, and **short** (less than 1 cm) **fruiting pods.**

FLOWERS WITH FOUR REGULAR PARTS

Wildflowers with Alternate Divided Leaves; flowers white to rose....

Meadow Bitter Cress

(Cardamine pratensis L.)

MUSTARD FAMILY
Cruciferae

OTHER NAMES: Field Bitter Cress; Cuckoo Flower; Lady's Smock

DESCRIPTION: A hairless perennial plant from a short rootstalk, 15-50 cm high with deeply lobed to **divided leaves,** the lower with 5-15 stalked rounded leaflets which soon wither, the **upper with many narrow linear divisions.** Flower cluster dense with several large and showy 1.5-2.5 cm wide **white to rose coloured flowers.** Petals with darker veins and 2-3 times longer than the sepals. Mature **fruiting pods 13-4 cm long** and **very narrow.**

HABITAT: Wet places; especially along creeks and in thickets: Meadow-Marsh and Willow/Bog Birch communities; along streams, lakeshores, and floodplains in the Churchill area.

FLOWERING: July: usually early in the month

COMMENTS: Occasional in the Churchill area and around Hudson Bay, this conspicuous plant has the largest flowers of any of the mustard relatives in the region. It often reproduces from leafy buds or plantlets at the base of the parent plant rather than by seeds, especially in the high arctic. Cultivated as an ornamental and salad plant in parts of Europe, the young basal leaves are sometimes eaten as a cress.

RANGE: Circumpolar arctic-subarctic plant: found all around Hudson and James bays.

FLOWERS WITH FOUR REGULAR PARTS

Shrubs with Alternate Entire Deciduous Leaves....

452
552 *Alpine Bilberry/Blueberry*

HEATH FAMILY

(*Vaccinium uliginosum* L.)

Ericaceae

OTHER NAMES:	Bog Whortleberry, Bilberry or Blueberry; Arctic or Alpine Blueberry
DESCRIPTION:	**Low**, 10-50 cm high **much-branched shrub** with thick **dull-green oval**, 1-2.5 cm long **deciduous leaves**, pale and finely veined beneath. The **bell-shaped** 5-7 mm long **pink or white flowers** grow in groups of 2-4 in the axils of the leaves. **Fruits are edible blue or black 6-7 mm wide berries** with a bloom.
HABITAT:	Dry to moist peat and moist gravel areas: common everywhere around Churchill in Hummocky Bog, White Spruce, and Stable Dune communities and on the outcrop ridge.
FLOWERING:	Late June to the end of July: berries not usually ripe until mid- to late August
COMMENTS:	The 'blueberry' of the North, this common small shrub produces delicious sweet and juicy berries. They make excellent jam and pies and also dry well, having been used as dried berries in many ways by native peoples. Northern residents complain about our higher southern berry bushes saying that they prefer to be able to lie down and pick their berries – which they can do for all the northern species. Best places for these berries in the Churchill region include Heath communities on the outcrop ridges and lichen-heath areas on the gravel ridges. But keep your eyes open for polar bears while you pick!
RANGE:	Circumpolar arctic-alpine, subarctic-northern boreal- montane species: occurs all around Hudson and James bays with the possible exception of the eastern side of James Bay.

126

FLOWERS WITH FOUR REGULAR PARTS
Shrubs with Opposite Entire Leaves....

452 *Canada Buffaloberry*

(Shepherdia canadensis (L.) Nutt.)

OLEASTER FAMILY
Elaeagnaceae

OTHER NAMES: Soapberry

DESCRIPTION: A 0.5-2 m high shrub with **brown scurfy branches** and opposite **leathery oval or ovate leaves.** The 2-5 cm long **leaves** are deep green above while the **lower sides** are **covered with a mixture of soft white hairs and distinctive spots of brown scales.** Flowers are unisexual, the separate sexes borne on different plants. Thus only some of the shrubs produce the 3-5 mm reddish yellow berry-like fruits. **Flowers appear before or just with the leaves,** have 4 sepals and no petals, are **yellowish green** and are clustered in the leaf axils.

HABITAT: Dry calcareous or slightly saline soils in open woods and along banks: Sandy Foreshore, Stable Dune and White Spruce communities; outcrop and gravel ridges.

FLOWERING: Very early: by the middle to end of June at the latest. Usually in bloom at the edges of melting snowbanks on the ridges and along the edge of the bay and Churchill River as soon as the ice has gone out.

COMMENTS: One of the earliest plants to bloom at Churchill, usually just after the Purple Saxifrage. It is common in most well drained habitats and occurs in a dwarfed 'bonsai' form at many places along the coast, growing tightly up against the lee side of a rock or almost flat against the sand and gravel of the beach ridges.

Birds and other animals eat the berry-like fruits and native people used to eat great quantities of them, especially in southern areas. Large amounts were dried for winter use and then cooked with buffalo meat, hence one of the common names. The other common name, Soapberry, comes from the bitter or astringent taste of the berries. This is caused by saponin, a chemical which produces a soap-like foam. The berries are much better after a frost and many native people still consider them a delicacy when whipped up with a little sugar into a foamy or creamy mass and served as a dessert topping.

RANGE: North American boreal to subarctic species; wide ranging, nearly to slightly above treeline: occurs from a latitude just north of Churchill south around both sides of Hudson and James bays.

Wildflowers with Opposite Entire Leaves; white flowers with deeply notched petals and 3 styles....

522 *Long-Stalked Stitchwort*

PINK FAMILY
Caryophyllaceae

(*Stellaria longipes* Goldie)

OTHER NAMES:	Long-stalked Chickweed or Starwort
DESCRIPTION:	Smooth fragile more or less tufted perennial, 2-25+ cm tall. Leafy stems bear opposite entire **lanceolate** to **oval, distinctly keeled leaves** which are 4-30 mm long and 1-4 mm wide. **Flowers** one to few, on long stalks at the tip of the stem, **with 5 more or less deeply divided** 4-8 mm long **white petals (which often look like 10 narrow ones** unless closely checked); 5 oval shorter sepals; 10 stamens and **3 styles.** Fruit an oval, dark, shiny capsule about 9 mm long.
HABITAT:	Weedy; general in a variety of habitats from dry sand to damp marsh: Ledge and Crevice communities on the outcrop ridge and disturbed gravel on beaches and ridges throughout the Churchill area.
FLOWERING:	Late June or early July
COMMENTS:	Some botanists separate this chickweed into several species but most consider it one very variable group. The plant is common on beaches including those at Cape Merry and Fort Prince of Wales. The scientific name *Stellaria*, comes from the Latin for "star", a much more appropriate name to my mind than chickweed or stitchwort. The flowers look like tiny white stars and their notched petals and opposite leaves are completely distinctive. The other common names come from their uses as fresh winter food for chickens (and people!) and poultices (stitchwort – a plant to stitch up a wound or sore). Many are hardy enough to grow year round in mild climates and all are good sources of vitamin C and mineral elements. They can be eaten raw or cooked as greens.
RANGE:	Wide ranging circumpolar arctic-alpine, boreal-montane species complex: occurs in one form or another all around Hudson and James bays.

Churchill
June 20, 1981

Stellaria longipes

NOTE: Several other species of *Stellaria* occur in the Churchill/Hudson Bay region. The only ones you are likely to encounter are the LOW CHICKWEED (*Stellaria humifusa* Rottb.) and the NORTHERN STITCHWORT or STARWORT (*S. calycantha* (Ledeb.) Bong.) which are occasionally found near the Bay, and the LONG-LEAVED STITCHWORT (*S. longifolia* Muhl.) which is common in freshwater Meadow-Marsh communities. The Low Chickweed is a **brownish matted plant** with **small oval fleshy leaves** and prefers open areas in **salt marshes** while the Northern Stitchwort or Starwort is much larger, often lacks petals, has individual stems and **non-fleshy lanceolate leaves** and grows **under willows** on beach and gravel ridges. The Long-Leaved Stitchwort looks like the Long-Stalked Stitchwort but has **leaves** which **taper toward both ends**, flower clusters with many flowers from the leaf axils, and petals no longer than the sepals. Three styles separate the stitchworts from the closely related Alpine Chickweed which has 5 styles.

131

FLOWERS WITH FIVE REGULAR PARTS

Wildflowers with Opposite Entire Leaves; white flowers with notched petals, free sepals, and 5 styles....

522 *Alpine Chickweed*

PINK FAMILY
Caryophyllaceae

(*Cerastium alpinum* L.)

OTHER NAMES: Mouse-ear Chickweed

DESCRIPTION: **Softly hairy or woolly**, often glandular, **matted** perennial **plant**, 5-20 cm tall. Stems bear opposite entire oval to lanceolate leaves which are about 1 cm long and 5 mm wide. **Flowers** 1-6, **showy**, on weak 1-4 cm long flowering stems. They have **5 shallowly notched** 1-1.3 cm broad **petals**, five 0.5-0.7 cm long oval, free green sepals with transparent margins; 10 stamens and **5 styles**. Fruit a 0.8-2 cm long slender capsule with 10 nerves.

HABITAT: Rocky sandy or gravelly places, also frequent on manured soils near bird cliffs and human settlements: Ledge, Crevice and Dry Peat communities on the outcrop ridge; sand dunes and disturbed gravel on beaches, ridges, and roadsides.

FLOWERING: Late June to early August: peak usually early July

COMMENTS: This is the largest chickweed in our region, fairly common on beaches and among the rocks on Cape Merry, at Fort Prince of Wales, and near the town centre. It can be distinguished from the closely related Long-Stalked Stitchwort (pg. 130) by its larger flowers with less deeply notched petals, 5 styles, and extreme hairiness. Its scientific name, *Cerastium*, comes from the Greek word *cerastes* which means "horned", a reference to the slender, often curved, capsule.

RANGE: Amphi-Atlantic arctic species: occurs only from Churchill north and west around the northern end of Hudson Bay, missing from the eastern and southern parts of the Bay and from James Bay.

Cerastium alpinum

FLOWERS WITH FIVE REGULAR PARTS

Wildflowers with Opposite Entire Leaves; white flowers with notched petals and fused ribbed sepals....

522 *Arctic Bladder-Campion*

(Melandrium affine J. Vahl.)

PINK FAMILY
Caryophyllaceae

OTHER NAMES: Mountain Cockle; Arctic Lychnis

DESCRIPTION: Erect, **somewhat glandular sticky,** 5-20 cm tall, usually branched or tufted perennial **plant** from a strong taproot. **Leaves** opposite, broadly lanceolate and entire, **mostly basal** but stems have 2-3 pairs of smaller, narrower leaves. **Flowers usually 3** (I-2), borne on erect flower stalks. **Petals 5, milky white, shallowly notched** and distinctly exserted from the mouth of the oval **slightly inflated** 8-12 mm long **bell-shaped calyx that has distinct purple green veins or ribs.** Styles 5; stamens 10; fruit a dry capsule containing many small (I-1.5 mm wide) narrowly winged seeds.

HABITAT: Rock crevices; moist sand, gravel, or stony places and near animal dens: Ledge and Crevice communities on the outcrop ridge and disturbed gravel on ridges and roadsides.

FLOWERING: Late June through July: peak usually early to mid-July

COMMENTS: This small bladder-campion is fairly common in crevices on the outcrop ridge east of Churchill and along the gravel ridges near Akudlik and elsewhere in the region. Its ribbed and inflated calyx, separate notched white petals and opposite leaves make it easy to identify and show its close relationship with the more common chickweeds.

RANGE: Circumpolar wide ranging arctic-alpine species: occurs along most of the eastern coast of Hudson Bay and at scattered locations along the western coast: apparently missing from James Bay except along the northwestern coast.

NOTE: A closely related species, the NODDING LYCHNIS or COCKLE *(Melandrium apetalum* (L.) Fenzl) is found in open wet tundra communities around most of Hudson and James bays. It can be distinguished from the Arctic Bladder-Campion by its **smaller size, single nodding flower with** short included **lilac petals,** and **strongly inflated calyx** which resembles a miniature Japanese lantern.

FLOWERS WITH FIVE REGULAR PARTS

Wildflowers with Opposite Entire Broad Fleshy Leaves; inconspicuous white flowers with entire petals....

Sea-Purslane/Seabeach Sandwort

(Honckenya peploides (L.) Ehrh.)

PINK FAMILY
Caryophyllaceae

OTHER NAMES: Sea Chickweed, Sea Sandwort

DESCRIPTION: A low matted fleshy smooth perennial with **much branched and freely rooting stems deeply buried in sand.** Leaves **yellow green,** opposite, sessile, 5 to over 20 mm long, oval but with a pointed tip. Small almost inconspicuous **flowers,** in leafy clusters at the tips of stems or in the axils of the upper leaves, have **5 green sepals** which are 4-7 mm long, ovate to lanceolate, slightly longer and **much wider than** the alternating, spatula-shaped **5 (occasionally 6) white petals.** Flowers functionally unisexual, male plants having flowers with 8 or 10 stamens and a poorly developed ovary; female plants having flowers with smaller petals, undeveloped stamens and a single pistil with a 3 parted style. Fruit a 6-12 mm wide globe-shaped leathery capsule.

HABITAT: Sandy seashores; rarely on inland lakeshores; Sandy Beach and Foreshore communities; gravel roadsides and ridges close to the coast.

FLOWERING: Late June to early August

COMMENTS: Seabeach Sandwort is one of the small group of northern **halophytes** (''salt-plants'') which can tolerate both salt water and unstable sandy soils. It grows very close to the bays, often with Seaside Lungwort and Sea Lime Grass. Its seaside habitat and succulent yellow green leaves make it easy to identify and the small white flowers are almost always present if you look closely. Good places to look for it at Churchill are beaches at the town centre, Fort Prince of Wales, and Bird Cove.

The fleshy young shoots are edible and may be eaten raw as a salad, cooked as a pot herb, or preserved as a pickle or sauerkraut. The plant has been used as fodder for pigs and sheep in some areas.

RANGE: Circumpolar low arctic maritime species; occurs all around Hudson and James bays.

FLOWERS WITH FIVE REGULAR PARTS

Wildflowers with Opposite Entire Oval Leaves; small white flowers with entire petals....

Blunt-Leaved Sandwort

(*Moehringia lateriflora* (L.) Fenzl)

PINK FAMILY
Caryophyllaceae

OTHER NAMES: Grove Sandwort

DESCRIPTION: Low erect perennial plant, 10-25 cm tall, with **weak slightly hairy stems** from a slender rootstalk. Stems bear 2-5 pairs of thin sessile opposite oval to oblong, 1-3 cm long, blunt **pale green leaves. Flower 1** (2 to several) in an open few-flowered cluster **on long slender pedicel. Petals white and entire**, 3-6 mm long, about twice as long as the blunt sepals, usually 5 but sometimes both sepals and petals 4. **Styles 3**, stamens 10 (rarely 8), fruit a 3-7 mm long oval capsule with many small shiny black seeds.

HABITAT: Edges of moist woodlands and thickets; sheltered gravel or mossy shores: mostly open White Spruce and poplar forests or under willows in our region.

FLOWERING: Mid-July to early August

COMMENTS: This delicate little relative of the chickweeds or starworts is occasionally found in open moist but well drained protected sites. I have most often found it under White Spruce trees along the 'esker' and gravel ridges near the Churchill River and at Twin Lakes. It is a boreal forest species which reaches its northern limit at Churchill and is more common under poplar trees and mixed forests south along the Bay. Its 5 unnotched white petals, thin oval opposite leaves, and sheltered habitat preference make it easy to identify.

RANGE: Circumpolar boreal species: found on Hudson Bay only from Churchill south and east to, and all around, James Bay.

FLOWERS WITH FIVE REGULAR PARTS
Wildflowers with Opposite Entire Leaves; blue purple (rarely white)
flowers over 1 cm wide....

522 ## *Star Gentian*

(*Lomatogonium rotatum* (L.) Fries)

GENTIAN FAMILY
Gentianaceae

OTHER NAMES: Marsh Felwort

DESCRIPTION: An erect slender purplish green annual or biennial plant with simple or branched 5-30 cm tall stems. **Leaves opposite sessile and entire**, 1-5 cm long; basal ones spatula-shaped, upper ones oval to linear. **Showy bluish purple (rarely white) flowers 1-3 cm wide**, borne singly or in clusters in the axils of the leaves. Corolla deeply divided into 5 (rarely 4) widely spreading petals, each with a pair of tiny scale-like structures at their base; the 2-5 much smaller calyx lobes united only at the base; stamens 5, attached at the base of each petal; pistil 1. Fruit an oval 0.5-2.5 cm long pointed capsule containing many small seeds.

HABITAT: Seashores, freshwater marshes, and stream banks: Salt-Marsh and Meadow-Marsh communities and along stream banks.

FLOWERING: Late July through August

COMMENTS: This beautiful little wildflower is one of my favourites and is locally abundant in the Churchill region. It does resemble a small blue star and usually shows up dramatically against the shorter plants of the salt marshes and bare gravel where it grows. Good places to find it are along the banks of the Churchill River near the pumphouse, in moist gravel west of Akudlik, and in the salt marsh at Sloop's Cove. It is another of the showy late-blooming plants which reward the late summer traveller to Churchill and Hudson Bay.

RANGE: Circumpolar (with large gaps) subarctic-boreal-montane species: known to occur from the southern Northwest Territories south around the coasts of Hudson and James bays to about halfway up the eastern side of Hudson Bay. May well be present but not recorded on other parts of the bays because of its late season blooming period.

Lomatogonium rotatum

522 *Purple Saxifrage*

SAXIFRAGE FAMILY
Saxifragaceae

(*Saxifraga oppositifolia* L.)

OTHER NAMES:	Purple Mountain, Red-Flowered or Opposite-Leaved Saxifrage; French Knot Moss
DESCRIPTION:	Densely or loosely matted low perennial plant with crowded or trailing branches and **dull bluish green overlapping scale-like 4-ranked persistent leathery** bristly-ciliate, 2-6 mm long **leaves. Solitary flowers pale pink to deep purple** on very short stalks. Petals 5, oval to spatula-shaped, 4-10 mm long, much longer than the 5 oval, bristly-ciliate sepals; stamens 10; **pistil** one **with 2 distinct styles. Fruit** a 3-10 mm long capsule **with two slender beaks.**
HABITAT:	Moist calcareous gravels and heaths, rock crevices: exposed summits of gravel ridges; Dry Peat, Hummocky Bog, and Ledge and Crevice communities.
FLOWERING:	Late April (or as early as the snow starts to melt) to early July
COMMENTS:	This small saxifrage is the first real sign of spring at Churchill and elsewhere in the arctic. It is the first flower to appear, often blooming right at the edges of melting snowbanks on gravel ridges. Small clumps or cushions of its purple dot the ridges for a few weeks and then the willows, bearberries, and other early flowers appear. A few flowers can usually be found as late as early July in snow covered north- or east-facing crevices on the outcrop ridge but it is usually finished by early June on the gravel ridges.
	Purple flowers are unusual for a saxifrage, most species including those found in this region having white or yellow flowers. But the 5 petals, 5 sepals, 10 stamens and 2 styles are typical of the saxifrages and together with its matted form and small overlapping leaves make Purple Saxifrage easy to recognize.
RANGE:	Circumpolar wide ranging arctic-alpine species: occurs from Churchill north and east around Hudson Bay and most of James Bay but apparently missing on Hudson Bay between Churchill and James Bay.

522 *Salt-Marsh Sand Spurry*

PINK FAMILY
Caryophyllaceae

(*Spergularia marina* (L.) Griseb.)

DESCRIPTION: **Tiny fleshy annual** with simple or freely branching and spreading stems seldom over 5-7 cm long in our area. **Leaves** opposite, sparse, narrowly cylindrical, **very fleshy**, 6-20 mm long with small triangular stipules at their nodes. Flowers fairly numerous at the tips of stems or in the axils of the upper leaves. **Petals pink to white**, slightly shorter than the blunt, oval, 3-5 mm long green sepals. Stamens 2-5, **styles 3**, fruit an oval capsule as long as, or slightly longer than, the sepals.

HABITAT: Saline or brackish soils: occurs in the Salt-Marsh community.

FLOWERING: Late July through August

COMMENTS: This tiny salt-tolerant annual is common on the mud flats of salt marshes in August. It forms extensive colonies or mats, usually growing with Star Gentian and Northern Samphire. Good places to look for it around Churchill are at Bird and Sloop's coves. If you look closely you should be able to spot the small flowers set closely against the mud like tiny pink stars. The flowers and round fleshy leaves immediately identify the plant.

The generic name, *Spergularia*, comes from *Spergula* which in turn comes from the Latin word *spargere* – "to scatter". *Spergula* is the genus name of the European Corn Spurry, a quick growing annual closely related to Sand Spurry which is still grown as an early forage crop for domestic animals.

RANGE: Circumpolar non-arctic maritime and other saline area species with large gaps: occurs (with a very similar closely related species) from Churchill south and around both sides of James Bay. Apparently missing from the eastern and northwestern parts of Hudson Bay.

FLOWERS WITH FIVE REGULAR PARTS
Wildflowers with Opposite Entire Narrow Pointed Leaves; flowers with
5 white petals and 3 styles....

522 **Early Sandwort**

PINK FAMILY
Caryophyllaceae

(*Minuartia rubella* (Wahlenb.) Hiern.)

OTHER NAMES: Reddish Sandwort

DESCRIPTION: Small 2-10 cm tall **bluish green tufted, matted, or cushion-shaped perennial** plant from a long leathery taproot. Leaves crowded on basal shoots, narrow, stiff and sharp pointed, prominently 3-nerved and 2-8 mm long. **Thread-like flowering stems** barely emerge **above** the 'cushion' surface and bear 1 to several flowers at their tips. Sepals 5, lanceolate, 3-nerved, greenish purple, 2.5-5 mm in length, slightly longer than the **entire white petals** and shorter than the fruiting capsule; stamens 10; **styles 3.**

HABITAT: Dry usually calcareous sandy, gravelly, or rocky places: Ledge and Crevice communities on the outcrop ridge; gravel roadsides and ridges throughout the region.

FLOWERING: Late June through July

COMMENTS: This little sandwort is one of those plants which repay humility – you really have to observe it on bended knee. It is common in the gravel and peat-filled cracks (often growing with the Three-Toothed Saxifrage) on the outcrop ridge and on disturbed gravel throughout the Churchill area. Good places to find it are amid the rocks near the radar domes and on disturbed gravel near Akudlik. The tiny tufts of the plant are fairly easy to spot but the flowers are so small that you have to look very closely to see them.
The Early Sandwort is one of the hardiest of northern flowering plants, reaching nearly to the North Pole and all around Greenland. Several other less common sandworts occur around the bays. All are small plants similar in appearance and flower structure to the Early Sandwort and those at Churchill are listed in the Appendix.

RANGE: Circumpolar wide ranging arctic-alpine species: occurs all around Hudson and James bays except apparently between Churchill and the northwestern corner of James Bay.

146

FLOWERS WITH FIVE REGULAR PARTS

Wildflowers with Opposite Entire Narrow Leaves; flowers with 5 entire white petals and 4 or 5 styles....

522 ## *Pearlwort*

PINK FAMILY
Caryophyllaceae

(*Sagina nodosa* (L.) Fenzl)

OTHER NAMES: Knotted Pearlwort; Knotted Spurrey

DESCRIPTION: A small tufted perennial, 5-15 cm high, with several slender, often branched, stems which are erect or more commonly lie flat on the ground. Stems bear opposite narrow pointed leaves, 5-20 mm long and clustered at the base, much smaller, scale-like and well separated along the stem. **Stem leaves bear clusters of bulb-like tiny leaves in their axils which look like 'knots'** and which can drop off and root to form new plants. **Flowers** are usually **solitary** at the ends of the stems with 5 green, oval, 2-4 mm long sepals; **5 conspicuous 6-8 mm long entire white petals;** 10 stamens and **4 or 5 styles.** Fruit an oval capsule longer than the sepals.

HABITAT: Damp rocky, gravelly, or peaty soils: Meadow-Marsh communities; beaches of freshwater ponds and lakes; moist disturbed areas on gravel ridges and roadsides.

FLOWERING: Late July through August

COMMENTS: Pearlwort is locally abundant on moist gravel areas in the Churchill region and is one of those plants which reward close attention to the ground. The relatively large white flowers at the ends of the long slender 'knotty' stems are unmistakeable and form startling displays on bare gravel areas. A good place to look for it is near Akudlik but it is a late-season bloomer and nearly impossible to find earlier than mid-July.

Its generic name, *Sagina*, comes from the Latin word for "fodder" or "fattening" and a closely related genus is still planted in Europe as an early forage for sheep. Our attractive little Pearlwort is far too small and scattered to make a good feed for anything.

RANGE: Amphi-Atlantic low arctic species: occurs nearly all around Hudson and James bays south of about 63°N latitude.

NOTE: There are two or three other species of Pearlworts found occasionally around Hudson and James bays, although not at Churchill. All are small tufted or matted plants with short narrow opposite pointed leaves; 4-5 (or 0) white petals and as many styles as sepals (4 or 5).

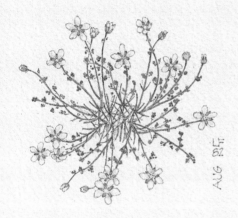

AUG
LH
82

Sagina nodosa

FLOWERS WITH FIVE REGULAR PARTS

Wildflowers with Opposite Deeply 3-lobed Leaves; solitary yellow flowers....

523
723
724

Yellow Anemone

(Anemone richardsonii Hook.)

BUTTERCUP FAMILY
Ranunculaceae

OTHER NAMES: Richardson's Anemone

DESCRIPTION: Slender delicate perennial plant from thin threadlike horizontal rootstalks which bear individual leaves and flowering stems (6-25 cm high) at some distance from each other. '**Basal' leaves round to kidney-shaped** in outline, 2-5 cm wide, **long petioled** and **3 (to 5) lobed** no more than 3/4 of the way to the midrib; lobes shallowly divided and sharp tipped. Stem leaves 2-3, sessile and thus appearing opposite or whorled; 3-lobed and sharply toothed. **Flowers solitary,** 1.5-3 cm wide, **golden yellow with only** a **single series of 5 (4 to 7)** oval **sepals present; petals lacking; stamens and pistils many.** Fruits many small smooth 5-8 mm long achenes with long curved beaks, forming a globe-shaped cluster.

HABITAT: Moist sheltered slopes, thickets, and snowbeds; under willows and in moss around edges of freshwater pools on the outcrop ridge and inland lakes and streams; Willow/Bog Birch and Black Spruce Bog communities.

FLOWERING: Late June to late July; peak usually early July

COMMENTS: This is the only yellow-flowered northern anemone, most being white to reddish in colour. It is locally common at Churchill under willows near water and good places to find it are the Cape Merry road, near the 'Radar' domes, and along the Churchill River near the pumphouse.
The Yellow Anemone often grows in mossy bogs next to the very similar Lapland Buttercup (pg. 180). It looks like a buttercup at first glance but has only the single series of coloured 'petals' while buttercups have an additional outer series of green sepals. Look for the green sepals, smaller petals, and lack of stem leaves to distinguish the buttercup from the anemone. Anemones are closely related to buttercups; both contain irritating and **poisonous** substances and should be handled with care.

RANGE: Eastern Asian, North American, and western Greenland subarctic-low arctic-montane species; occurs along most of the eastern and western sides of Hudson Bay but apparently missing from all of James Bay, the region between York Factory and James Bay, and the northern islands.

FLOWERS WITH FIVE REGULAR PARTS

Wildflowers with Opposite Divided Leaves with Broad Lobes; a single
white flower....

524
534
544
724

Small Wood Anemone

(*Anemone parviflora* Michx.)

BUTTERCUP FAMILY
Ranunculaceae

OTHER NAMES: Northern Anemone

DESCRIPTION: Delicate perennial plant with long slender branched rootstalks which end in **rosettes of shiny dark green leaves** surrounding solitary, 7-35 cm tall, flowering stems. Basal leaves long-petioled, the oval, 1-4 cm wide blades divided completely or nearly so into 3-lobed and bluntly toothed parts. Stem leaves 2-3, sessile or nearly so and thus appearing opposite or whorled, divided into 3 narrow lobes which are again shallowly toothed or lobed. **Flower solitary,** 2-3 cm wide, with a single series of **5 (4 to 7) sepals** which are **pure white above, silky hairy and tinged with blue or rose beneath; petals lacking; stamens and pistils many.** Fruits many small beaked densely woolly achenes in an oval, 6-13 mm wide cluster.

HABITAT: Wet to dry calcareous soils: Ledge and Crevice communities on the outcrop ridge; mossy areas along streambanks and under White Spruce.

FLOWERING: July through mid-August

COMMENTS: This beautiful little anemone is not common in the Churchill region but has been found in crevices on Cape Merry, along streams under White Spruce near Akudlik, and at Twin Lakes. Similar plants are the common Cloudberry (pg. 198) which has both sepals and petals and **alternate** toothed stem leaves, and some of the white-flowered saxifrages (pgs. 178 & 200) which have both sepals and petals and only 10 stamens and 2 pistils.

Anemones appear to take their common and scientific names from the original Greek and Latin word for these plants, a Semitic name for Adonis, a mythical youth from whose blood the crimson-flowered anemone of the Orient is said to have sprung. Another possible source for the name is the Greek words for "daughter of the wind", a reference to the legend that anemones open only when a wind is blowing and to the fact that many species depend on wind for distribution of their long feathery seeds. Anemones are close relatives of the buttercups and, like them, contain **poisonous** and irritating substances. Handle them with care.

RANGE: North American-eastern Asian low arctic-boreal-alpine species: occurs from Churchill south around Hudson and James bays and up the entire eastern side of Hudson Bay.

FLOWERS WITH FIVE REGULAR PARTS

Wildflowers with Opposite (sometimes Alternate) Divided Leaves;
aquatic plant with white flowers....

524
544 ## *Large-Leaved Watercrowfoot*

(*Ranunculus aquatilis* L.)

BUTTERCUP FAMILY
Ranunculaceae

OTHER NAMES: White or Large-Leaved Water Buttercup, White Watercrowfoot

DESCRIPTION: Soft perennial **aquatic plant** with slender elongated stems floating under and upon the surface of the water, often forming thick mats. **Leaves opposite, or alternate** but so **finely divided** as to appear opposite, usually all underwater, the blades very soft, about 2.5 cm long on stalks 1.3-2 cm long and finally divided **into forked, hair-like segments.** Floating leaves, when present, less finely divided. **Small white,** 0.5-2 cm wide **flowers** float on the water or are held about 2.5 cm above the surface on slender stalks. 5 petals 2-3 times longer than the 5 green sepals; 5-25 stamens and 5-35 pistils. Fruits achenes, 1-2 mm long, beakless or with very short beaks, borne in an 8-10 mm wide round cluster.

HABITAT: Shallow water in ponds and slow streams: freshwater pools and streams, Meadow-Marsh community.

FLOWERING: Mid-July through August

COMMENTS: One of the few truly aquatic plants to grow well beyond the northern tree limit, this small buttercup is common throughout the Churchill area. The Small Yellow Watercrowfoot (pg. 202), an abundant aquatic in similar habitats, has bright yellow flowers and deeply lobed rather than finely divided leaves. All buttercups have an acrid and **poisonous** juice and should be handled with care to avoid skin irritation.

RANGE: Circumpolar boreal-arctic species: occurs as several varieties all around Hudson and James bays.

NOTE: The only other white-flowered aquatic buttercup in the region is the much larger and rarer PALLAS'S BUTTERCUP (*Ranunculus pallasii* Schlecht.) which has been found only once or twice at Churchill and a few other places around Hudson Bay. Like the Watercrowfoot, it also grows in shallow freshwater habitats but can easily be differentiated by its **large white flowers** (2-2.5 cm wide), which often have more than 5 petals, and its **basal long-petioled fleshy leaves** which have a short, oval 1-to-3-lobed blade.

524 *Cut-Leaved Anemone*

(*Anemone multifida* Poir.)

DESCRIPTION: Tufted 15-50 cm tall perennial plant from a strong many-headed taproot. Flowering stems 1-7, they and the leaves silky hairy. **Basal leaves long petioled**, the blades 1.5-8 cm long and **2-4 times divided into very narrow lobes.** Stem leaves similar but smaller, usually 3, sessile or nearly so and thus appearing opposite or whorled. Flowers 1 (2-3) on long stalks, **sepals** usually 5, 5-15 mm long, **creamy white or sometimes red or purple** in colour forms, silky hairy on the outside. **Petals lacking; stamens and pistils many;** fruits **many small woolly achenes** in a **globe-shaped**, 8-18 mm long **cluster.**

HABITAT: Dry calcareous slopes, river banks, or lakeshores: Open and Stable Dune communities; gravel ridges.

FLOWERING: July: early to mid-month at Churchill

COMMENTS: This tall anemone is common on sand throughout the Churchill area. Good places to look for it are near Fort Prince of Wales and the wrecked Lambair plane. The coloured sepals tend to fall off quickly making identification somewhat difficult. However **no other wildflower** in the area **has such finely divided leaves and** such a **round woolly fruiting cluster.**

All anemones contain **poisonous** substances when fresh and should be handled with care. On drying, some of these substances are converted to slightly less toxic ones which were historically used to treat everything from headaches to measles. I wouldn't recommend that you try it!

RANGE: North American (to South America) boreal-prairie species: occurs from Churchill south around Hudson and James bays; apparently missing from most of the eastern and northwestern sides of Hudson Bay but recorded for both the northwestern and northeastern corners.

JULY 20 1957

Churchill

Anemone multifida

FLOWERS WITH FIVE REGULAR PARTS

Wildflowers with Alternate Entire Mostly Basal Leaves; single pure white flowers with veined petals....

532
542

Northern Grass-Of-Parnassus

(*Parnassia palustris* L. var. *neogaea* Fern.)

SAXIFRAGE FAMILY
Saxifragaceae

OTHER NAMES: Common or Large Grass-of-Parnassus; Bog Star

DESCRIPTION: Smooth perennial plant, 10-40 cm tall, with a cluster of **long petioled heart-shaped** entire 1-2.5 cm wide **leaves** at the base of the erect unbranched flowering stem(s) and a **single** smaller clasping **leaf at**, or below, the **middle of the stem. Flowers one per stem** with 5, 0.8-1.5 cm long, **pure white petals with** 5-9 **contrasting veins**, the **petals** being about **twice the length of** the 5 green **sepals.** Stamens 5, alternating with the petals and **5 gland tipped staminodia** (sterile stamens) which look like tiny fringes tipped with golden balls at the base of the petals. Fruit an oval dry capsule about 1 cm long containing many small seeds.

HABITAT: Wet calcareous soil: upper Salt-Marsh and Damp Dune Hollow communities; in saline areas on outcrop ridge; on disturbed moist to wet gravel throughout the Churchill region.

FLOWERING: Late July through August

COMMENTS: This exquisite wildflower is a real treat for the mid- to late season northern visitor. The translucent white petals with contrasting veins and golden staminodia make it an excellent subject for photography. It is common throughout the Churchill region and elsewhere around the bays on moist sand and gravel.

The Grass-of-Parnassus takes both its scientific and common names from Mt. Parnassus in Greece. The plants were probably dedicated or sacred to the Muses who were believed to live on the snowcapped mountain.

RANGE: Circumpolar boreal-subarctic-montane species: occurs all around Hudson and James bays except the far northern islands and shores.

NOTE: A smaller relative, the SMALL GRASS-OF-PARNASSUS (*Parnassia kotzebuei* Cham. & Schlect.), is somewhat less common but still easily found in most of our region. It blooms earlier than the Northern Grass-of-Parnassus (early to late July), has smaller flowers with **petals equal to the sepals**, shorter petioles on its leaves and **no leaf on** the flowering **stem.** It sometimes grows in the same habitats as the Northern but prefers more peaty soils and can even be found in bogs.

Parnassia palustris

Wildflowers with Basal Entire Spatulate Leaves; few flowers borne in an umbel....

532 *Greenland Primrose*

PRIMROSE FAMILY
Primulaceae

(*Primula egaliksensis* Wormskj.)

DESCRIPTION:	Slender perennial plant with stems 3-20 cm tall; **leaves in a basal rosette**, entire oval to spatulate in shape, to 6 cm in length, the petiole as long as or longer than the thin smooth green blade. **Flowers**, 1-9 **in an umbel**, 5-9 mm across **with 5 deeply notched lilac to white petals, a yellow centre and tube;** calyx lobes glandular hairy; fruit a small, many-sided capsule.
HABITAT:	Meadows and wet calcareous shores especially near the sea: Salt-Marsh, Damp Dune Hollow and Meadow-Marsh communities near the shore; saline pools, ledges, and crevices on outcrop ridge; freshwater Meadow-Marsh and rich Hummocky Bog communities; gravel edges of ponds and streams.
FLOWERING:	July: (late June to early August)
COMMENTS:	This small primrose is common in salt marshes and other moist areas along the coast and on inland streams and lakes. It is a confusing little plant because the flowers vary in colour from pure white (most common) to a deep lilac colour – often right next to each other. However it always has the 5 notched petals and yellow flower centre characteristic of the primroses. Its close relative, the Strict or Erect Primrose (pg. 174), which grows in similar habitats, has **toothed leaves, shorter petioles** and **no hairs or glands on the calyx.** Both the common and scientific names of the primrose come from the Latin *primus* "first" and refer to the early spring flowering of many of the larger and showier European species.
RANGE:	Wide ranging North American subarctic-alpine species: occurs all around Hudson and James bays except for the far northern islands.

Churchill
June 22 '81

Primula incana

Wildflowers with Basal Entire Leaves; many pink flowers in a dense head....

532 ***Thrift***

(Armeria maritima (Mill.) Willd.)

LEADWORT FAMILY
Plumbaginaceae

OTHER NAMES: Sea-Pink

DESCRIPTION: Grass-like perennial plant, often forming dense tussocks, from a branched woody rootstalk with a **basal rosette of** narrow (3 mm) **linear greyish green** partly evergreen **fleshy** glandular **leaves**, 2-15 cm long. **Flowers** many, **rose pink** to occasionally white **in dense globe-shaped** 1.5-3 cm wide **heads** at the ends of 5-30 cm tall scapes. Corolla about 8 mm wide, of 5 nearly separate petals; stamens and calyx lobes 5; **each flower subtended by a papery nearly transparent bract.** Fruit dry and one-seeded, remaining enclosed by the persistent calyx.

HABITAT: Wide range of habitats but most common on coarse saline soils and cliffs along coasts, rare inland on moist gravel; sand and gravel ridges near the coast.

FLOWERING: Mid-July to mid-August

COMMENTS: Unfortunately this attractive little coastal plant with its head of pink or white paper-like flowers doesn't occur at Churchill. However it is common both north of Churchill and along the eastern side of the bays and is included here for those lucky enough to visit these areas. The dense almost clover-like head and narrow basal greyish green leaves are absolutely distinctive – nothing else looks anything like the Sea-Pink. It is used as an edging in formal gardens in Britain and other parts of Europe where it is a common northern coastal plant.

RANGE: Wide ranging mostly coastal circumpolar arctic-subarctic species; occurs around most of Hudson and James bays with apparent gaps on the western side of James Bay and along the Manitoba coast from Ontario to north of the Seal River. Not present at Churchill or York Factory.

FLOWERS WITH FIVE REGULAR PARTS

Wildflowers with Basal or Alternate Entire Leaves; many small white to pinkish flowers....

532
542

Alpine Bistort

(*Polygonum viviparum* L.)

BUCKWHEAT FAMILY
Polygonaceae

OTHER NAMES: Viviparous Knotweed; Alpine Smartweed

DESCRIPTION: 4-30 cm tall perennial plant from a short **often twisted starchy rootstalk.** Single erect stem has a few narrow alternate entire, 3-10 cm long, basal leaves pointed at the tip and tapering into long petioles, and 1-3 much smaller sessile upper leaves. **Stems above leaf nodes** are **sheathed by** a characteristic translucent brown structure called an **ochreae** which is 1 cm or longer above the lower leaves and open along one side. **Spike narrow,** 3-8 cm long; upper **flowers** 3-5 mm wide **with 5 white to pinkish sepals, no petals** and **several projecting stamens; lower flowers produce tiny reddish to dark purple bulblets** that sometimes sprout into tiny leafy plants on the parent plant. Fruits seldom formed, the triangular-capped bulblets serving the purpose of seeds.

HABITAT: Turfy to rocky, dry to very moist areas, often associated with nitrogen rich soils near animal dens, bird cliffs, or human campsites: general throughout the Churchill and Hudson Bay regions, especially on moist peat over gravel and near the coast.

FLOWERING: Early July to late August

COMMENTS: This small knotweed is common throughout the region, often growing in large colonies. Its elongated spike of tiny whitish flowers and small bulblets is completely distinctive. Many parts of this plant and its relatives are edible and have been used as food by northern peoples. Bulblets, young roots, and leaves are eaten raw while older roots and leaves are tougher, have more tannic and oxalic acid and are usually boiled. The crisp and nutty-flavoured rootstalk was a choice delicacy of the Inuit who preserved it by freezing or in seal oil. Ptarmigan, lemmings, and other small mammals and birds also eat the bulblets and other parts of the plant.

RANGE: Circumpolar widely distributed arctic-alpine species: occurs all around Hudson and James bays.

FLOWERS WITH FIVE REGULAR PARTS
Wildflowers with Basal Entire Leathery Leaves; flowers borne
from different points....

532 *Large-Flowered Wintergreen*

(*Pyrola grandiflora* Radius)

WINTERGREEN FAMILY
Pyrolaceae

OTHER NAMES: Arctic Pyrola, Wintergreen, or Shinleaf

DESCRIPTION: Perennial plant from slender rootstalks with a **basal rosette** of long petioled **smooth shiny leathery evergreen** and nearly entire **leaves.** Leaf blades thick and round, 1-4 cm wide, often with conspicuously lighter veins. 5-9 fragrant **creamy white to pink flowers** borne in an elongated cylindrical raceme on a 5-20 cm tall scape. Individual flowers 1.2-2 cm wide with **long downward curving** persistent **styles** and **yellow anthers** on threadlike filaments. Fruit a many-seeded capsule.

HABITAT: Dry to moist well drained sheltered areas: under willows on coastal beaches; Ledge and Crevice communities on the outcrop ridge; in sheltered hollows or under willows on moist peat inland.

FLOWERING: Late June to early August: peak usually early to mid-July

COMMENTS: This common and extremely attractive wildflower often grows in large colonies under or near willows along the coast. Its masses of creamy white to pink flowers and sweet scent are a treat during its peak bloom. Cape Merry, Fort Prince of Wales, and Bird Cove are good places to look for it in the Churchill area.

All pyrolas contain a drug related to aspirin and poultices of the leaves have been used to reduce the swelling and pain of bruises and wounds. Such leaf plasters were referred to as shin plasters and provided one of the common names of this group, their evergreen leaves providing the other.

RANGE: Circumpolar wide ranging arctic-subarctic-alpine species: occurs all around Hudson and James bays with a few apparent gaps (York Factory region; eastern James Bay).

NOTE: The PINK WINTERGREEN (*Pyrola asarifolia* Michx.) is a southern pyrola similiar to the Large-Flowered found occasionally and reaching its northern limit at Churchill. It grows inland in sheltered locations under willows or White Spruce sometimes with its larger relative. It can be recognized by its **smaller crimson to pale pink flowers** which have **red to pink anthers.**

533
733

Seaside Buttercup

BUTTERCUP FAMILY
Ranunculaceae

(*Ranunculus cymbalaria* Pursh)

OTHER NAMES: Seaside Crowfoot; Northern Seaside Buttercup

DESCRIPTION: Low tufted somewhat fleshy perennial plant with **slender runners which root freely** at the nodes. **Leaves** mostly basal and **long-petioled**, the 0.5-2.5 cm wide **blades kidney- to oval-shaped** with many large blunt teeth or shallow lobes. Flowering stems leafless, 2-20 cm tall, bearing one (to 4) **flowers with 5** (to 12) **narrow bright yellow**, 2-5 mm long **petals,** 5 slightly shorter yellow green sepals, **8-30 stamens** and **many pistils on a cylindrical center.** Fruits many small grooved beaked achenes.

HABITAT: Moist usually saline clay or sand: Salt-Marsh, Foreshore, Damp Dune Hollow and Saline Pool communities along the coast; inland very occasionally on moist peat or sand on the gravel ridges.

FLOWERING: Mid-July to mid-August

COMMENTS: This coastal buttercup is not uncommon although never abundant. Most of our plants are the tiny northern variety, only 2-3 cm tall with small three-toothed leaves. Good places to look for them at Churchill include the salt marshes and sandy beaches near Bird and Sloop's coves.

The generic name *Ranunculus* comes from the Latin word for "small frog", a reference to the marshy or aquatic habitats of many of the species. All buttercups are acrid and **poisonous** and should be handled with care.

RANGE: Circumpolar boreal-subarctic species with large gaps: occurs on the western side of Hudson Bay from near the Northwest Territories/Manitoba border south around James Bay to slightly up the eastern side of Hudson Bay.

FLOWERS WITH FIVE REGULAR PARTS

Wildflowers with Basal Toothed Leaves; a single white to light
pink waxy flower....

533 *One-Flowered Wintergreen*

(Moneses uniflora (L.) Gray)

WINTERGREEN FAMILY
Pyrolaceae

OTHER NAMES: One-Flowered Pyrola; Single Delight; Single-Flowered Wintergreen; Shy Maiden; Waxflower; Wood Nymph

DESCRIPTION: A small delicate perennial herb, 5-10 cm high, from a slender creeping rootstalk. **Leaves nearly round**, finely toothed, **almost evergreen**, 1-3 cm long including the short petiole and **borne in pairs or whorls at the base of the stem. One nodding** open **fragrant white** or pale pink **waxy looking flower** borne **at the top of the short stem.** Petals 5, 6-9 mm long; stamens 10, opposite the petals in pairs; style prominent, greenish, the stigma with five narrow conspicuous green lobes. Fruit an erect small brown capsule.

HABITAT: Moist mossy areas, usually under trees or shrubs: moist moss under willows and Black and White Spruce trees inland from the coast.

FLOWERING: Mid- to late July

COMMENTS: Widespread but never common inland in the Churchill region, this beautiful little wildflower should be looked for in moss carpets under White Spruce along the Goose Creek and Landing Lake roads. Its fragrant and lovely flower well repays a close look and/or photography. Its wide distribution and general attractiveness is echoed in its many common names. One of these, "Single Delight", is a direct translation of the generic name *Moneses* which comes from the Greek words *monos* ("single") and *hesis* ("delight"), a reference to the solitary flower.

RANGE: Widespread circumpolar boreal-subarctic species: occurs from the latitude of Churchill south around both sides of Hudson and James bays; reaches its northern limit at Churchill.

533 *Pygmyflower*

PRIMROSE FAMILY
Primulaceae

(*Androsace septentrionalis* L.)

OTHER NAMES: Rock Jasmine; Northern or Tooth-Leaved Androsace; Northern Fairy Candelabra

DESCRIPTION: Small annual or biennial herb, 2.5-15 cm tall, with a **basal rosette** of irregularly toothed, lanceolate, 1.3-3 cm long **sessile leaves** which are **often reddish green** in colour. The **few to several scapes from each rosette** end in an **open umbel of many very small white flowers with yellow centres.** Tiny corolla funnel-shaped, 3-5 mm wide, with 5 shallow rounded lobes and a flower tube that is constricted at the throat and extends just beyond the 5 triangular lobes of the calyx. Fruit a small round light brown few-seeded capsule.

HABITAT: Open, usually dry and chiefly calcareous rocky and sandy places: Sandy Foreshore, Open and Stable Dune communities; disturbed open areas on gravel ridges and roadsides.

FLOWERING: Mid-June to mid-August

COMMENTS: Often overlooked because of its small size, Pygmyflower is a little jewel of a wildflower. It is common to abundant along the coast and inland throughout the Churchill region. The Pygmyflower's clusters of flowers resemble miniature star bursts while individual flowers look like tiny primroses without the notched petals – not surprising since it belongs to the same family. As it blooms during the entire growing season, you should be able to find it at anytime throughout the summer and it well repays a close look at the ground.

RANGE: Circumpolar arctic-boreal-montane species: occurs all around Hudson and James bays except for the far northeastern section of Hudson Bay.

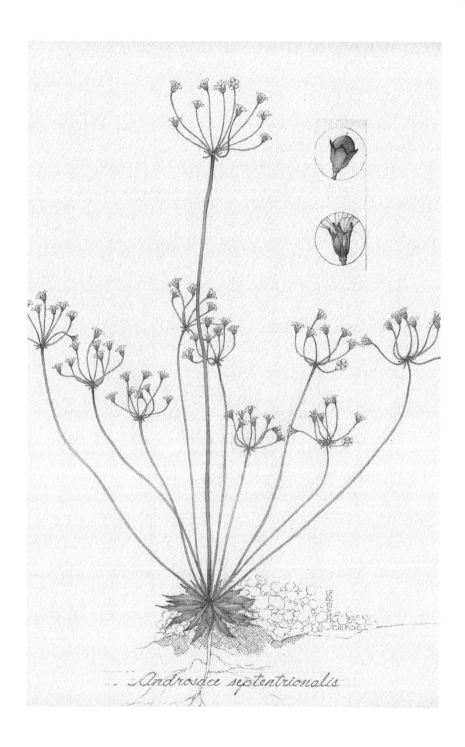

Androsace septentrionalis

FLOWERS WITH FIVE REGULAR PARTS
Wildflowers with Basal Toothed Leaves; 4 or more flowers
borne in an umbel....

533 *Erect Primrose*

(*Primula stricta* Hornem.)

PRIMROSE FAMILY
Primulaceae

OTHER NAMES: Strict Primrose

DESCRIPTION: Slender perennial herb with stems 5-30 cm tall. **Leaves** 2-6 cm long, in **a basal rosette**, with **toothed narrowly oval blades** that may be slightly mealy beneath and a winged petiole shorter than the blade. **Flowers** 5-9 mm wide, 1-8 **in an umbel, with 5 notched lilac to violet or white petals and a yellow centre and tube. Lobes of the calyx without hairs.** Fruit a small many-seeded capsule.

HABITAT: Moist places, preferably saline: Salt-Marsh, Damp Dune Hollow, and Stable Dune communities; saline pools and Ledge and Crevice communities on the outcrop ridge; moist, usually disturbed gravel inland.

FLOWERING: Mid-June to mid-July

COMMENTS: This small but very attractive primrose is common on sandy and rocky areas along the coast, much less common on disturbed gravel inland. It is very similar to the lilac-flowered form of its close relative, the Greenland Primrose (pg. 160) which often grows with or close to it. Both have basal rosettes of leaves and umbels of lilac or white flowers with notched petals and yellow centres and tubes. But the Greenland Primrose has entire leaves with much longer petioles, no hairs on its calyx, and usually white flowers. Both primroses are striking little plants, often present in surprising numbers along the coast and presenting excellent subjects for photography, especially when found in rock crevices on the outcrop ridge.

RANGE: North American-Greenland-European low arctic-subarctic species: occurs all around Hudson and James bays except for the northwestern corner and far northern islands.

FLOWERS WITH FIVE REGULAR PARTS

Wildflowers with Basal Toothed Leaves; more than 4 flowers from different points....

533 *One-Sided Wintergreen*

(*Pyrola secunda* L.)

WINTERGREEN FAMILY
Pyrolaceae

OTHER NAMES: One-Sided Pyrola

DESCRIPTION: Small slender perennial herb, to 10 cm tall in our area, from slender creeping rhizomes; **basal rosette of** slightly **leathery, fresh to yellow green,** oblong ovate and usually **pointed leaves** with small rounded teeth. Petioles usually much shorter than the 0.5-2 cm long blades. **Flowers few,** creamy white to greenish yellow, scentless, **in a distinctly one-sided raceme** on the scape. The 5 oval **petals** are 4-5 mm long and **form a nearly closed bell** which is longer than broad. The slender, **straight style** has a distinct flattened tip and **extends well out beyond the petals.** It is much longer than the 2.5-5 mm wide capsule.

HABITAT: Moist to dry moss or peat in sheltered areas: especially under willows or spruce trees in our area.

FLOWERING: July to early August

COMMENTS: This small wintergreen is common at Churchill. A good place to find it is under willows along the roadsides and dikes near Akudlik. The generic name *Pyrola* is Latin for "small pear", the pear being *pyrus*, and refers to the shape of the leaves of many of the species. More information on the genus can be found in the account on the Large-Flowered Wintergreen (pg. 166).

RANGE: Circumpolar low arctic-boreal-subalpine species: occurs from Churchill south around Hudson and James bays to about latitude 55°N on the eastern side of Hudson Bay.

NOTE: The related and similar-sized LESSER WINTERGREEN (*Pyrola minor* L.) is uncommon at Churchill but occurs occasionally there and along the southern coast of Hudson and James bays. It grows in woods and snow drift depressions and can be told from the One-Sided by the **cylindrical arrangement of** its white to pink **flowers,** its short straight **style** which is **enclosed within the petals,** and its oval, usually blunt-tipped leaves.

FLOWERS WITH FIVE REGULAR PARTS

Wildflowers with Mostly Basal Three-Toothed Leaves; white flowers with coloured spots....

533
543 ***Three-Toothed Saxifrage***

(*Saxifraga tricuspidata* Rottb.)

SAXIFRAGE FAMILY
Saxifragaceae

OTHER NAMES: Prickly Saxifrage

DESCRIPTION: Loosely matted tough nearly evergreen perennial herb, often forming **large flat cushions of branching stems.** The **rigid leathery** 1-2 cm long **leaves** are **brownish green, often tinged with red or purple,** narrowly oblong **with 3 obvious sharp teeth at their tips** and closely crowded, the dead and withered leaves remain below the live ones on the stem. Flowering stems 6-15 cm tall from the tips of the branches with a few small widely spaced alternate leaves. **Flowers several** to many in an open branched cluster, each **with 5 oval** 6-7 mm long **creamy white petals spotted with coloured dots,** usually yellow at the base and shading to red at the tips. There are 5 short broadly triangular sepals, **10 stamens,** and **2 styles.** Fruit a cone-shaped 5-8 mm long **capsule with 2 small divergent beaks.**

HABITAT: Dry, rocky, and gravelly places: occurs in dry habitats throughout the Churchill region, from Sandy Foreshore communities along the coast to eroded and open areas on the gravel ridges.

FLOWERING: Late June to early August

COMMENTS: This tough little saxifrage is common to abundant throughout the Churchill region and other parts of Hudson Bay. It grows on some of the driest and most exposed places along the coast and inland ridges, forming large mats of leathery three-pointed leaves. The flowers are the typical attractive 5-petals-with-spots ones of the family and they and the three-toothed leaves (they **are** prickly!), make the plant easy to recognize. The Three-Toothed Saxifrage is indeed a "rock-breaker", as the Latin generic name implies, and one of its favourite habitats is nooks and crannies of the outcrop ridge or cliffs.

RANGE: Wide ranging North American (Greenland) arctic-alpine species: occurs all around Hudson and James bays with the possible exception of the southernmost tip of James Bay.

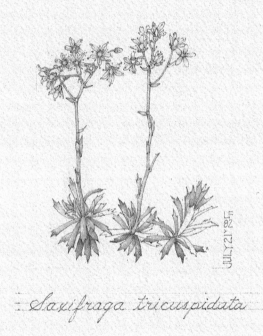

Saxifraga tricuspidata

733
734

Lapland Buttercup
(*Ranunculus lapponicus* L.)

BUTTERCUP FAMILY
Ranunculaceae

DESCRIPTION: Terrestrial perennial herb with slender white creeping **stems deeply buried in moss** and freely rooting at the nodes. Leaves basal, long-petioled, solitary or a few together, the blade deeply 3-lobed to divided, the lobes broadly oval in shape and coarsely toothed. **Flowers solitary**, on 5-25 cm high flowering stems, **sweet scented**, about 1 cm in diameter, **with 3 sepals, 6-10 pale yellow to whitish petals and numerous stamens and pistils.** Fruiting cluster globe-shaped, of 3-15 achenes, their bodies slightly longer than their slender hooked beaks.

HABITAT: Damp moss, often under willows or in sphagnum bogs: fresh Meadow-Marsh, Sphagnum Bog and Muskeg communities.

FLOWERING: Late June to mid-July

COMMENTS: This is one of the least common of the buttercups in the Churchill region but very attractive with its bright yellow flower against the green moss. You are almost certain to find it if you go 'bogging' in the sphagnum bogs along Goose Creek or Landing Lake roads in early July. The only plant you are likely to confuse it with is the Yellow Anemone (pg. 150) which has large deeply lobed opposite leaves on the stem, larger flowers, and no sepals. This whole group is acrid and **poisonous** and should be handled with care.

RANGE: Nearly circumpolar (large gaps) wide ranging low arctic-subarctic species: found all around Hudson and James bays.

534 *Egede's Cinquefoil*

(*Potentilla egedii* Wormskj.)

ROSE FAMILY
Rosaceae

OTHER NAMES: Pacific Silverweed or Argentine

DESCRIPTION: Small often tufted perennial herb from a short thick rootstalk which supports a rosette of once-pinnately divided leaves from which come **smooth** long slender freely rooting **flowering runners.** The **compound leaves** are 2-20 cm long with 2-9 pairs of oval deeply sharp toothed usually widely spaced leaflets **with grey to white undersides.** The **single rose-like bright to pale yellow flowers** are 1-3 cm wide and borne on smooth leafless pedicels from the rosette or nodes of the runners. Petals 5, sepals 5 with 5 smaller sepal-like bracts alternating with them, **stamens 10-30** and **pistils many** on a 'head' in the centre of the flower.

HABITAT: Halophyte; grows in colonies to just above the high tide mark on muddy or sandy flats: Salt-Marsh, Damp Dune Hollow, Ledge and Crevice, and Saline Pool communities on the seaward side of the outcrop ridge.

FLOWERING: Late June to mid-August

COMMENTS: This attractive low cinquefoil is common in saline areas along the coast. Good places to look for it around Churchill are among the rocks near the town centre, at Fort Prince of Wales, and at Bird Cove. Its inter-connected mats and runners, small rose-like yellow flowers, and pinnately divided leaves are unmistakeable. All cinquefoils contain large amounts of tannin and many have been used as antiseptics, astringents, and tonics as well as to tan leather. The generic name, *Potentilla*, reflects these uses and means "powerful little one" in Latin. Its common and scientific names honor Hans Egede, the father of modern Greenland.

RANGE: Circumpolar arctic-subarctic species of seacoasts: found all around Hudson and James bays with occasional gaps.

NOTE: SILVERWEED (*Potentilla anserina* L.), a widespread closely related and very similar cinquefoil, occurs occasionally at Churchill and along southern Hudson and James bays but grows inland on fresh-water sites. It has larger and longer leaves with more leaflets than Egede's Cinquefoil and **densely hairy runners and leaves.**

534 *Buck-Bean*

(*Menyanthes trifoliata* L.)

BUCK-BEAN FAMILY
Menyanthaceae

OTHER NAMES: Bog-Bean; Marsh Trefoil; Water Shamrock

DESCRIPTION: Coarse perennial **aquatic or marsh herb** from a stout submerged scaly rootstalk. **Bluish green** fairly **thick leaves** are **divided into 3 oval** 5-10 cm long **leaflets at** the **tip of a long petiole.** Flowers few to many in a raceme at the tip of a separate 10-40 cm tall scape. Individual **flowers star-like,** 1-1.5 cm across, **white** or purple tinged, **with** a 6-9 mm long floral tube and **5 (rarely 6) long-fringed or bearded petal lobes.** Fruit a round light brown capsule containing a few shiny seeds. Leaves and flowers extend separately 10-30 cm above the surface of the water.

HABITAT: Freshwater bogs, marshes, and shallow lakes; margins of ponds and lakes on inland gravel ridges and peat areas.

FLOWERING: July

COMMENTS: This striking aquatic plant is not common near Churchill but can be found along the edges of the lakes east of Akudlik and in bog pools along the Landing Lake Road. Once spotted Buck-Bean is easy to identify by its cluster of star-shaped white flowers with bearded petals and long stemmed 3-parted clover-like leaves. Buck-Bean has been used by native peoples and northern Europeans as an all purpose medicinal plant to treat a variety of ills. Its generic name is Greek for "flower of the month" and refers to both the duration of its beautiful shaggy flowers and its beneficial effects on menstrual pain. The recent common name comes from the German *Bocksbohen* which means "Goat's Beans" and was transliterated into the English "Buck-Bean".

RANGE: Wide ranging circumpolar boreal-subarctic-montane species: occurs from near the latitude of Churchill south around both sides of Hudson and James bays; reaches its northern limit at Churchill.

Menyanthes trifoliata

distylis
5 stamens

Churchill

LF.82
JULY 18

FLOWERS WITH FIVE REGULAR PARTS
Wildflowers with Alternate Entire Leaves; terminal yellow flowers and
2-beaked capsules....

542 *Yellow Marsh Saxifrage*

(*Saxifraga hirculus* L. s. lat.)

SAXIFRAGE FAMILY
Saxifragaceae

OTHER NAMES:	Bog Saxifrage
DESCRIPTION:	More or less tufted perennial herb, often with short runners. Basal leaves alternate entire smooth oblong, 1-4 cm long, usually clustered and overlapping. Flowering stems erect, 15-25 cm tall, bearing curly reddish hairs above and several narrow, sessile leaves. **Flowers usually 1** (to 4), 1.5-3 cm wide and nodding at first **with 5 oval pale yellow petals that often have orange spots** near their bases and are about twice as long as the 5 oval and reddish fringed sepals which become reflexed below the fruits. **Stamens 10; styles 2 and short;** fruit an 8-12 mm long dry **capsule with 2 slightly spreading short beaks.**
HABITAT:	Wet and mossy freshwater tundra areas: Wet Meadow, Hummocky Bog, Willow/Bog Birch Thicket and Black Spruce/Larch Muskeg and Bog communities.
FLOWERING:	Mid-July to late August: peak usually in early August
COMMENTS:	This attractive wildflower is one of the late-season yellow-flowered saxifrages, most other species having purple or white flowers and blooming much earlier. All have the distinctive saxifrage flower pattern of 5 petals, 5 sepals, 10 stamens and 2 pistils, often with dots of contrasting colour spotting the petals. The exquisite flowers and mainly arctic distribution of the Yellow Marsh Saxifrage make it truly a northern treat. The only other plant you are likely to confuse it with is the Yellow Mountain Saxifrage (pg. 188) which blooms at the same time. That is a low mat-forming plant with trailing stems and sessile leaves which grows on sandy and gravelly sites rather than on peat or moss. The Yellow Marsh Saxifrage is relatively common in bogs and meadow-marshes in the Churchill region and should be looked for particularly in the White Spruce bogs near Akudlik and hummocky bogs near Bird Cove.
RANGE:	Circumpolar arctic-subarctic-montane species: occurs all around Hudson and James bays except the southern part of James Bay.

July 15 '81
Churchill

L.F.

Saxifraga hirculus

FLOWER WITH FIVE REGULAR PARTS

Wildflowers with Alternate Entire Leaves; terminal yellow flowers
and two-beaked capsules....

542 *Yellow Mountain Saxifrage*

(*Saxifraga aizoides* L.)

SAXIFRAGE FAMILY
Saxifragaceae

OTHER NAMES: Golden Saxifrage

DESCRIPTION: **Low matted perennial herb** with several stems radiating out from a single rootstalk. Leaves smooth sessile light green, somewhat fleshy, 0.5-1.5 cm long, alternate, and linear, the basal ones clustered or overlapping slightly. Flowering stems 5-30 cm tall, branched, with 1-20 (usually 4-5) flowers and several widely scattered leaves. Flowers erect, 5-8 mm wide, with **5 oval yellow petals (usually with orange dots)**, 5 shorter triangular calyx lobes, 10 stamens and **two styles.** **Fruit an obviously 2-beaked dry capsule** divided nearly to the base.

HABITAT: Moist usually calcareous gravel, sand, or clay; occasionally moist peat: Sandy Foreshore, Damp Dune Hollow and Hummocky Bog communities; moist shallow peat and disturbed gravel on ridges, around the edge of ponds and along roadsides.

FLOWERING: Mid-July to late August: peak late July or early August

COMMENTS: This attractive late-season saxifrage is common in a variety of habitats in the Churchill region. It grows in low ground-hugging colonies and is difficult to spot until it blooms. Then the numerous yellow flowers show up clearly. Check for it in late July on disturbed gravel along the Launch and Goose Creek roads, the ridges east of Akudlik, and the fossil beach ridges and upper salt-marshes at Bird Cove. Most saxifrages are arctic and mountain plants, few reaching south into the boreal forest zone. Their name comes from the Latin *saxum* ("a stone") and *frangere* ("to break"). It alludes to both the habitat of many species, which do grow in rocks, and the early 'doctrine of signatures' medicinal use in which the small bulblets borne by some species were believed to dissolve kidney and bladder stones. The only other yellow-flowered saxifrage that you are likely to confuse with this plant is the Yellow Marsh Saxifrage (pg. 186). Although it blooms at the same time, it is much taller (15-25 cm), has larger flowers (to 8 cm wide), petioled lower leaves and grows inland on moist peaty or mossy areas.

RANGE: Amphi-Atlantic arctic-alpine species: occurs all around Hudson and James bays.

Saxifraga azoides

FLOWERS WITH FIVE REGULAR PARTS
Wildflowers with Alternate Entire Leaves; tiny yellow green flowers and red fruits....

542 *Northern Comandra*

SANDALWOOD FAMILY
Santalaceae

(Geocaulon lividum (Richards.) Fern.)

DESCRIPTION:
Low, 10-30 cm high, smooth perennial herb from narrow creeping brown to red underground rootstalks. Stems erect, unbranched, bearing alternate entire lanceolate **blue to yellow green leaves** that are 1-3 cm long and **have a distinctive network of veins beneath.** The **small bronze to yellow green flowers** are star-shaped, about 4 mm wide and **occur in sessile clusters** of 2-4 in the **axils of** the **middle leaves.** Sepals 5, united to form the bell-like calyx of the flower; petals lacking, stamens 5 and opposite the lobes of the calyx, style short and cone-shaped. **Fruit** one (rarely two) **red, fleshy and drupe-like, 6-8 mm wide** and with a single large seed.

HABITAT:
Moist mossy but well drained woods: mossy areas under White Spruce on the outcrop and gravel ridges.

FLOWERING:
Late June through mid-July: fruits ripe in early August

COMMENTS:
Although this small boreal plant is near its northern limit, it is present in fair numbers under most White Spruce trees in the Churchill area. It requires some protection as it is one of the few northern representatives of a family composed mainly of tropical trees and shrubs. Most of its relatives are semi-parasites, able to manufacture their own food but absorbing water and minerals from a host plant through root connections, but it is not known if this is true of the Northern Comandra. The small red fruits are listed as edible by one source but I have never tried them and the large seed would make them hardly worth the effort. This plant is easiest to spot when its fruits are ripe but the tiny flowers are worth looking for in early July. Not many plants grow directly under White Spruce trees and your chances of finding the Northern Comandra are good if you look there.

RANGE:
Boreal-subarctic North American species: occurs from just north of Churchill south around both bays to about halfway up the eastern side of Hudson Bay.

FLOWERS WITH FIVE REGULAR PARTS

Wildflowers with Alternate Entire Narrow Leaves; large pure white flowers with unveined petals....

542 **Lewis' Wild Flax**

FLAX FAMILY
Linaceae

(*Linum lewisii* Pursh)

OTHER NAMES: White Flax

DESCRIPTION: A smooth perennial herb with several erect 15-60 cm tall stems from a stout rootstalk. Stems densely leafy with alternate linear 1-2.5 cm long sessile leaves. The **large 2-3.5 cm wide white flowers** are **borne at** or near the **tips of the stem**, 1 flower opening each day and **soon dropping** its **petals**. **Petals 5, pure white and translucent**; sepals 5, green, 3-6 mm long; stamens 5, joined into a tube at the base with teeth-like staminodia between. Fruit a small round 5 mm wide capsule.

HABITAT: Dry calcareous sandy, gravelly, and rocky slopes: occurs on the Sandy Foreshore, Open and Stable Dune communities and very occasionally on dry exposed sites on the inland gravel ridges.

FLOWERING: July: usually early to mid-month

COMMENTS: A close relative of cultivated flax, Lewis' Wild Flax is relatively uncommon at Churchill. The best place to find it is along the sides of the gravel road just east of the wrecked Lambair plane. Individual flowers only open for 1 day and drop their petals by late afternoon so the best time to find the plant in bloom is mid-day. Only the white-flowered form occurs around Hudson and James bays, the more common blue-flowered plant occurring on dry prairie sites throughout southern Manitoba and further west.

Flax of course has been grown for centuries, both for the fibres of its stem, used to make linen and other forms of cloth, and the oil from its seeds. We don't know whether this wild species was used in this way by native people or settlers but it may well have been.

RANGE: North American endemic of prairies to subarctic slopes (including the more common blue-flowered form); a close relative occurs in similar habitats across Asia and Europe: our white-flowered form occurs from Churchill south around both bays to slightly up the eastern side of Hudson Bay.

542 *Seaside Lungwort*

BORAGE FAMILY
Boraginaceae

(*Mertensia maritima* (L.) S.F. Gray)

OTHER NAMES: Sea-Lungwort; Oysterleaf; Seaside Smooth-Gromwell; Northern Shorewort

DESCRIPTION: Smooth perennial herb with trailing stems that radiate out from a small taproot to form a circular rosette from 5 to nearly 100 cm wide. The **fleshy** alternate entire **leaves** are a **characteristic bluish colour** and usually have tiny round dots or projections on their surfaces. Stems are purplish and often bear the 1-7 cm long spatula-shaped leaves in two rows. The many 3-10 mm long flowers are borne in open clusters at the ends of stems and have a **bell-shaped flower tube which starts pink then changes to blue** as the flower ages. Sepals 5, fused into a deeply 5-parted calyx; stamens 5, attached to the flower tube near its top; style narrow and not projecting beyond the petals. Fruit 4 smooth nutlets about 5 mm long which have a spongy outer coat that becomes inflated, allowing them to be dispersed by water.

HABITAT: Halophyte; grows only on sandy to shingly sea beaches: Foreshore communities just above the high tide mark at Churchill.

FLOWERING: Late June to late August: peak about mid-July

COMMENTS: Seaside Lungwort is one of a small group of halophytes or "salt plants" that can grow in or close to Hudson Bay and other oceans. It is found occasionally on sand or gravel beaches in the Churchill region, usually along with Sea-Purslane and Sea Lime Grass. These salt-tolerant plants grow as colonies or clustered plants just above the high tide mark, the first flowering plants you find next to the bay. Good places to find it at Churchill are the beaches near Fort Prince of Wales and the town centre. The characteristic blue green leaves, pink to blue flowers, and radiating stems make it easy to identify. One of its common names, "Oysterleaf", comes from the salty-fishy flavour of the leaves, but I can't really recommend it as an edible plant.

RANGE: Nearly circumpolar arctic-subarctic species of seacoasts: occurs all around Hudson and James bays.

FLOWERS WITH FIVE REGULAR PARTS

Wildflowers with Alternate Entire Leaves; a single deep blue flower....

Alpine Bluebell

(Campanula uniflora L.)

BLUEBELL FAMILY
Campanulaceae

OTHER NAMES: Arctic Dwarf Harebell

DESCRIPTION: A dwarf perennial herb with 1 to several ascending, unbranched, 3-30 cm tall leafy stems from a fleshy taproot. The stout stems bear numerous dark green alternate leathery entire (a few small teeth may be present) leaves which are clustered and spatula-shaped near the base, widely spaced smaller and narrower towards the top. **A single deep blue narrowly bell-shaped flower, often nodding when young, is borne at the tip of the stem.** Corolla 5-13 mm long and 4-8 mm wide, the 5 pointed lobes about as long as the floral tube which is enclosed by the 5 narrow lobes of the calyx. It has an **inferior ovary** which becomes an erect 1-2 cm long capsule with many small seeds.

HABITAT: Calcareous turfy, stony, or gravelly ridges and cliffs: Ledge and Crevice communities on the outcrop ridge and eroded turf and gravel patches on gravel ridges.

FLOWERING: Early to mid-July

COMMENTS: This attractive small bluebell is unfortunately uncommon to rare in the Churchill region, reaching its southern limit at the Churchill River. It has been found only on the beach and outcrop ridges between Sloop's Cove and Fort Prince of Wales and on Cape Merry. Because of its small size (most of our plants are under 10 cm), it is hard to spot but the single dark blue bell-shaped flower is absolutely distinctive. Even its generic name *Campanula* comes from the Latin word for "little bell" and refers to the shape of the flower.

RANGE: Circumpolar wide ranging high arctic-alpine-montane species with a large gap in northern Asia: occurs from Churchill north and east around Hudson Bay as far south as the northeastern corner of James Bay.

543 *Cloudberry*

(*Rubus chamaemorus* L.)

ROSE FAMILY
Rosaceae

OTHER NAMES:	Baked-Apple Berry
DESCRIPTION:	Low perennial herb from creeping rootstalks, the 5-20 cm high erect simple stems with 1-3 **broad dark green alternate leathery 3-5-lobed leaves** with distinct petioles, 2-7 cm wide blades, and coarse to fine teeth on the lobes. **Flowers solitary and white**, 1-2.5 cm wide, borne at the tip of the stem. Plants male or female, only the style or stamens functioning in an individual flower although the other is usually present in a reduced and non-functional form. The large **raspberry-like** edible **fruits** borne on female plants are hard and deep red when young, becoming juicy and **amber yellow when ripe.**
HABITAT:	Moist peat bogs, usually in mosses or lichens: general on organic soils in the Churchill area, from damp mossy areas on the outcrop ridges to Black Spruce/Larch muskegs and bogs inland.
FLOWERING:	Late June to mid-July: fruits usually ripe in early August
COMMENTS:	This tasty yellow relative of the raspberry is common in the Churchill region. The fruit keeps through the winter without the addition of sugar and makes a very good jam. The taste is supposed to be similar to that of baked apples, hence the common name, but I personally find it a bit insipid. It is the earliest berry to ripen at Churchill, with the exception of the rare wild strawberry or Stemless Raspberry, and a good place to find early berries is on the pressure ridges around the edge of Landing Lake. Later they are abundant on the outcrop ridges between Cockle's Point and Sloop's Cove. Cloudberries were the favourite native fruit of the Inuit who preserved them in seal oil.
RANGE:	Wide ranging circumpolar low arctic-montane species: occurs all around Hudson and James bays.

FLOWERS WITH FIVE REGULAR PARTS

Wildflowers with Alternate Lobed Leaves; several white flowers....

543 *Tufted Saxifrage*

(Saxifraga caespitosa L.)

SAXIFRAGE FAMILY
Saxifragaceae

OTHER NAMES: Tufted Alpine Saxifrage

DESCRIPTION: Low perennial glandular-hairy herb forming **dense cushions or mats**; persistent basal shoots 1-20 cm long are thickly covered with withered dead leaves below the living ones and form a compact rosette. **Leaves soft, spatula-shaped**, 0.5-3 cm long, **deeply palmately-lobed**, the lobes narrow rounded and spreading. Flowering stems erect, 1-20 cm tall, with 1-6 small, often entire, alternate leaves and 1-7 flowers on stout pedicels. The **white**, 3-11 mm long, oval **petals have** distinct veins but **no coloured spots**; the 5-lobed calyx is shorter than the petals and often purple; there are 10 stamens and 2 styles. Fruit a globe-shaped **capsule with 2 short beaks.**

HABITAT: Rocky, gravelly, or sandy areas: Ledge and Crevice communities, and on moist gravel areas adjacent to the outcrop ridge.

FLOWERING: Late June through July

COMMENTS: This small saxifrage is uncommon at Churchill. It has only been found a few times in moist gravel and crevices on the outcrop ridges along the coast at Bird Cove and the town centre. The 5 petals, 10 stamens and 2 styles mark it as a saxifrage and its short-petioled softly hairy leaves and unspotted white petals point directly to this species.

RANGE: Circumpolar arctic-alpine species: occurs all around Hudson and James bays as one variety or another.

NOTE: The similar, but even less common, ALPINE BROOK SAXIFRAGE (*Saxifraga rivularis* L.) grows in damp to wet shaded crevices on the outcrop ridge. It is known only from near Fort Churchill in our immediate area and has **smaller white or pink-tinged flowers** than the Tufted and a few smooth long-petioled **kidney-shaped basal leaves** with broad notched lobes.

Saxifraga caespitosa

JUNE 30 1947 CHURCHILL

Wildflowers with Alternate Deeply Lobed Leaves; small yellow flowers....

543
544
744

Small Yellow Watercrowfoot

BUTTERCUP FAMILY

(*Ranunculus purshii* Richards.)

Ranunculaceae

OTHER NAMES:	Small Yellow Water-Buttercup; Gmelin's Buttercup or Watercrowfoot
DESCRIPTION:	**Aquatic or semiaquatic** perennial herb with branched creeping or floating stems which root at the nodes. Underwater **leaves** 1-3 cm wide, **divided into 3 main lobes** which are **subdivided into long narrow segments;** floating leaves usually smaller with wider lobes. The few **flowers emergent** at the tips of stems or in axils of upper leaves with **5 (to 7) golden yellow** 3-6 mm long **petals, 5 shorter** greenish yellow **sepals,** and **many stamens and styles.** Fruit a 5 mm wide globe-shaped cluster of small achenes with distinct beaks.
HABITAT:	Shallow freshwater ponds and wet bogs: from semi-saline pools along the coast and river estuary to freshwater lakes, ponds, and streams inland.
FLOWERING:	July: usually mid- to late month
COMMENTS:	This small watercrowfoot is common in the ponds of the Churchill region, especially near the river estuary. Its bright yellow flowers and alternate leaves distinguish it from the white-flowered and usually opposite-leaved Large-Leaved Watercrowfoot or Buttercup (pg. 154) which is abundant in similar habitats. Both species often form masses of floating intertwined leaves with the small bright flowers sticking up out of the water above them. All buttercups have an acrid and **poisonous** juice and should be handled with care.
RANGE:	Nearly circumpolar subarctic-boreal-montane range for the species complex: occurs from the northwestern corner of Hudson Bay south and east around James Bay to slightly up the eastern side of Hudson Bay.

FLOWERS WITH FIVE REGULAR PARTS

Wildflowers with Alternate Divided Leaves; yellow flowers over 1 cm wide....

Northern Buttercup

(Ranunculus pedatifidus Sm.)

BUTTERCUP FAMILY
Ranunculaceae

DESCRIPTION: Tufted slightly hairy perennial herb from a short fibrous base which bears a few erect slender simple or slightly forking, 10-30 cm tall, flowering stems. **Basal leaves long petioled,** the blades cordate in outline and **deeply to shallowly palmately-divided into** 5-9 **narrow entire lobes.** Stem leaves sessile or nearly so, completely divided into 1 to 3 narrow lobes. **Flowers showy,** one to several, 1-2.5 cm wide, the 5 (0-7) round **pale to bright yellow** petals about twice as long as the 5 sepals which are thinly grey-hairy on their backs. **Stamens and pistils many;** fruits many small (2 mm) achenes with slender curved beaks borne in a nearly round 1 cm tall fruiting cluster.

HABITAT: Calcareous gravelly, sandy, or grassy places, usually moist: moist disturbed gravel and peaty areas near the coast and on the outcrop ridge.

FLOWERING: Late June to mid-July

COMMENTS: This showy buttercup is locally abundant in early July on moist gravel and under willows near Fort Prince of Wales, on Cape Merry, and elsewhere along the outcrop ridge. It is a highly variable species having one prairie variety which has only sepals. The normal alpine and arctic plant looks at first glance much like a cinquefoil but has shinier yellow petals which are distinctly veined on their backs and have no notches at their tips. All buttercups have an acrid **poisonous** juice and should be handled with care.

RANGE: Circumpolar arctic-alpine-grassland species complex: occurs all around Hudson and James bays.

204

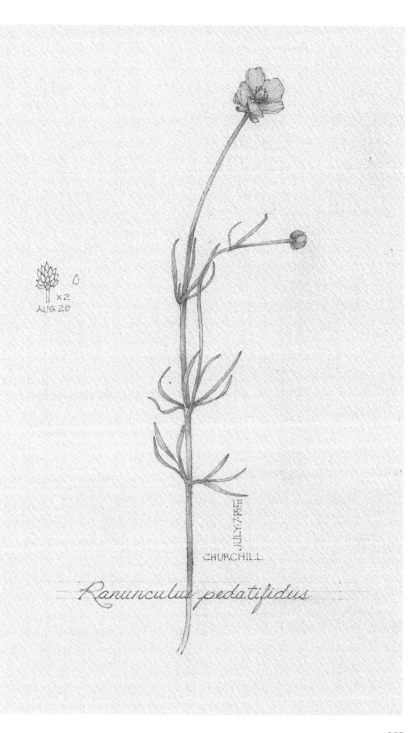

×2
AUG 20

JULY 7 1984

CHURCHILL

Ranunculus pedatifidus

FLOWERS WITH FIVE REGULAR PARTS

Wildflowers with Alternate Divided Leaves; 3 leaflets and pink flowers....

Stemless Raspberry

(*Rubus acaulis* Michx.)

ROSE FAMILY
Rosaceae

OTHER NAMES: Arctic Bramble; Dewberry

DESCRIPTION: **Dwarf tufted** unarmed perennial **herb** from a small rootstalk; stems 3-20 cm tall with a few alternate **leaves**, their blades **divided into 3**, 1.5-5 cm long, **coarsely toothed leaflets.** Flowers usually **single, large fragrant and showy**, with 5, 1-2 cm long, spatula-shaped **pink to red petals**, 5 triangular shorter green sepals, and many stamens and styles. **Fruit a** fairly small very **sweet aromatic red raspberry.**

HABITAT: Damp peat and sand: Damp Dune Hollow, White Spruce scrub, and Moist Heath communities near the coast; under willows along rivers and lakes inland.

FLOWERING: Late June to late July: peak usually in mid-July

COMMENTS: Locally common on moist peat and sand throughout the Churchill region, this small thornless raspberry is prized for its marvelously sweet and flavourful red berries and attractive flowers. The berries are similar to those of the southern white-flowered Dewberry and like them never seem to occur in large enough numbers to pick for preserves but are a delicious 'on-the-spot' treat. Good places to find them are under willows along the Churchill River at the Goose Creek pumphouse and along the edge of the salt marshes at Bird Cove. Raspberries were named after a sweet red French wine called *raspis* but I don't know whether the wine was actually made from the berries.

RANGE: Nearly circumpolar subarctic-boreal-montane species complex: occurs down the western side of Hudson Bay from near the Northwest Territories/Manitoba border to James Bay: apparently missing from most of the eastern side of Hudson and James bays.

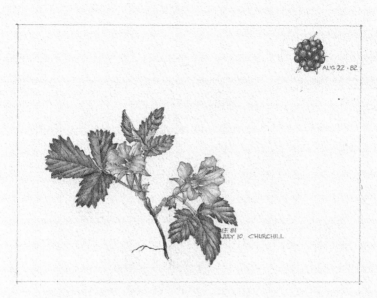

Rubus acaulis

FLOWERS WITH FIVE REGULAR PARTS
Wildflowers with Alternate Divided Leaves; 3 leaflets and yellow flowers....

544 *Snow Cinquefoil*

(Potentilla nivea L.)

DESCRIPTION: Low loosely tufted perennial herb from a stout brown base and taproot, the alternate mostly **basal leaves palmately-divided into 3** (rarely 5) 1-3 cm long oval **deeply toothed leaflets** which are **silvery hairy beneath** and usually **smooth and dark green above.** Flowering stems branched, sparsely hairy, 4-30 cm high bearing 3-15 **pale yellow rose-like flowers with** 5 wide 5-9 mm long **shallowly notched petals** which are much longer than the 5 triangular calyx lobes which alternate with 5 narrow bracts; **20 stamens and many pistils.**

HABITAT: Dry calcareous rocks and slopes; Stable Dune communities; Ledge and Crevice communities on the outcrop ridges; disturbed gravel roadsides and ridges.

FLOWERING: Late June through July

COMMENTS: The Snow Cinquefoil is the commonest three-leaved cinquefoil found at Churchill. It is widespread but never abundant and good places to find it are Cape Merry and other outcrop ridges along the coast and disturbed gravel near Akudlik. Its leaves and stems are reported to be particularly good sources of vitamin C.

The only plant you are likely to confuse it with is the Beautiful Cinquefoil (pg. 216) which is also common on dry and disturbed areas in the region. However it has 5 rather than 3 leaflets (you may have to look closely to determine this as the bottom two tend to be quite small) which are deeply lobed rather than toothed, shorter flowering stems, and narrower petals which are only slightly longer than the sepals. The whole plant tends to be more compact and silky hairy than the Snow Cinquefoil.

RANGE: Circumpolar (with gaps) arctic-subarctic-alpine species complex: occurs as one variety or another all around Hudson and James bays except for the region between Churchill and the southern part of James Bay.

NOTE: The only other three-leaved cinquefoil you are likely to find at Churchill is the less common and weedy ROUGH CINQUEFOIL (*Potentilla norvegica* L.) which reaches its northern limit there. It occurs on disturbed areas on the upper beaches, ridges, and roadsides and is a larger, coarser plant. It can be told from the Snow Cinquefoil by its **lack of silvery hairs, larger leaves, leafy stems,** and **small petals** which barely exceed the sepals. Several other palmately 3 to 5-lobed cinquefoils occur elsewhere around Hudson and James bays but are either very uncommon or lacking at Churchill. They are difficult to separate from the Snow Cinquefoil so if you find one which doesn't quite fit that description, check with one of the technical floras listed in the reference section if you want to track it down. The cinquefoils are recognized as one of the most 'difficult' (to separate and identify) groups in the north and one authority calls them a "devilish combination".

FLOWERS WITH FIVE REGULAR PARTS

Wildflowers with Alternate Lobed to Divided Leaves; small white
flowers in umbels....

543
544

Water-Hemlock

(*Cicuta mackenzieana* Raup)

PARSLEY FAMILY
Umbelliferae

OTHER NAMES: Mackenzie Water-Hemlock; Cowbane

DESCRIPTION: Stout perennial herb to over 1 m high with smooth hollow stems from a short stout **chambered rootstalk**. Leaves alternate with large basal sheaths, **doubly pinnately divided**, the **leaflets 5-8 cm long and usually less than 5 mm wide with sharply toothed edges.** Tiny white flowers borne in a distinctive 'umbel of umbels' 3-8 cm wide, the 9-21 rays of the primary umbel each bearing a secondary umbel (umbellet) whose 50 or more rays each end in a flower. Individual flowers 2-4 mm wide with 5 white petals, a shorter 5-toothed calyx, 5 stamens which alternate with the petals and a single pistil with two styles. The dry oval 2-2.5 mm long two-chambered fruit is characteristic of the Parsley Family.

HABITAT: Freshwater marshes and wet areas: Meadow-Marsh community; along edges of streams, ponds, and lakes in water to 50 cm deep.

FLOWERING: Late July through August

COMMENTS: All parts of this plant are **DEADLY POISONOUS** and all white-flowered umbel-bearing plants with divided leaves should be treated with extreme caution. Fortunately none of the water-hemlocks are that common at Churchill for they are close relatives of the hemlock used to poison Socrates and even a small part of the plant can cause severe illness or death. Water-Hemlock occurs occasionally in marshes and along streams on the Goose Creek Road and elsewhere, and around pools on the outcrop ridge. It should be admired from a respectful distance.

RANGE: Western North American subarctic-boreal species: occurs from Churchill south to the tip of James Bay reaching its eastern limit there.

NOTE: Two very similar plants, one **poisonous** the other **non-poisonous**, also occur at Churchill and a few other places along southwestern Hudson and James bays. They grow in the same wet freshwater habitats, often along with the Water-Hemlock. The **poisonous** BULB-BEARING WATER-HEMLOCK (*Cicuta bulbifera* L.) has **narrower leaflets** than the regular Water-Hemlock and bears **small bulblets in the axils of** the smaller **upper leaves.**

The **non-poisonous** look-alike is the WATER-PARSNIP (*Sium suave* Walt.), whose **leaves** are **divided only once** into entire unlobed leaflets instead of twice into narrower sub-leaflets like those of the water-hemlock. These leaf patterns are sometimes hard to determine and the Water-Parsnip is so similar in appearance to the Water-Hemlocks in other ways that the best rule is to never nibble on, or unnecessarily handle, an umbel-bearing white-flowered marsh plant.

FLOWERS WITH FIVE REGULAR PARTS

Wildflowers with Alternate Divided Leaves; small white flowers from different points....

Yarrow

SUNFLOWER FAMILY
Compositae

(Achillea nigrescens (E. Mey.) Rydb.)

OTHER NAMES: Milfoil; Flumajillo; Sneezeweed; Nosebleed

DESCRIPTION: **Somewhat aromatic** perennial herb from a creeping branching rootstalk which bears 20-60 cm high stems with al ternate **several times pinnately-divided leaves**, the sub divisions narrow and 1-1.5 cm long. **Flowers in small heads in a branching flat topped cluster, the heads from dif ferent points.** What look like small flowers with 5 (4-6) white petals are actually many small individual flowers of 2 types – a 'composite head'. The 5 'petals' are **ray flowers with** a single strap-shaped 3-notched **white corolla** while the 'flower' centre is made up of small **yellow tubular disc flowers.** Below the flower head is a series of overlapping light green bracts with straw-coloured to black fuzzy edges. Fruits small smooth achenes.

HABITAT: Open moist to dry, sandy or gravelly areas, often on disturbed ground: general in the Churchill region especially on Sandy Upper Beach and Stable Dune communities as well as disturbed gravel on ridges and roadsides.

FLOWERING: July to at least mid-August

COMMENTS: The northern variety of this common weedy species is abundant at Churchill and elsewhere around the bays. It is very hairy and the bracts below the flower head have dark brown to black edges. The introduced 'true' yarrow is smooth and has straw coloured bract edges. Many of the common names of this wildflower, such as Milfoil (''thousand leaf'') and Plumajillo (''little feather'') refer to its finely divided leaves while others refer to its reputed medicinal properties. It is one of the most ancient of the healing herbs, the generic name *Achillea* having been used by Hippocrates, the Greek 'Father of Medicine'. The reference is to Achilles who is said to have used it to heal his warriors. It is an antiseptic and aids skin formation as well as having been used in the treatment of flu, colds, high blood pressure, tooth aches, and many other ailments.

RANGE: Circumpolar boreal-arctic species complex including a widespread weedy colonizer and several native varieties: occurs in one form or another all around Hudson and James bays except for the northwestern sector of Hudson Bay and far northern islands.

FLOWERS WITH FIVE REGULAR PARTS

Wildflowers with Alternate Divided Leaves; more than 3 pinnate leaflets and red/purple flowers....

544 *Marsh Cinquefoil*

ROSE FAMILY
Rosaceae

(*Potentilla palustris* (L.) Scop.)

OTHER NAMES: Marsh Five-Finger; Purple Cinquefoil

DESCRIPTION: Perennial herb from long creeping reddish to dark brown somewhat woody rootstalks which bear 20-50 cm high stems with alternate pinnately-divided leaves, the lower with long petioles and 5-7 oval to oblong 2-7 cm long coarsely sharp-toothed leaflets, the upper short-stalked with 3-5 smaller leaflets. The **conspicuous purple flowers** are about **2 cm wide**, solitary or a few together in the axils of the upper leaves, the **five broad pointed sepals dark purple** and **overshadowing the five brownish purple** much shorter and narrower **petals. Stamens many and deep purple, styles many** on a hairy central cylinder and fruits many small plump achenes with lateral beaks.

HABITAT: Aquatic or semi-aquatic in wet marshes and bogs: freshwater Meadow-Marsh communities and edges of inland peaty lakes, ponds, and bog pools.

FLOWERING: Late July through August

COMMENTS: This attractive late-blooming aquatic wildflower is not common in the Churchill area but occurs in some of the lakes along the road between the airport and town and in a number of bog ponds along the Landing Lake and Goose Creek roads. Its purple 5-petaled star-shaped flower is distinctive but the plant is usually growing in deep enough water that you risk wet feet to get at it. All other cinquefoils in the region (there are many) are yellow-flowered and none of them are true aquatics.

The Siberian Inuit used the dried leaves to make a favourite tea. Most of the cinquefoils contain tannin-like compounds and have been used for treating intestinal upsets, surface cuts, and burns and the Marsh Cinquefoil probably has similar properties.

RANGE: Circumpolar wide ranging boreal-subarctic species: occurs all around Hudson and James bays except for the far northern islands.

214

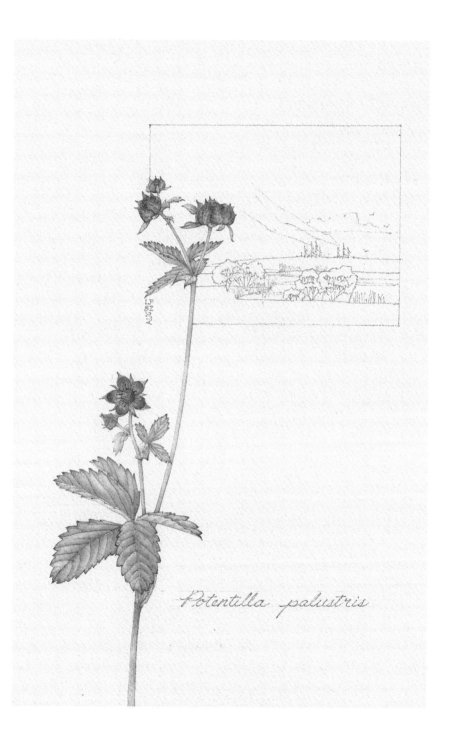

Potentilla palustris

FLOWERS WITH FIVE REGULAR PARTS

Wildflowers with Alternate Divided Leaves; pinnate leaflets and yellow flowers....

Beautiful Cinquefoil

ROSE FAMILY
Rosaceae

(*Potentilla pulchella* R. Br.)

OTHER NAMES: Bright Cinquefoil

DESCRIPTION: Low compact perennial herb, 2-15 cm high, with a long taproot and several branches from a thick base which is covered with persistent dark brown leaf bases. **Leaves** alternate, **mostly basal, pinnately-divided into 3 large leaflets and 2** (rarely 4 or none) **smaller lower ones** all of which are divided into narrow pointed lobes which reach less than halfway to the mid-rib. **Whole plant** is **densely silvery silky-hairy** especially lower surfaces of the leaflets. Flowering stems often not much longer than the leaves, bearing 1-6 **pale yellow rose-like flowers.** Calyx lobes 5, narrowly triangular and alternating with the 5 shorter bracts below; **petals** about 5 mm long, scarcely to somewhat longer than the calyx lobes, **narrow and shallowly lobed; many stamens and pistils.**

HABITAT: Sand, gravel, and dry tundra, often near the coast: Open Dune, Damp Dune Hollow and Stable Dune communities; Ledge and Crevice communities on the outcrop ridges; gravel ridges and roadsides.

FLOWERING: Late June through July

COMMENTS: This little cinquefoil with its dense cluster of silvery hairy leaves is as beautiful as its Latin and common names imply. It is fairly common at Churchill and elsewhere along the coast, especially on present-day and fossil beaches. The only plant you are likely to confuse it with is the Snow Cinquefoil (pg. 208) which is nearly as silvery-hairy but has only 3 leaflets (check carefully to be sure), teeth rather than deep lobes on the leaflets, and much wider and longer petals. Both other common cinquefoils with pinnately-divided leaves, the Prairie Cinquefoil and the Branched Cinquefoil (pg. 218) are much less hairy and have larger leaflets completely divided into long narrow widely-spaced lobes.

All of the yellow-flowered cinquefoils without runners tend to grow in well drained disturbed habitats but careful attention to leaflet number and shape, hairiness, and flower size should allow you to sort them out – at least as far as it is possible to do so!

RANGE: Circumpolar (with large gaps) arctic-subarctic species: occurs all around Hudson and James bays.

Potentilla pulchella

JULY 28 '77 CHURCHILL

Wildflowers with Alternate Divided Leaves; pinnate leaflets and yellow flowers....

544 *Branched Cinquefoil*

ROSE FAMILY
Rosaceae

(*Potentilla multifida* L.)

OTHER NAMES: Cut-Leafed Cinquefoil

DESCRIPTION: Spreading to erect perennial herb, 15-30 cm tall, from a stout **many-headed brown base** with a long **taproot. Basal leaves with 7 leaflets**, stem leaves with 5-7 leaflets, the leaflets nearly completely divided again into narrow, widely spaced segments with the edges rolled under. The segments are **dark green above** and **densely short white-hairy beneath.** The many tiny **rose-like flowers** are **borne in leafy branched clusters,** the 5 nearly round **yellow petals** 4-6 mm long **with a shallow notch** at the tip. They alternate with 5 slightly shorter and broader triangular sepals which alternate with 5 short linear bracts and are covered with soft white hairs. **Stamens and pistils many.**

HABITAT: Sandy shores and waste places to rocky ledges: Coastal Sand communities; gravel ridges and roadsides.

FLOWERING: July to mid-August

COMMENTS: This yellow-flowered cinquefoil with the finely divided leaves is common on sandy beaches and gravel areas in the Churchill region. A good place to find it is on the disturbed gravel areas near Akudlik.

RANGE: Circumpolar (with large gaps) wide ranging boreal-subarctic species complex: occurs from Churchill south to the southern tip of James Bay.

NOTE: The very similar but less common PRAIRIE CINQUEFOIL, (*Potentilla pennsylvanica* L.), occurs in similar habitats and locations around the bays. It is very difficult to tell from the Branched at first glance (or even second) but has **leaflets** which are **less deeply divided** into broader lobes and **pale green to sparsely greyish beneath** instead of densely white hairy. It also has slightly shorter petals, 2-4 mm long rather than 3-6, but as you see they can overlap and your plant is sure to have 3-4 mm long petals. Unfortunately, they also often grow right next to each other but at least both are easy to recognize as cinquefoils with their miniature rose-like flowers and finely divided leaves.

FLOWERS WITH FIVE REGULAR PARTS

Dwarf Shrubs with Alternate Entire Evergreen Leaves; leaves less than 1 cm long and pink star-shaped flowers....

Alpine Azalea

(*Loiseleuria procumbens* (L.) Desv.)

HEATH FAMILY
Ericaceae

OTHER NAMES: Trailing Azalea

DESCRIPTION: A creeping much-branched **mat-forming dwarf shrub** with small (8 mm), leathery elliptical short-stalked opposite **evergreen leaves with rolled margins.** Pink 5 mm wide star-shaped flowers occur in terminal clusters of 2-5 and have 5 sharp-tipped lobes on a floral tube of about the same length. **Fruit** a small plump **purple brown capsule surrounded by** the persistent deeply **5-lobed dark red calyx.**

HABITAT: Peaty or rocky exposed areas and mountain summits, usually on acid soils: Dry Heath, White Spruce scrub, Ledge and Crevice communities on outcrop ridge; dry Hummocky Bog and Lichen-Heath communities; open White Spruce forest on dry peat.

FLOWERING: Mid-June to late July

COMMENTS: Mats of this tiny beautiful shrub are locally common on dry peat in the Churchill area, usually associated with Crowberry and Alpine Bilberry. Good places to look for it are along the outcrop ridge between Churchill and the airport, especially near the wrecked Lambair plane and also near Launch. Though difficult to spot because of its low height and small flowers, the miniature pink stars of the flowers amply repay a careful search in late June or early July. The Alpine Azalea is closely related to the more open-flowered members of the Heath family such as the Labrador Teas and Lapland Rose-Bay.

RANGE: Incompletely circumpolar low arctic-alpine species: occurs around most of Hudson and James bays except for the region from south of Churchill to the southern tip of James Bay.

FLOWERS WITH FIVE REGULAR PARTS

Dwarf Shrubs with Alternate Entire Evergreen Leaves; leaves over 1 cm long and white flowers....

552
652 **Dwarf Labrador Tea**

HEATH FAMILY
Ericaceae

(*Ledum decumbens* (Ait.) Lodd.)

OTHER NAMES: Narrow-Leafed Labrador Tea; Labrador Tea; Hudson's Bay Tea; Marsh Tea

DESCRIPTION: Low 6-50 cm high **aromatic evergreen shrub with densely hairy twigs** bearing conspicuous scaly buds in winter. **Leaves linear** alternate, 10-25 cm long, **leathery with rolled margins, dark green above** and **rusty to white woolly beneath,** fragrant when bruised. **Spicy small white flowers** are borne **in** terminal **umbel-like clusters** with 5 oval spreading and separately deciduous petals and a very small 5-toothed calyx. **Stamens usually 10, pedicels** of the flower and capsule **bent into a hook** at tip; **fruit a persistent brown capsule.**

HABITAT: Moist to dry peat and dry rocky places: Heath and Ledge and Crevice communities on outcrop ridge; Hummocky Bog and Lichen-Heath communities.

FLOWERING: Late June to early August

COMMENTS: This small heath species is common to abundant in the Churchill region. It is most frequent on damp exposed peaty areas on the outcrop ridge, usually associated with Mountain-Avens, Dry-Ground Cranberry, and Alpine Azalea.

RANGE: Circumpolar arctic-subarctic species: occurs around Hudson and James bays except from south of York Factory to the southern tip of James Bay.

NOTE: The very similar true LABRADOR TEA (*Ledum groenlandicum* Oeder) is relatively uncommon at Churchill, found on wetter and more acid inland sites than the Dwarf Labrador Tea, almost always in association with Black or White Spruce. It is taller than the Dwarf, with much wider leaves (6 X longer than wide versus 12 X longer for the Dwarf) and usually has only **8 stamens** and **curved rather than hooked flower pedicels.** It is boreal rather than arctic in distribution, occuring around the southern half of Hudson Bay and all of James Bay.

Although called a tea and used for that purpose by early settlers, both Labrador Teas contain ledol, a **poisonous** substance causing cramps and paralysis, and should not be used as a beverage.

FLOWERS WITH FIVE REGULAR PARTS

Dwarf Shrubs with Alternate Entire Evergreen Leaves; leaves over 1 cm long and pink bell-shaped flowers....

552 **Bog-Rosemary**

(*Andromeda polifolia* L.)

HEATH FAMILY
Ericaceae

OTHER NAMES: Marsh Andromeda or Andromeda; Common Bog-Rosemary

DESCRIPTION: **Dwarf wiry shrub,** 3-42 cm high, with slender erect branches from a horizontal base; **leaves** alternate **evergreen narrow,** 1-4 cm long, smooth, the **edges rolled under,** greyish to bluish green on top, **usually whitened beneath.** The **bright pink urn- or bell-shaped flowers** are 4-8 mm long and **borne in small nodding umbels** at the tips of the branches. The corolla has 5 short lobes or teeth and the persistent calyx is of 5 short distinct reddish sepals. Fruit a dry relatively persistent pinkish capsule.

HABITAT: Moist to dry peat and the edges of pools: Stable Dune community; Heath, White Spruce scrub, and Ledge and Crevice communities on outcrop ridge; Hummocky Bog, Lichen-Heath, White Spruce forest, Black Spruce/Larch Muskeg and Bog communities inland.

FLOWERING: Mid-June to late July: peak usually early July

COMMENTS: This attractive little heath species is abundant to common on most peaty areas in the Churchill region. It is easily recognized by its typical blueberry-like bell-shaped pink (rarely white) flower and long narrow rosemary-like leaf. Although small it is abundant enough to form a pink carpet on some areas, usually just after the Lapland Rose-Bay and Mountain Avens have finished blooming. True Rosemary is an unrelated member of the Mint Family.

This is another plant which should not be nibbled on as it **contains a toxin** that causes low blood pressure, breathing difficulties, and intestinal upsets.

RANGE: Circumpolar boreal-subarctic, low arctic-alpine species: occurs all around Hudson and James bays except for the far northern islands.

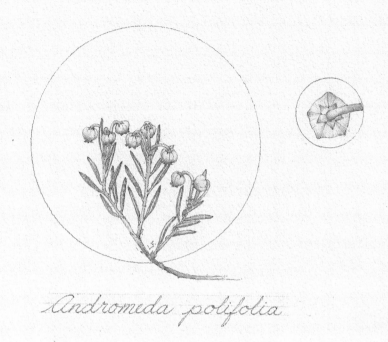

Andromeda polifolia

FLOWERS WITH FIVE REGULAR PARTS

Dwarf Shrubs with Opposite Entire Evergreen Leaves; leaves over 1 cm long and pinkish purple saucer-shaped flowers....

552 ***Bog Laurel***

(*Kalmia polifolia* Wang.)

HEATH FAMILY
Ericaceae

OTHER NAMES:	Pale or Purple Laurel
DESCRIPTION:	**Dwarf shrub,** 10-30 cm tall, with erect slender somewhat branching stems which bear smooth lanceolate leathery nearly sessile 1-3 cm long opposite or sometimes whorled **leaves** which are **dark green above** and **whitened beneath. Showy pinkish purple flowers,** 1.2-2 cm across, are borne in small clusters on slender red pedicels at the ends of the branches. The **saucer-shaped corolla** is shallowly 5-lobed but **10-keeled, each keel a pocket with 1 stamen** tucked into it under tension. As the flowers open the stamens may simply pop out of the petal pouches or they may be dislodged by an insect entering the flower and spray pollen onto it. Fruit a dry red to brown capsule.
HABITAT:	Bogs, damp mossy hummocks, and peaty soils: Hummocky Bog, Bog, or Muskeg communities; wet peat around ponds.
FLOWERING:	Late June through July
COMMENTS:	This small shrub is uncommon around Churchill but can easily be spotted when its striking flowers are present. It always occurs on peat, usually with live sphagnum moss and well inland from the coast. Look for it in this kind of habitat along Goose Creek Road near the cottage development and on the 'esker'. The flowers look like tiny oriental paper lanterns and the 'bent bow' arrangement of the stamens is great fun to play with in the open flowers. Poke a pen or stick at the filament and watch the stamen pop up! A beautiful flower which has an ingenious pollination mechanism. It is, however, not a good plant to nibble on as close relatives are known to be **poisonous** to animals.
RANGE:	North American boreal-subarctic species: occurs around all of James Bay and all of Hudson Bay except for the far northern coastal areas.

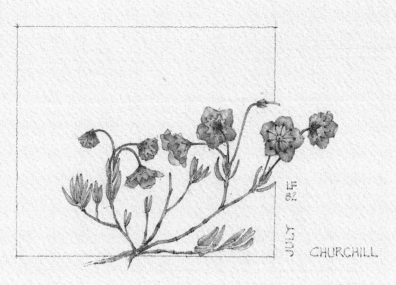

Kalmia polifolia

FLOWERS WITH FIVE REGULAR PARTS

Dwarf Shrubs with Alternate Entire Evergreen Leaves; leaves over 1 cm long
and deep purple cup-shaped flowers....

552 **Lapland Rose-Bay**

(R*hododendron lapponicum* (L.) Wahlenb.)

HEATH FAMILY
Ericaceae

DESCRIPTION: **Dwarf much branched shrub** rarely more than 30 cm high forming depressed mats or tiny spreading bushes; 0.5 to 2 cm long, elliptical to oval, alternate nearly sessile **leaves** are **dark green above** with **rust-coloured scaly hairs beneath** and **resin dots on both sides.** Fragrant showy royal purple flowers are 1-2 cm broad, **bell- to cup-shaped**, and **borne in a 1-5 flowered umbel** at the ends of the branches. Fruit a persistent brown capsule.

HABITAT: Open stony or gravelly tundra, usually calcareous or at least non-acid soils: Stable Dune communities; Heath, White Spruce scrub, and Ledge and Crevice communities on the outcrop ridge; Hummocky Bog, Lichen-Heath and White Spruce communities on peat and gravel ridges.

FLOWERING: Early June to mid-July: usually peak near late June

COMMENTS: This small showy-flowered shrub is, to my mind, the most distinctive and characteristic plant of the Churchill region. Abundant to common everywhere near the coast, it forms broad purple carpets over many ridges and bogs in late June or early July. It often grows with Mountain-Avens, which blooms at about the same time, and the white of the.Avens makes a stunning floral combination with the purple of the Rose-Bay. The Lapland Rose-Bay is Manitoba's only native rhododendron, a genus which is usually large shrubs or small trees. Although the plant is small, the flowers are comparatively large and typical of the genus in shape and colour. Many of the larger rhododendrons are grown as ornamentals in more moderate climates but the Lapland Rose-Bay is a true northerner and does not survive transplanting to warmer and drier climates.

RANGE: Circumpolar arctic-alpine species with large gaps in Eurasia, wide ranging in North America: occurs all around Hudson and James bays although not abundant in some southern areas.

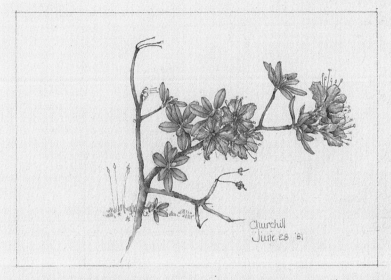

Churchill
June 28 '81

Rhododendron lapponicum

FLOWERS WITH FIVE REGULAR PARTS

Dwarf Shrubs with Alternate Toothed Deciduous Leaves; bell-shaped whitish flowers and juicy berries....

553 *Alpine Bearberry*

(*Arctostaphylos alpina* (L.) Spreng.)

HEATH FAMILY
Ericaceae

DESCRIPTION: Creeping or trailing densely branched dwarf shrub whose 10-20 cm long **branches** are usually **covered with reddish to greyish papery shredding bark and old dead leaves** or their bases. The thin eventually deciduous **strongly net-veined** alternate and toothed **leaves** are 1.5-5 cm long **with** spatulate to oblanceolate blades which narrow down into **a winged petiole** and are often tinged with purple or red, **turning bright red in the fall.** The 4-5 mm long **whitish to yellow green bell-shaped flowers** are borne in small clusters at the ends of the branches, appearing before or with the new leaves. Fruit is a 6-10 mm wide **juicy black berry**, edible but insipid.

HABITAT: Dry areas of bare mineral soil or open spots in heaths and among rocks: all dry habitats on outcrop and gravel ridges in our area.

FLOWERING: June to early July

COMMENTS: Alpine Bearberry is abundant along the coastal cliffs and ridges, often forming mats more than 1 meter wide. Along with its close relative the very similar Red Bearberry (see Note), it is responsible for most of the vivid patches of scarlet and purple in the fall tundra. Set against the gold of dwarf birches and willows, the Bearberries form intense almost overwhelming colour patterns which are a photographer's delight. Traces of these colours are often present in summer leaves, especially if the spring has been cold.

RANGE: Circumpolar subarctic-arctic-montane species: occurs all around Hudson and James bays with the possible exception of the western side of James Bay.

NOTE: RED BEARBERRY (*Arctostaphylos rubra* (Rehd. and Wils.) Fern.) is more common at Churchill than the Alpine but less widely distributed in our region as it does not occur along most of the eastern side of Hudson Bay. It grows on the Sandy Upper Beach and Stable Dune communities along the coast and on moist peat inland. Its flowers, leaves, and growth pattern are very similar to the Alpine Bearberry's but the Red tends to have **larger leaves** which are completely shed in the fall leaving the **stems bare** and of course **juicy red berries** rather than black. Intermediate plants are common however, and the two bearberries are very hard to distinguish unless there are ripe berries. They are in fact often considered varieties of the Alpine Bearberry rather than different species. Neither berry is a favourite with people because of their insipid taste and large seeds but all bearberries are fine in a pinch and

eagerly eaten by birds and wild animals.

The COMMON BEARBERRY or KINNIKINICK (*Arctostaphylos uva-ursi* (L.) Spreng.) is a typical boreal forest species which occurs around the southwestern sides of Hudson and James bays and reaches its northern limit at Churchill. It is uncommon at Churchill, found only on dry inland sites under White Spruce. It has the typical bearberry flower and matted growth form but 1-1.5 cm long **evergreen leathery leaves** and **dry mealy red berries.**

FLOWERS WITH FIVE REGULAR PARTS

Shrubs with Alternate Lobed Deciduous Leaves; smooth stems and clusters of 8-10 whitish flowers....

553 ## *Northern Black Currant*

(Ribes hudsonianum Richards.)

SAXIFRAGE FAMILY
Saxifragaceae

OTHER NAMES: Black Currant

DESCRIPTION: An erect 1-1.5 m high shrub with **smooth stems** and alternate or clustered **palmately 3-** (occasionally 5-) **lobed leaves** which are 2-8 cm wide, wider than long, more or less hairy on both sides and **pale and resinous-dotted beneath. Flowers borne in** ascending 8-10 flowered clusters in the **leaf axils**, the **petals whitish** and about 4 mm long. **Fruit** a somewhat bitter but edible **smooth juicy black berry**, 5-10 mm wide.

HABITAT: Moist woods, often along streams; ledges and crevices on the landward side of the outcrop ridge and amid boulders and on moist peat under White Spruce on the gravel ridges.

FLOWERING: Late June to mid-July; berries ripe late July to early August

COMMENTS: This smooth-stemmed black currant can be found occasionally in moist sheltered places in the rocks along the coast. Fort Prince of Wales, near the wrecked Lambair plane, and the Launch Road (under White Spruce) are good places to look for it. Its palmately-lobed leaves and small whitish flowers or developing berries make it easy to identify. The fruit is more bitter than most currants but is quite edible and can be used in any of the ways you would use the domestic varieties.

RANGE: North American boreal-montane species; occurs from about the latitude of Churchill south around both sides of Hudson and James bays.

NOTE: The only other smooth currant you are likely to find on the southern parts of Hudson and James bays is the SWAMP RED CURRANT (*Ribes triste* Pall.). It is much less common at Churchill than the Northern Black, having been found only on Cape Merry under willows along the edge of a pond and along an inland creek. It resembles the Northern Black Currant in leaf shape and size but has **smaller pink to purple flowers in drooping clusters** and **smooth bright red juicy edible berries** which are about 6 mm wide.

FLOWERS WITH FIVE REGULAR PARTS

Shrubs with Alternate Lobed Deciduous Leaves; prickly stems and small greenish white flowers in groups of 1-2....

553 ## Northern Gooseberry

(*Ribes oxyacanthoides* L.)

SAXIFRAGE FAMILY
Saxifragaceae

OTHER NAMES: Wild Gooseberry

DESCRIPTION: Low shrub, rarely over 50 cm tall, with **prickly** erect or prostrate **branches bearing** deciduous **palmately 3-5 lobed leaves**, the blades 3-4 cm broad, the lobes irregularly and bluntly toothed, the middle lobe seldom exceeding the side ones. **Flowers 1-2 in leaf axils with white to greenish purple sepals and petals** which are free for about one-half their length. **Fruit a smooth edible purplish black berry** about 1 cm wide.

HABITAT: Calcareous rocky hillsides or open stony areas: Sand and Cobble Beach and Dune communities along the coast; Ledge and Crevice communities on the outcrop ridge, and occasionally on dry open sites inland.

FLOWERING: Late June to mid-July: berries ripe in early August

COMMENTS: Northern Gooseberry is the only prickly deciduous shrub you are likely to find near the coast except for the uncommon Prickly Rose with its distinctive pink flower and red fruit. The Gooseberry grows absolutely flat against the ground on the beaches or in sheltered cracks or crannies in the rocks. Its fruit is excellent, very similar to the domestic gooseberry in size and flavour and often surprisingly abundant on the small shrubs. Berries can be used for jam, jelly, etc. in the same ways as the domestic ones and are very high in vitamin C. Not really common around Churchill, it can be found on Cape Merry, near Fort Prince of Wales, and on Bird Cove. It becomes abundant on fossil and present day beach ridges south of York Factory.

RANGE: Central and western North American boreal-subarctic species: occurs around Hudson and James bays from the southern Northwest Territories south around to the eastern side of James Bay.

NOTE: The only other prickly gooseberry found in our region is the SWAMP GOOSEBERRY or BRISTLY BLACK CURRANT (*Ribes lacustre* (Pers.) Poir.). It grows inland on moist mineral soil, usually along streams or lakes, and can be told from the Northern Gooseberry by its **bristly black berries, long clusters of pinkish flowers** and a centre leaf lobe which is noticeably longer than the side lobes.

234

554 *Shrubby Cinquefoil*

(*Potentilla fruticosa* L.)

ROSE FAMILY
Rosaceae

OTHER NAMES: Golden Hardhack; Yellow Tundra-Rose

DESCRIPTION: **Much branched deciduous shrubs** to 1.5 m tall but usually lower, **with shredding reddish brown outer bark** and pale, transparent sheathing stipules. Leaves pinnately-divided into 5-7 (rarely 3) narrow leaflets, 1.2-2.5 cm long, pointed at both ends, usually silky hairy on both sides, and alternate or more often clustered at the ends of branches. **Flowers yellow,** usually solitary in the axils of leaves, 1-3 cm wide and like miniature roses **with many stamens and pistils.** Fruit a cluster of very hairy achenes.

HABITAT: Very adaptable plant, grows on habitats ranging from exposed gravel to bogs and marshes but most often on calcareous soils: moist disturbed gravel and White Spruce forests on inland ridges; roadsides.

FLOWERING: Late July through August

COMMENTS: The only shrubby cinquefoil, this plant is uncommon at Churchill. The only place I have seen it is along the edge of the Goose Creek Road about 1 km east of the pumphouse. It is more common on beach ridges along the coast from York Factory southwards. The flower looks like a tiny yellow rose, all cinquefoils having these miniature rose-like flowers, usually yellow but sometimes white or purple in colour. Many other species, all herbs, occur at Churchill and several are described and illustrated elsewhere in this book.

The wild Shrubby Cinquefoil is the ancestor of all the attractive cultivated cinquefoil shrubs planted in cities like Winnipeg. They have been bred to be taller and bushier and have abundant white to flaming orange flowers. The common name 'cinquefoil' (''five-leaves'' in French) refers to the five-parted leaves of many species.

RANGE: Circumpolar boreal-subarctic-montane species with large gaps: occurs from the latitude of Churchill south all around Hudson and James bays.

632 ## *Bog Asphodel*

LILY FAMILY
Liliaceae

(*Tofieldia pusilla* (Michx.) Pers.)

OTHER NAMES: False or Scottish Asphodel; Featherling

DESCRIPTION: **Tiny perennial herb** seldom over 10 cm tall at Churchill, **with a basal tuft of short iris-like or sword-like leaves**, and a smooth **scape bearing** a small **raceme of whitish flowers.** The tiny 2 mm wide flowers have **6 stamens, 3 identical sepals and petals**, and a 3-parted style. Fruit is a 2-3 mm long greenish- to straw-coloured capsule.

HABITAT: Moist to dry acid to calcareous organic soils: Stable Dune, Wet Meadow, White Spruce Forest, Hummocky Bog communities; Heath community on the outcrop ridge.

FLOWERING: Late June to the end of July

COMMENTS: Generally abundant and locally occuring in very dense patches throughout the Churchill region except on saline, very wet, or very dry sites. The small white flower clusters are most noticeable on moist peaty areas associated with such dwarf shrubs as Alpine Bearberry, Bog-Rosemary, Mountain-Avens, Alpine Bilberry, and Snow Willow. While the individual flowers are tiny, the inflorescence is quite noticeable. The pattern of 3 or 6 flower parts along with a superior ovary place the Bog Asphodel squarely in the Lily Family, 1 of only 2 lily relatives found in the Churchill region.

RANGE: Circumpolar Northern Hemisphere arctic-alpine species: occurs all around Hudson and James bays.

642
632

Three-Leaved Solomon's-Seal

(Smilicina trifolia (L.) Desf.)

LILY FAMILY
Liliaceae

OTHER NAMES: Bog False Solomon's-Seal; False Solomon's-Seal

DESCRIPTION: Short slender perennial herb arising from a thin rootstalk, several stems often coming from the same one. 5 to 20 cm in height, usually around 10 cm in the Churchill region, bearing **3 (2-4) lanceolate lily-like alternate leaves.** The **few whitish flowers** (to 10) occur **in a raceme.** The flowers have **six 'petals' – actually 3 identical sepals and petals** – and **6 stamens** which bear purple or purple-dotted anthers. Fruit a green berry ripening to deep red.

HABITAT: Peat bogs, usually associated with sphagnum (peat) moss: most commonly found at Churchill on moist sphagnum hummocks in Black Spruce bogs and forests.

FLOWERING: July: usually early to mid-month

COMMENTS: Common in southern bogs, this small relative of the lilies is confined to acid bogs such as those found along the Goose Creek and Landing Lake roads in the Churchill region. It is usually associated with Black Spruce and other acid-loving plants such as Mossberry, Swamp Cranberry, and Labrador Tea. Locally abundant in such areas, the berries of the Three-Leaved Solomon's-Seal are presumably edible although there are no records of northern peoples making use of them. The berries of a close southern relative are called 'scurvy berries' and were widely used by central and western native peoples, presumably for their high vitamin C content.

RANGE: Eastern Siberian and North American boreal species: found up the western coast of Hudson Bay to the southern border of the Northwest Territories and all around James Bay.

Smilacina trifolia

611
632
642
811
832

Rushes

(*Juncus* spp.)

RUSH FAMILY
Juncaceae

Rushes are smooth grass-like plants which often bear only round stem-like or reduced sheath-like leaves. When regular grass-like leaves are present, they occur only in basal tufts or alternately along the stems. Flowering stems are round and solid, bearing tiny regular flowers with 6 similar brown or green petals and sepals (see illustrations in species accounts). Rush flowers look like tiny perfect brown lilies, often with bright pink or red stamens and styles, and these beautiful miniatures amply repay close observation with a hand lens.

Rush flowers are always at the tip of a stem but a projecting stem-like leaf often causes them to appear to be along the side. Fruits are many-seeded brown or greenish capsules.

Rushes are common in all wet and moist sites, both fresh and brackish. They often form dense nearly pure stands in salt marshes, wet meadows, shallow ponds, and along the edges of streams and lakes.

Included here are keys to and descriptions of 6 of the commonest rushes found at Churchill, 4 in detail and 2 as brief notes. None of them have any present day commercial or ethnic uses. A complete list of the rushes found at Churchill is given in the technical species list in the appendix. Rushes can be told from the closely related Wood-rushes (Genus L*uzula*) by the lack of hairs on their leaves and capsules with more than 3 seeds. They can be told from grasses and sedges by their 6-parted flowers, solid round stems, and many-seeded capsules.

SUBKEY TO THE COMMON RUSHES

11
32
42
11
32

Flowers Appearing Lateral (on the side of the stem); No Leaf Blades Present on the Stem

Flower cluster open, individual flowers on long pedicels; anthers longer than their filaments ....BALTIC RUSH
(*Juncus balticus*)

Flower cluster dense, individual flowers on short pedicels; anthers distinctly shorter than their filaments ....ARCTIC RUSH
(*Juncus arcticus*)

Flowers Appearing Terminal; Stems with Well-Developed Green Leaves from the Base or on the Stem

Small mat-forming annual; branched from base with alternate leaves and usually solitary flowers...TOAD RUSH
(*Juncus bufonius*)

Wiry erect perennials; unbranched from their base and with more than one flower per cluster;

Flowers in a single dense cluster; sepals and mature capsule pale or reddish brown; plant tufted ....WHITE RUSH
(*Juncus albescens*)

Flowers usually in several stalked clusters; sepals and mature capsules chestnut brown to darker; plants from rootstalks;

Flower clusters 1 to 3; sepals pointed; flat leaf extending 2-8 cm above clusters; seeds with tails ....CHESTNUT RUSH
(*Juncus castaneus*)

Flower clusters more than 3; sepals blunt; flat leaf, if present, to less than 1 cm above clusters; seeds without tails ....ALPINE RUSH
(*Juncus alpinus*)

FLOWERS WITH SIX REGULAR PARTS

Wildflowers with No Apparent or Basal Entire Narrow Leaves; brownish or greenish flowers....

611
632
832

Baltic Rush

(*Juncus balticus* Willd.)

RUSH FAMILY
Juncaceae

DESCRIPTION: Perennial herb with 20-50 cm high **stems arising in more-or-less regular rows from thick creeping scaly rhizomes. Bract extending** the stem usually **more than 4 cm long** and the **bladeless basal sheath leaf 8-15 cm** in length. Open flower cluster 2-8 cm long, the individual flowers borne on 3-10 mm long pedicels and having 6, 4-5 mm long, purplish brown sepals and petals. **Sharply tipped chestnut brown capsules** about 5 mm long containing numerous 0.8-1 mm long seeds.

HABITAT: Wet fresh to brackish ground mostly on bare calcareous sand, gravel, and clay: Damp Dune Hollow, Salt-Marsh, and Wet Meadow communities; moist gravel ridges; edges of rivers, ponds, and lakes.

FLOWERING: Mid- to late July: capsules usually mature by early August and remaining on the plant

COMMENTS: Common to abundant around Churchill. Flats along the Churchill River and the upper edges of Salt-Marsh communities such as those at Bird and Sloop's coves are good sites to find it.

RANGE: Circumpolar arctic-alpine-boreal species: found from just north of Churchill south around Hudson and James bays to about half-way up the eastern side of Hudson Bay.

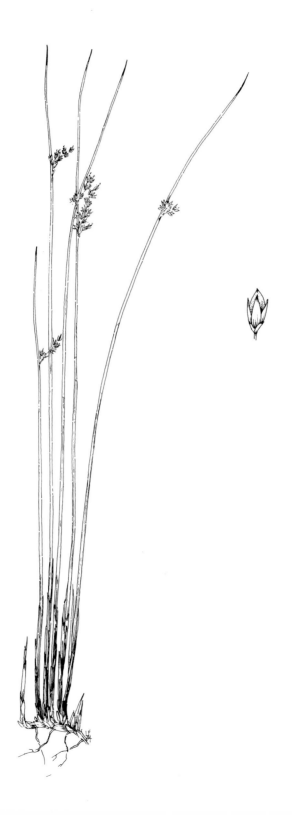

245

FLOWERS WITH SIX REGULAR PARTS

Wildflowers with No Apparent or Basal Entire Narrow Leaves; brownish or greenish flowers....

611
632
811

Arctic Rush

(*Juncus arcticus* Willd.)

RUSH FAMILY
Juncaceae

DESCRIPTION: Perennial herb with 10-50 cm high **stems** arising **in clusters or a row from stout creeping rhizomes. Bract extending stem usually 4 cm or less** long and the **bladeless reddish brown basal sheath 6-10 cm long.** Lateral flower cluster few-flowered but appearing as a dense clump because of the short or non-existent flower pedicels. Dark brown sepals and petals 2.5-3.5 mm long, 6 in total, the **blackish brown blunt-tipped capsules** about 3 mm long and containing numerous 1 mm long seeds.

HABITAT: Wet sand, gravel, and shores of lakes and rivers; often also on brackish or saline sandy shores and in tidal marshes: Sandy Foreshore and Damp Dune Hollow communities.

FLOWERING: Early to mid-July: ripe capsules usually present by the end of July and remaining on the plant

COMMENTS: Less common than the Baltic Rush, the Arctic occurs in similar habitats and communities and has in fact been combined with the Baltic by some botanists. It appears to prefer salt-marshes or other saline or brackish wet areas in the Churchill region and is abundant on the beach below the garbage dump.

RANGE: Circumpolar low arctic species: found generally around Hudson Bay except in the southern James Bay region.

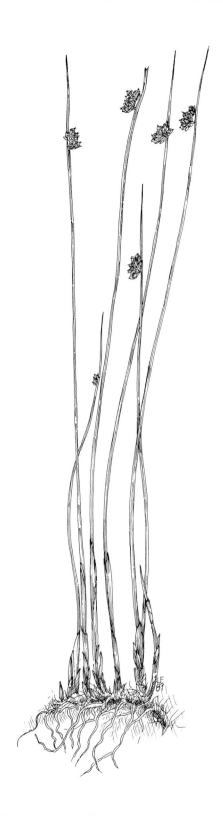

247

632
832

Alpine Rush

(*Juncus alpinus* Vill.)

RUSH FAMILY
Juncaceae

DESCRIPTION: Perennial herb with 10-45 cm tall **stems occuring in small tufts from a creeping rhizome** and **bearing 1 to 3 short stiff leaves with pinkish basal sheaths. 3-12 flowered clusters few to several at the tips of** stiffly erect **branches**, the **flowers sessile** or on very short pedicels. **Pale to dark brown sepals and petals** 2-3 mm long, 6 in total, similarly-coloured capsule 2.5-3.5 mm long and containing 0.5 mm long spindle-shaped seeds.

HABITAT: Wet calcareous or brackish gravel beaches and river banks: Meadow-Marsh community, pool edges, and disturbed roadsides in the Churchill area.

FLOWERING: July: mature capsules usually present by the end of July and remaining on the plant

COMMENTS: Most common along the Goose Creek Road.

RANGE: Circumpolar subarctic-boreal species common throughout northern North America and Eurasia: found in our region from the latitude of Churchill south all around Hudson and James bays.

249

FLOWERS WITH SIX REGULAR PARTS

Wildflowers with Basal Entire Narrow Leaves; brownish or greenish flowers....

632
832
Chestnut Rush

(*Juncus castaneus* Sm.)

RUSH FAMILY
Juncaceae

DESCRIPTION: Perennial herb with 10-40 cm tall **stems arising individually from slender short light brown rhizomes or runners** and with **well developed basal leaves.** The 1-3 flower clusters have 4-10 flowers each, these with 5-7 mm long **chestnut brown petals and sepals.** Beaked capsules 6-10 mm long, **chestnut to purplish black in colour,** containing 3 mm long seeds with slender white tails. Lowermost bract longer than the flower heads but flat rather than round and thus not appearing as a continuation of the stem.

HABITAT: Wet sand, clay, or gravel; often calcareous: outcrop ridge (pools and seeps); Meadow-Marsh and moist gravel ridge communities; and along lake shores and streams.

FLOWERING: July: mature capsules remaining on the plant

COMMENTS: Common in the Churchill area, the Chestnut Rush is found in moist freshwater sites on most of the rock and gravel ridges as well as in wet meadows along the Churchill River.

RANGE: Circumpolar wide ranging arctic-alpine species: found all around Hudson Bay and James bays except the southern James Bay region.

NOTE: WHITE RUSH (*Juncus albescens* [Lange] Fern.) is an uncommon but beautiful little perennial rush with a **single head of whitish or pinkish flowers** on a short (under 10 cm) stem. It has several narrow basal leaves, 2-3 mm long petals and sepals, and is found in damp dune hollows and wet areas on the rock ridges in July. North American arctic-alpine species: occurs all around Hudson and James bays. See drawing on pg. 253.

TOAD RUSH (*Juncus bufonius* L.) is the only annual rush at Churchill. Common on disturbed sand and gravel, this tiny plant forms extensive mats along the shores of the Churchill River and in the middle salt marsh zone. Its small size (usually under 5 cm), single flowers, late blooming date (late July through August), and mat-forming habit make it easy to recognize. Cosmopolitan, non-arctic weedy species: occurs from Churchill south to the southern coast of James Bay. See drawing on pg. 253.

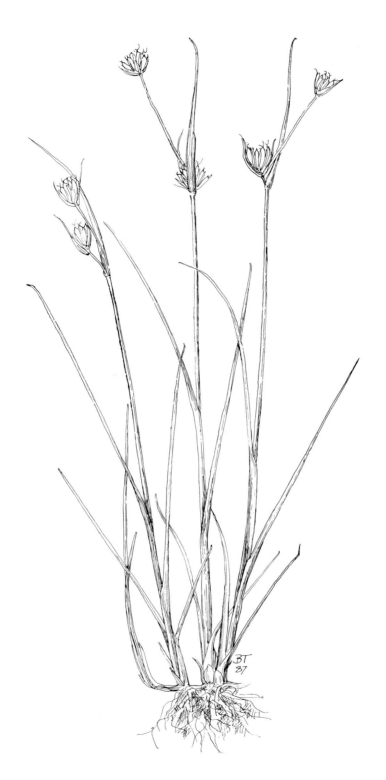

251

FLOWERS WITH SIX REGULAR PARTS

Wildflowers with Basal Entire Narrow Leaves; brownish or greenish flowers....

632
832

White Rush

RUSH FAMILY
Juncaceae

(*Juncus albescens* (Lange) Fern.)

An uncommon but beautiful little perennial rush with a single head of whitish or pinkish flowers on a short (under 10 cm) stem. It has several narrow basal leaves, 2-3 mm long petals and sepals, and is found blooming in July on wet areas in the rock ridges and damp sand and gravel inland. North American arctic-alpine species: occurs all around Hudson and James bays.

632
832

Toad Rush

RUSH FAMILY
Juncaceae

(*Juncus bufonius* L.)

The only annual rush at Churchill. Common on disturbed sand and gravel, this tiny plant forms extensive mats along the shores of the Churchill River and in the middle salt marsh zone. Its small size (usually under 5 cm), single flowers, late blooming date (late July through August), and mat-forming habit make it easy to recognize. Cosmopolitan non-arctic weedy species: occurs from Churchill south to the central coast of James Bay.

FLOWERS WITH SIX REGULAR PARTS

Wildflowers with Alternate Entire Narrow Leaves; brownish or greenish flowers....

642
842 ## Northern Wood-Rush

(*Luzula confusa* Lindeb.)

RUSH FAMILY
Juncaceae

DESCRIPTION: Perennial **grass-like plants with soft white hairs along the edges of leaves, leaf sheaths,** and **bracts** of the flower clusters. **Tufted** 10-30 cm high **stems** bear **2 to 3 short 1-3 mm wide alternate leaves.** Basal sheaths of leaves dark brown to purple shiny, often persisting for many years. **Flower clusters dense on relatively short branches.** Flowers like a tiny lily with 6 identical brown 2.5-3 mm long sepals and petals. Fruit a **red brown capsule with 3 smooth seeds.**

HABITAT: Dry peaty, turfy, or rocky places: Lichen-Heath and Ledge and Crevice communities of the outcrop ridge.

FLOWERING: Late July to early August: mature capsules remaining on the plant.

COMMENTS: Fairly common at Churchill. Outcrop ridges at Bird Cove and west along the shore of the bay are good places to look for it. Flowers are very small and it is often difficult to see the parts clearly.

RANGE: Circumpolar wide ranging arctic-montane species: found from Churchill north around to and down the eastern side of Hudson Bay.

NOTE: The SMALL-FLOWERED WOOD-RUSH (*Luzula parviflora* (Ehrh.) Desv.) is a taller, more robust relative of the Northern which occurs around the southern part of Hudson Bay and James Bay. Occuring occasionally in July on moist gravel and peaty areas along streams, under willows, and on disturbed gravel roadsides, it has wide **6-10 mm leaves** and small **flower clusters at** the **end of long drooping branches.**

711
742

Arrow-Leaved Colt's-Foot

SUNFLOWER FAMILY
Compositae

(*Petasites sagittatus* (Banks) A. Gray)

OTHER NAMES: Sweet Colt's-Foot; Butterbur; Arrow-Leaved Butterbur

DESCRIPTION: Perennial herb from thick creeping rootstocks with **scaly-bracted flowering stems which usually appear before and separate from the leaves.** This makes it difficult to associate leaves and flowers and thus to identify the plant so it is here keyed by its leafless flowering stems. **Leaves large** (to 30 cm long), long-stalked and basal, **dark green and smooth above, densely white woolly beneath, triangular** to narrowly arrow-shaped with wavy or coarsely toothed edges. **Flower stems stout,** 15-50+ cm high and **long hairy, bearing** a **dense** terminal **cluster of** 10-20, 1-2 cm long, **fragrant white daisy-like compound flower heads** composed of outer strap-shaped ray flowers and central tubular disk flowers. Fruiting heads clusters of small ribbed achenes, each bearing a tuft of 15-30 mm long tan-coloured hairs called a **pappus.**

HABITAT: Wet alluvial flats or marshy tundra beside freshwater pools and streams, usually on calcareous soils: Damp Dune Hollow and edges of Salt-Marsh and Meadow-Marsh communities; moist gravel and peat around pools on the outcrop and gravel ridges and some of the large lakes.

FLOWERING: Mid- to late June: usually in fruit and leaves developing in early July

COMMENTS: While not really common at Churchill, the Arrow-Leaved Colt's-Foot is not hard to find and usually grows in large patches. Good places to find it are the ponds just west of Fort Prince of Wales, salt-marshes near Sloop's Cove, ponds on Cape Merry, moist streamsides near Akudlik, and the shores of Christmas and Farnworth lakes. No other marsh plant has such a stout stem with white daisy-like flowers and the fragrance of a large patch is almost strong enough to make you dizzy. The young leaves and stems are edible and can be used raw as a salad or cooked as a pot herb. Ashes of the dried leaves provided a valuable salt substitute for several tribes of inland native peoples.

RANGE: North American boreal-subarctic-montane species: occurs from about latitude 60°N south around Hudson and James bays and on the northeastern corner of Hudson Bay.

722 *Alpine Arnica*

(*Arnica alpina* (L.) Olin)

SUNFLOWER FAMILY
Compositae

DESCRIPTION: Tufted 10-50 cm high perennial herb from slender scaly rootstalks which form **basal rosettes** of nearly **sessile, entire long narrow leaves.** Stem has 2-5 pairs of smaller leaves and supports **erect showy sunflower-like heads with a distinct central disk.** Flower heads mostly solitary but sometimes 1-4 smaller lower ones present; the outer ligulate ('strap-shaped') or **ray flowers bright yellow,** 1.5-3 cm long and distinctly toothed at the tips; the **small central disk flowers darker yellow** with yellow anthers. Seeds small achenes with a **bristly pure white pappus** which aids in wind distribution. Entire plant more-or-less hairy especially the bracts below the flower heads.

HABITAT: Open, well drained areas, usually dry but including river banks and flood plains: Open and Stable Dune communities; Ledge and Crevice communities on the outcrop ridge; gravel ridges and disturbed roadsides and waste places.

FLOWERING: Early July to at least mid-August: peak usually mid-to late July

COMMENTS: Alpine Arnica is an extremely showy and relatively common wildflower at Churchill, the only large yellow sunflower-like plant to occur there. It grows in large patches and shows up vividly on the ridges and beaches during July. Especially good places to look for it are near Fort Prince of Wales and on the sandy beaches along the coast road between the town and airport and across from the airport.

RANGE: Circumpolar wide ranging arctic-alpine species: occurs from Churchill south around Hudson Bay to the southern tip of James Bay.

Arnica alpina

JULY·19·82

CHURCHILL

FLOWERS WITH SEVEN OR MORE REGULAR PARTS

Dwarf Shrubs with Basal Entire Leaves....

732
752
White Mountain-Avens

ROSE FAMILY
Rosaceae

(*Dryas integrifolia* M. Vahl)

OTHER NAMES: Mountain-Avens, Arctic Avens; Entire-Leafed Mountain-Avens; White Dryad; Dryas

DESCRIPTION: A **low mat-forming subshrub** with woody freely-rooting branches. **Leaves leathery simple** petioled nearly entire and usually **with inrolled margins.** They remain on the plant until new leaves form, are **dark green above** and **densely white-hairy beneath**, and have blades which are 8-28 mm long, 3-7 mm wide, and distinctly broadest below the middle. **Flowers solitary on leafless stalks with 7-10** (to 20) 1+ cm long **white petals, numerous stamens and pistils.** Fruits dry achenes with long feathery tails which are often twisted together as a long cone in the maturing fruiting heads.

HABITAT: Open calcareous rock and gravel areas, sometimes on bare moist soil: Open and Stable Dune communities; Ledge and Crevice communities and clearings in the White Spruce scrub on outcrop ridges; exposed areas on outcrop and gravel ridges and the Hummocky Bog community.

FLOWERING: Mid-June to early August: peak usually early July

COMMENTS: One of the most widespread and abundant wildflowers in the Churchill area, Mountain-Avens forms large mats on beaches and the outcrop and gravel ridges. It usually provides one of the most spectacular seasonal flower displays, carpeting the ridges and beaches with white, often with, or just after, the rose purple Lapland Rose-Bay. This plant requires calcareous soils and is one of the most important colonizers and stabilizers of marine beaches and gravel areas in the arctic, seldom being found far inland. Mountain-Avens takes its generic name from the mythical dryads, the Greek tree-nymphs, because of a fancied resemblance of the leaves of some species to tiny oak leaves. The mature fruiting heads provide as spectacular a display as the flowers, clusters of long feathery fruits glistening like silk on the ridges. The White Mountain-Avens is the territorial flower of the North-west Territories.

RANGE: Widespread basically North American (Greenland) arctic-alpine-montane species: occurs all around Hudson and James bays.

Dryas integrifolia

FLOWERS WITH SEVEN OR MORE REGULAR PARTS

Wildflowers with Basal Lobed Leaves; flowers yellow, more than 1 cm wide....

Lacerate Dandelion

(*Taraxacum lacerum* Greene)

SUNFLOWER FAMILY
Compositae

OTHER NAMES: Ragged or Greenland Dandelion

DESCRIPTION: This wildflower is easy to recognize because it so closely **resembles** the **Common Dandelion** of yards and waste places. It is, however, a native species, not an introduced weed, and can be told by its **shallowly lobed leaves** which have no teeth on the lobes. Leaves of the Common Dandelion tend to be lobed completely to the mid-rib, especially near the base, and to have coarse teeth on the lobes. Dandelions are perennial herbs with **milky juice.** They arise from a stout taproot, have a basal rosette of leaves and solitary flowering heads on leafless hollow stems. The **flower head** is composed entirely of tiny yellow ligulate ("strap-like") or ray flowers and therefore **has no distinct centre** such as that of daisies and sunflowers. **Fruits dry achenes with a** distinctive tuft of whitish hairs called a **pappus** which helps disperse the seeds on the wind.

HABITAT: Open dry to moist places, often on mineral soil near the sea but also frequent near animal burrows, bird cliffs, and human settlements: Open and Stable Dune communities; dry heath and gravel areas on outcrop and gravel ridges; disturbed roadsides and waste places.

FLOWERING: July to mid-August: peak usually near mid-July

COMMENTS: Although the introduced weedy Common Dandelion (*Taraxacum officinale* Weber) has occasionally been found at Churchill and other settlements along Hudson Bay, the native Ragged Dandelion is much more common in our region. Good places to find it are sandy beaches below the Churchill town centre and east along the coast. The young leaves and taproots are edible and those of the Common Dandelion have been used as potherbs, emergency food supplies, and a coffee substitute.

RANGE: Widespread North American (Greenland) arctic-subarctic species: occurs sporadically around Hudson and James bays, apparently missing on the western side of James Bay and southwestern coast of Hudson Bay.

NOTE: Two other species of native dandelions occur at Churchill but both are much less common than the Lacerate. See complete species list in the Appendix and technical floras for more information on them.

FLOWERS WITH SEVEN OR MORE REGULAR PARTS

Wildflowers with Alternate Entire Linear Leaves; slender purple stems and white daisy-like flowers....

Rush Aster

SUNFLOWER FAMILY
Compositae

(Aster junciformis Rydb.)

DESCRIPTION:	Slender glandless erect little-branched 20-40 cm tall **purple-stemmed perennial** herb from a threadlike creeping root stalk. **Leaves linear clasping** 2-8 cm long, entire and **with an obvious network of veins. Flower heads daisy-like,** one to a few, 1.5-3 cm wide **with white to light purple ray** and **yellow disk flowers. Bracts below** the **flower heads in 3 distinct rows** and **uniformly green.** Fruits small achenes with a white **pappus.**
HABITAT:	Wet places and bogs: Salt-Marsh, Black Spruce/Larch Muskeg and Bog communities; disturbed moist gravel.
FLOWERING:	August: usually early in the month
COMMENTS:	This late-blooming aster has been listed as uncommon but you can find it at several places around Churchill if you visit the area in late July or August. Good places to look for it are upper edges of salt marshes along the lower Churchill river and around pools and streams near Akudlik. The only other white-flowered daisy-like plants you are likely to confuse it with are the Arctic Daisy (pg. 274) which has fleshy lobed leaves and the Sea-Shore Chamomile (pg. 276) which has very finely divided leaves. Both species also have much larger flowers.
RANGE:	Wide ranging North American boreal-montane species: known in our region only from Churchill and the southern and western coast of James Bay.

FLOWERS WITH SEVEN OR MORE REGULAR PARTS

Wildflowers with Alternate Entire or Mostly Basal Toothed Leaves; many clustered yellow daisy-like flower heads....

742
743 *Alpine Goldenrod*

(*Solidago multiradiata* Ait.)

SUNFLOWER FAMILY
Compositae

OTHER NAMES: Northern or Rocky Mountain Goldenrod

DESCRIPTION: A **slender-stemmed hairy** 5-40 cm tall **perennial** herb with 1 to several stems from a short woody and divided rootstalk. **Leaves spatulate or oblanceolate** in shape, **sessile, mostly basal** or much larger at the base, alternate and conspicuously veined, usually with a few large teeth. The **8-15 flower heads usually densely clustered**, each head about 1 cm high **with 10-18 short yellow ray flowers** and **many central yellow disk flowers**. Pappus of achenes white to tan.

HABITAT: Open meadows, sheltered peaty depressions, and dry rocky slopes: Sandy Foreshore, Open and Stable Dune, Ledge and Crevice communities; gravel ridges and roadsides, occasionally under White Spruce.

FLOWERING: Mid-July to late August

COMMENTS: Found throughout the Churchill area, the Alpine Goldenrod is most common on the coastal dunes and gravel ridges in late July and early August. It is the only goldenrod you are likely to encounter along Hudson Bay and the only slender yellow-flowered daisy-like plant with unlobed stem leaves. The generic name, *Solidago*, comes from the Latin verb meaning "to fasten together", a reference to the wound healing properties which some goldenrods were believed to possess.

RANGE: Wide ranging low arctic-boreal-montane species: occurs nearly all around Hudson and James bays except along the coast of the Northwest Territories.

266

FLOWERS WITH SEVEN OR MORE REGULAR PARTS

Wildflowers with Alternate Toothed Leaves; yellow daisy-like flower heads and coarse hollow stems....

743 *Marsh Ragwort*

(Senecio congestus (R.Br.) DC.)

SUNFLOWER FAMILY
Compositae

OTHER NAMES: Marsh Flea-Wort; Mastodon Flower

DESCRIPTION: Annual or biennial herb, usually with a simple **stout hollow stem** which can reach 100 cm in height. Leaves alternate sessile entire to irregularly toothed 3-15 cm long and present along the stem. **Entire plant**, especially stem and flower clusters, **densely yellowish brown hairy. Flower heads numerous,** 1-3 cm wide, **in several dense terminal and lateral clusters, daisy-like with pale yellow ray and disk flowers.** Pappus pure white and much longer than the 2-4 mm long smooth achenes.

HABITAT: Wet mud or marshy areas, especially near the sea or around the edges of freshwater ponds: Damp Dune Hollow, Salt- and Meadow-Marsh communities; shores of ponds and lakes and wet disturbed gravel areas.

FLOWERING: July: to mid-August

COMMENTS: This coarse weedy plant is common in the Churchill area where it tends to grow in large localized patches. Good places to find it are the salt marshes at Bird Cove, ponds by the grain elevator, and marshes along Goose Creek Road. It is easily distinguished from other ragworts and goldenrods by its coarse stem and extreme hairiness. The young leaves and flowering stems of the Marsh Ragwort are edible and may be used in salads or as a potherb. It is normally an annual, dying after flowering and producing seeds, but in the high arctic, plants on which the flowers are killed by early frosts may flower again and produce seeds the following year.

RANGE: Circumpolar (incompletely) arctic-subarctic-boreal species: found all around Hudson and James bays.

Wildflowers with Alternate Mostly Basal Toothed Leaves; lobed stem leaves
and a few yellow daisy-like flower heads....

743 ## *Balsam Groundsel*

(*Senecio pauperculus* Michx.)

SUNFLOWER FAMILY
Compositae

DESCRIPTION: A slender stemmed fibrous-rooted short-lived nearly smooth 20-50 cm tall perennial herb with a small **basal rosette of long petioled** 2-8 cm long **oval toothed leaves.** Stem leaves smaller sessile alternate and deeply lobed. **Flower heads** 1-6 (to 10), **widely spaced,** similar in size, 1-3 cm wide, and **daisy-like with a few pale yellow 6-12 mm long ray flowers, many yellow to orange central disk flowers,** and a **single row of** 4-9 mm high **involucral bracts.** Fruits ribbed achenes with a soft white pappus.

HABITAT: Wet often calcareous or saline places: Coastal Beach, fresh and saline Meadow-Marsh communities; margins of ponds and wet gravel areas, especially disturbed roadsides and ridges.

FLOWERING: Late July through August

COMMENTS: The only *Senecio* likely to be encountered on Hudson Bay except for the ubiquitous Marsh Ragwort (pg. 268) from which it can easily be told by its slender stem, basal leaves, and general lack of hairiness. Good places to look for it at Churchill, where it is relatively common, include the coast near Bird Cove and roadsides along the Goose Creek Road.

The only other plant you are likely to confuse the Balsam Groundsel with is the Alpine Goldenrod (pg. 266) which has more, smaller, and closely-clustered flower heads and entire stem leaves.

RANGE: Wide ranging North American boreal-subarctic-montane species: occurs from Churchill south all around Hudson and James bays.

FLOWERS WITH SEVEN OR MORE
REGULAR PARTS

Wildflowers with Alternate Entire Leaves; white to purple
daisy-like flowers....

742 *Tall Fleabane*

(*Erigeron elatus* (Hook.) Greene)

SUNFLOWER FAMILY
Compositae

OTHER NAMES: Fleabane or Wild Daisy; Blue Fleabane

DESCRIPTION: Slender slightly hairy perennial herb, 5-20 cm high, from a small **basal rosette of oblanceolate** 2-7 cm long **leaves. Stem leaves** 3-8, shorter than the basal ones, linear to oblanceolate in shape and **never longer than the flower stalks.** The 1 to 8 **daisy-like flower heads** (usually only 1 or 2 in our plants) are 1-2 cm wide and **have** very short and usually **inconspicuous,** 1-3 mm long, **white to pink purple ray** ('petals') and larger **yellow central disk** flowers. **Floral bracts** are 4-8 mm high, long pointed, and **in a single row** as opposed to asters whose bracts are always in more than 1 overlapping row.

HABITAT: Moist sand and gravel, bogs, and open boggy woods: Stable Dune, freshwater Meadow-Marsh, Hummocky Bog, and White Spruce communities; disturbed moist gravel on ridges.

FLOWERING: Late July through August

COMMENTS: This small late-blooming daisy is relatively uncommon at Churchill although the most common of the local fleabanes. It has been seen on disturbed gravel near Akudlik and under White Spruce near Goose Creek as well as on several gravel ridges in the area. It can easily be distinguished from the Rush Aster (pg. 264) by its inconspicuous rays and single series of floral bracts. The common name for fleabanes comes from the old belief that the dried flowers would drive fleas from a dwelling.

RANGE: Wide ranging North American boreal-montane species: occurs from the latitude of Churchill south around both sides of Hudson and James bays.

NOTE: Two other fleabanes which you might encounter at Churchill are both much less common than the Tall. The HIRSUTE or HAIRY FLEABANE (E. *lonchophyllus* Hook.) is very similar to the Tall except for its **much longer leaves** which overtop the flowering heads. The WILD DAISY (E. *hyssopifolius* Michx.) has **much longer purple rays** and many short narrower stem leaves. Both species have been found more abundantly elsewhere along the western sides of Hudson and James bays. Two other fleabanes occur occasionally along the northern and eastern coasts of Hudson Bay, the DWARF (E. *eriocephalus* J. Vahl.) and the LOWLY (E. *humilis* Grah.). These are sturdy **hairy single-headed plants with long purple rays** and they grow on dry slopes or along the edges of snow banks.

272

FLOWERS WITH SEVEN OR MORE REGULAR PARTS

Wildflowers with Alternate Lobed Fleshy Leaves; white daisy-like flower heads....

743 *Arctic Daisy*

(*Chrysanthemum arcticum* L.)

SUNFLOWER FAMILY
Compositae

OTHER NAMES: Arctic Chrysanthemum

DESCRIPTION: Perennial herb, 6-20 cm high, from a creeping rootstalk with long **fleshy mostly basal alternate** 2-12 cm long **wedge-shaped leaves** which taper into the petiole and have 3-5 large teeth or lobes at the tip. **Flower heads daisy-like and showy,** usually solitary, 2-5 cm across **with** long **white** often notched **ray flowers** and **short yellow disk flowers.** Bracts below the flower head have conspicuous black tips.

HABITAT: Moist muddy or gravelly coastal saline areas: Salt-Marsh, Sandy Foreshore, Beach, and Damp Dune Hollow communities; rock crevices in cliffs near the coast.

FLOWERING: July to mid-August

COMMENTS: The showy Arctic Daisy is common all along the coast at Churchill. Especially good places to look for it include the beach and rocks below the town centre, on Cape Merry, and near Fort Prince of Wales. The only plant you are likely to confuse it with is the Sea-Shore Chamomile (pg. 276) which also has a large white daisy-like flower and grows in similar habitats. However the Sea-Shore Chamomile has very finely divided leaves, quite different from the fleshy broadly-lobed ones of the Arctic Daisy. Fleshy leaves are one way in which plants have adapted to growing in soils with high concentrations of salt and many seacoast plants have them.

RANGE: Incompletely circumpolar low-arctic species with many gaps: occurs all around Hudson and James bays.

FLOWERS WITH SEVEN OR MORE REGULAR PARTS

Wildflowers with Alternate Finely-Divided Leaves; white daisy-like flowers....

Sea-Shore Chamomile

(*Matricaria ambigua* (Ledeb.) Kryl.)

SUNFLOWER FAMILY
Compositae

OTHER NAMES: Scentless Mayweed or Chamomile; Corn Feverfew

DESCRIPTION: A short-lived **smooth and scentless** perennial herb with erect simple or branched stems, 10-30 cm high, bearing **leaves finely pinnately-divided into very narrow segments. Flower heads daisy-like**, one to several per stem, **showy**, 3-5 cm wide **with long white ray flowers** and **short yellow disk flowers.** Bracts below the flower head have a green centre and dark brown edge.

HABITAT: Moist sandy places by the sea shore sometimes becoming weedy on disturbed areas: upper Salt-Marsh, Sandy Foreshore, upper Beach and Damp Dune Hollow communities; disturbed moist gravel and sandy areas such as roadsides.

FLOWERING: Mid-June to late August

COMMENTS: This showy daisy-like wildflower is common along the coast at Churchill. Good places to look for it are the beaches below the wrecked Lambair plane, marshes at Bird Cove, and disturbed roadsides along the Goose Creek Road. The generic name *Matricaria* comes from either the Latin word for "mother" or the one for "womb" and refers to supposed medicinal properties of some of the European species. The only plant you are likely to confuse it with is the Arctic Daisy (pg. 274) which has a very similar flower head and also grows along the coast but has fleshy slightly lobed leaves.

RANGE: Incompletely circumpolar arctic species with many gaps: occurs at least sporadically all around Hudson and James bays.

Matricaria ambigua

277

FLOWER PARTS INDISTINGUISHABLE
OR NONEXISTENT

Wildflowers with No Apparent Leaves; tiny fleshy jointed plant of salt marshes....

811 *Northern Samphire*

(Salicornia borealis Wolff & Jeffries)

GOOSEFOOT FAMILY
Chenopodiaceae

OTHER NAMES: Slender Glasswort; Sand-Fire; Saltwort; Chickenclaws; Pigeon-Foot; Marsh Samphire

DESCRIPTION: **Tiny annual herb** reduced to a **fleshy cylindrical stem with opposite branches, seldom** reaching **4 cm in height and 5 mm in width** in our region. Leaves reduced to tiny opposite scales at the nodes. Internodes of stem swollen into joints, each having a transparent-edged collar at the upper end. Inconspicuous tiny green flowers are embedded in the stems on the upper joints.

HABITAT: Saline areas: Salt-Marsh community.

FLOWERING: Late July through September: does not appear until mid-July or later

COMMENTS: This tiny late-season annual is found occasionally on open tidal mud-flats in the lower Salt-Marsh communities on both sides of the Churchill River. Good places to find it are Sloop's and Bird coves. You have to look closely at the mud but it usually grows in large clumps and, once spotted, its fleshy branches can't be mistaken for anything else.

The Northern Samphire has only recently (1986) been recognized as a species distinct from the EUROPEAN ·or RED SAMPHIRE (S. *europea* L.) and was described from plants found at La Perouse Bay, just east of Churchill. The larger and more abundant Red Samphire has a long history of human use in Europe and Asia. It was used in the manufacture of glass because of its high proportion of mineral salts and is still eaten raw as a salad, cooked as a green, or pickled. Its scientific name comes from the Latin words for "salt" (*sal*) and "horn" (*cornu*) and aptly describes this salt-tolerant plant with horn-like branches. Its smaller relative, the Northern Samphire, has the same characteristics but on a miniature scale.

RANGE: Newly described species presently recorded only from the western side of Hudson Bay: occurs from the Knife River delta north of Churchill to the Broad River between Cape Churchill and the Nelson River. A different species, perhaps a variety of the European Samphire, grows along James Bay.

FLOWER PARTS INDISTINGUISHABLE
OR NONEXISTENT

Wildflowers with No Apparent Leaves; vertically ribbed stems; cone-like spore-bearing structures....

811
823

Common Horsetail

(*Equisetum arvense* L.)

HORSETAIL FAMILY
Equisetaceae

OTHER NAMES: Field Horsetail; Bottlebrush; Shave-Grass; Scouring Rush.

DESCRIPTION: Perennial rush-like non-flowering plants from a dark felt-covered rootstalk which produces **2 kinds of vertically ribbed hollow jointed stems.** Fertile stems produced early in spring, **straight, unbranched, light brown to pinkish,** 10-25 cm tall with 4-6 nodes, each **with** a transparent **leaf-sheath tipped with 8-12 dark narrow teeth.** Reproductive spores borne in **blunt, cone-like structures at the tips** of the fertile stems which die back after the spores are shed.

Sterile green shoots appear after the fertile shoots. They are 15-30 cm long **and have whorls of jointed side branches at each node** and green leaf-sheaths, again with small dark teeth. Both kinds of stems are very rough to the touch.

HABITAT: Grows in a wide variety of moist habitats but prefers disturbed sandy areas: Stable Dune and Meadow-Marsh communities; moist gravel roadsides and ridges; edges of rivers and ponds.

FLOWERING: Late May through June for fertile stems: spores usually shed by early July. Sterile green stems appear in late June to early July.

COMMENTS: The sterile stems of the primitive but successful Common Horsetail form the dense green carpets often seen along moist gravel roadsides during July and August. The pale fertile stems are thick there during June but soon wither and disappear.

The characteristic roughness of the stems results from their high silica concentration and they have been used to scour pots and pans and to polish everything from mussel shells and arrows to pewter and fine woodwork. The plant also contains powerful chemicals and infusions have been used to rid the hair of undesirable insects, to aid in the healing of wounds and sores, and as a mouthwash. Not a good plant to nibble on!

RANGE: Widespread circumpolar arctic-alpine, boreal-montane species: occurs all around Hudson and James bays.

NOTE: The SWAMP or WATER HORSETAIL or PIPES, (*Equisetum fluviatile* L.) is the only other large horsetail you are likely to find at Churchill and in the southern part of Hudson and James bays. It grows in shallow water in lakes, ponds, marshes, and bogs, its round straight stems often reaching nearly a metre in height. **Fertile and sterile stems are similar, both green, and either unbranched or with clusters of short whorled branches at the nodes** that are surrounded by a large green leaf-sheath with 15-20 fine dark teeth. **Fertile stems have 1-2 cm long spore-bearing 'cones' at their tips.**

FLOWER PARTS INDISTINGUISHABLE
OR NONEXISTENT

Wildflowers with No Apparent Leaves; vertically ribbed stem; cone-like spore-bearing structures under 1 cm long....

Variegated Horsetail

(*Equisetum variegatum* Schleich.)

HORSETAIL FAMILY
Equisetaceae

OTHER NAMES: Northern Mottled Scouring-Rush

DESCRIPTION: Small perennial rush-like non-flowering plant from a smooth dark creeping often buried rootstalk which produces **evergreen, vertically ribbed, hollow, jointed stems.** Stems seldom over 20 cm tall and 3 mm wide in our region, erect, tufted and unbranched with 6-8 flat topped ribs. **Leaves reduced to sheaths around each joint,** these short, rather loose, **green at base with a black band at the top** and **6-8 white-edged teeth with black centres.** Reproductive spores borne in pointed cone-like structures at the tips of stems; **'cones' 5-10 mm long.**

HABITAT: Damp often calcareous sandy and peaty shores and bogs: occurs generally in moist sand and peat in our region especially in the Stable Dune and Meadow-Marsh communities and on moist spots on the gravel ridges.

FLOWERING: Late July through September for female 'cones'

COMMENTS: This small horsetail and its close relative, the Dwarf Scouring-Rush (See NOTE), are common throughout the Churchill region but often overlooked because of their small size and lack of flowers. Their ribbed and jointed stems, lack of leaves, and tiny 'cones' show their primitive status and relationship to the giant coal-forming species of the past. They feel rough because of their high silica content but are far too small to serve as scouring or polishing pads as do their larger relatives.

RANGE: Widespread circumpolar arctic-alpine, boreal-montane species: occurs all around Hudson and James bays.

NOTE: DWARF SCOURING-RUSH (*Equisetum scirpoides* Michx.) is also circumpolar in distribution and is found occasionally around both bays. It is even smaller than the Variegated Horsetail, seldom reaching 10 cm in height and 1 mm in width, and prefers to **grow buried in mossy hummocks.** It has only **3 pointed teeth on the leaf-sheath,** which is black at its base, and the tiny **black 'cone'** is only **2-5 mm in length.**

FLOWER PARTS INDISTINGUISHABLE OR NONEXISTENT

Wildflowers with No Apparent Leaves; flowers with no petals in a single spike at tip of stem....

Creeping Spike-Rush

(*Eleocharis palustris* (L.) R. & S.)

SEDGE FAMILY
Cyperaceae

OTHER NAMES: Common, Swamp, and Marsh Spike-Rush

DESCRIPTION: Perennial **superficially rush-like dense colony-forming plants** from a stout freely branching rootstalk; stems 20-40 cm tall, 2-3 mm wide, solitary and unbranched, **leaves reduced to basal reddish brown sheaths** surrounding the stem, these **with a distinctly angled upper edge.** Flowers small and inconspicuous, **sepals and petals replaced by 6 tiny barbed bristles, each flower subtended by a single overlapping brown scale.** Flower spike 0.5-1.5 cm long and 2-3 mm wide; fruit a 1.5-1.7 mm long **achene topped by a triangular hat-like structure.**

HABITAT: Shallow freshwater marshy areas: general in Meadow-Marsh communities and along the muddy edges of ponds and streams in the Churchill area.

FLOWERING: Young flower spikes appear in late June to early July: ripe seed present by late July to early August

COMMENTS: Creeping Spike-Rush is such a common marsh and wet area plant in the Churchill/southern Hudson Bay region that you are almost certain to come across it. Its round rush-like stem, basal leaf sheaths, and sedge-like spike of flowers make it simple to identify.

RANGE: Widespread nearly worldwide species: occurs from latitude 62°N on the western side of Hudson Bay south around James Bay to slightly up the eastern side of Hudson Bay.

NOTE: Several other species of spike-rushes occur in our region. The only one you are likely to encounter is the common NEEDLE SPIKE-RUSH (*Eleocharis acicularis* (L.) R. & S.), a tiny version of its larger relatives. It forms large mats on sandy or muddy shores all around both bays with **3-6 cm tall stems** and **3-4 mm long flower spikes.** It often has sterile stems without the flower spikes but these tiny green needles can be identified by the **brownish leaf-sheaths at their bases** and their underground tubers.

FLOWER PARTS INDISTINGUISHABLE
OR NONEXISTENT

Wildflowers with No Apparent Leaves or Leaves Reduced to Basal Nearly
Bladeless Sheaths; sepals and petals replaced by short bristles....

811
832

Tufted Bulrush

(*Scirpus caespitosus* L.)

SEDGE FAMILY
Cyperaceae

OTHER NAMES: Tufted Club-Rush; Deer-Grass

DESCRIPTION: Small, 10-30 cm tall, **densely tufted perennial herb forming hard tussocks.** Stems slender **wiry grey green,** vertically lined or ribbed, and **bearing persistent overlapping brown leaf sheaths at their base and 1 or 2 green sheaths with a short blade** (to 1.5 cm) **on the lower stem.** Flowers 6-7, borne in a **single** 3-6 mm long narrowly oval brownish **spike** at the tip of the stem; **sepals and petals replaced by 6 inconspicuous straight bristles** which seldom reach over 4 mm in length; each flower subtended by a light brown to straw-coloured pointed scale. Fruit a 2 mm long sharply pointed achene.

HABITAT: Peaty soil and wet places: occasional in Stable Dune (moist depressions) and Meadow-Marsh communities; around ponds on the outcrop and gravel ridges.

FLOWERING: Young flower spikes in late June to early July: seed usually shed by early August

COMMENTS: Tufted Bulrush is a fairly common bog or marsh plant in the Churchill region, Landing Lake being one good place to find it. Its abundant basal brown leaf-sheaths, blades on the stem sheaths, and lack of a 'hat' on the achene distinguish it from the spike-rushes which it closely resembles. Its generic name is that of the bulrush of ancient times while the specific name *caespitosus* comes from the Latin word for "tufted".

RANGE: Nearly circumpolar subarctic-montane species: occurs all around both bays except for the far northern islands and northwestern coast of Hudson Bay.

Scirpus caespitosus L.

FLOWER PARTS INDISTINGUISHABLE
OR NONEXISTENT

Wildflowers with Whorled Entire Leaves; marsh or aquatic plants....

822 *Common Mare's-Tail*

(*Hippuris vulgaris* L.)

MARE'S-TAIL FAMILY
Haloragaceae

DESCRIPTION: Stout unbranched **smooth** perennial **aquatic plants** from submerged rootstalks, usually growing in large clumps. **Stems emergent**, 10-50 cm tall, **bearing whorls of 6-12, narrow pointed** 1-6 (8) cm long **leaves which equal or exceed the internodes.** Emergent leaves firm, submerged leaves longer, softer, and translucent. Tiny perfect flowers lacking sepals and petals are borne in the axils of the leaves, producing tiny green nut-like fruits.

HABITAT: Shallow ponds, lakes, and streams; usually freshwater but occasionally saline; in mud: general in our region in shallow ponds, around lakes, and along streams; occasional in upper edges of Salt-Marsh community.

FLOWERING: Plants appear and flower in July: seed usually dispersed by early August

COMMENTS: Mare's-Tail is a common and attractive plant and its whorls of emergent entire leaves make it easy to identify. It is a lovely subject for photography, often growing in clusters in still pools which reflect the intricate pattern of its leaves against the water. Its scientific and common names both come from the Greek word for "horse" (*Hippos*) and "tail" (*oura*) but it is not related to the plants commonly called horsetails which grow in similar habitats. The horsetails (Genus *Equisetum*, pgs. 280-82) are primitive non-flowering plants with ribbed stems and no true leaves.

RANGE: Widespread circumpolar arctic-alpine, boreal-montane species: occurs all around Hudson and James bays.

NOTE: A close relative of the Common Mare's-Tail, the FOUR-LEAVED MARE'S-TAIL (*Hippuris tetraphylla* L.f.) is also common in salt marshes in parts of our region. It has **whorls of 4 (6) firm oval** 1-1.5 cm long **leaves** which are **shorter than the internodes** and often borne on a reddish stem. It has been recorded from all around James Bay and along the southern and far northern coasts of Hudson Bay.

Hippuris vulgaris   *Hippuris tetrophylla*

FLOWER PARTS INDISTINGUISHABLE OR NONEXISTENT

Wildflowers with Whorled Finely-divided Leaves; aquatic or marsh plants....

824 *Spiked Water-Milfoil*

(Myriophyllum exalbescens Fern.)

WATER-MILFOIL FAMILY
Haloragaceae

DESCRIPTION: Perennial, **usually submerged, aquatic or marsh plant** with slender usually branched stems from a long creeping rootstalk. **Stems** 1-3 mm wide, 15-100 cm long, **purple when fresh, drying white, bearing whorls of 3 or 4** 1.2-3.0 cm long **soft leaves that are divided into 6-11 pairs of threadlike segments. Tiny purplish flowers are borne in** an erect interrupted **spike** 2-8 cm long **that projects above the water** and has female flowers at its base, perfect flowers in the middle, and male flowers at the top. The 4 tiny purple sepals and petals are largest but soon shed in the male flowers. Fruits 4 small round shallowly-grooved nutlets from each flower.

HABITAT: Shallow still mostly calcareous freshwater lakes, ponds and streams: general in shallow water away from the coast in our region; sometimes occurs in brackish streams on the tidal flats of salt marshes.

FLOWERING: Late-season: leaves appear by early July, flower spikes in August

COMMENTS: You may be more familiar with this common aquatic plant than you realize as varieties of this and other species are some of the commonest plants grown in freshwater aquariums. They can survive a wide range of water temperatures· and chemistries which accounts for their broad geographical distribution and great usefulness in aquariums. The submerged whorled finely-divided leaves easily separate the Spiked Water-Milfoil from the alternate entire-leaved pondweeds (Genus *Potamogeton*) with which it tends to grow. All of these submerged water plants provide valuable food for waterfowl, aquatic insects, and fish.

RANGE: Nearly worldwide boreal-temperate species: occurs around both bays, north to about 62°N latitude on the western and 56°N latitude on the eastern sides of Hudson Bay.

FLOWER PARTS INDISTINGUISHABLE
OR NONEXISTENT

Wildflowers with Basal Entire Fleshy Linear Leaves; plant under 10 cm tall with short dense flower clusters....

832 *Seaside Plantain*

(Plantago juncoides Lam.)

PLANTAIN FAMILY
Plantaginaceae

OTHER NAMES: Goose-Tongue

DESCRIPTION: Small short-lived perennial herb from a thick root with a **basal rosette of many linear pointed fleshy leaves,** 2-3 mm wide and 5-10 cm long. **Flowering stems dark purple** leafless usually slightly longer than the leaves, **bearing** a dense **1-2 cm long spike of brownish flowers** at the tip. Tiny 3 mm wide flowers have 4 dry brown sepals and 4 similiar petals joined at their bases, 4 (2) stamens, and long hairy styles and are subtended by a tiny bract. Fruit a small capsule with several winged seeds.

HABITAT: Seacoasts, salt marshes, and inland salt springs: occurs along the coast in moist sandy beach areas, Salt-Marsh and Ledge and Crevice communities, and saline pools on the outcrop ridge.

FLOWERING: Late June through July

COMMENTS: This small plantain is common in salt marshes and on the out-crop ridge throughout our region. Good places to look for it are below the town centre and at Bird Cove. Its tiny narrow fleshy leaves and small brownish spike of flowers make it easy to recognize. Although small, the rosettes of this plant can be boiled and eaten as a green. Close relatives such as the common broad-leaved weedy plantain of yards and gardens have long been used as food plants and to treat a variety of illnesses.

RANGE: Circumpolar and South American coastal and inland saline areas: occurs nearly all around Hudson and James bays except for the northwestern and east-central parts of Hudson Bay.

FLOWER PARTS INDISTINGUISHABLE
OR NONEXISTENT

Wildflowers with Basal Entire Fleshy Linear Leaves; over 10 cm tall
elongated flower clusters....

832 *Seaside Arrow-Grass*

(*Triglochin maritima* L.)

ARROW-GRASS FAMILY
Scheuchzeriaceae

DESCRIPTION:	Stout perennial plant, usually 20-50 cm tall, from short rootstalks. **Leaves basal clustered fleshy linear or rush-like,** to 30 cm long, **half-round in cross section with transparent sheaths at their bases,** these usually covered by persistent light-coloured old leaf bases. Flower stem taller than leaves, flower cluster at tip, 4-5 cm long when young, greatly elongating in fruit. **Flowers tiny,** 3-4 mm wide, **with 3 greenish sepals and petals,** 3(6) stamens, and a round 6(3) parted ovary. Mature **ovary splits into 6(3) segments which have** round bases and **small recurved beaks.**
HABITAT:	Saline or alkaline flats, marshes, or river meadows: occurs generally in moist to wet saline to freshwater habitats especially in Salt-Marsh and Meadow-Marsh communities and in and around saline pools on the outcrop ridge.
FLOWERING:	Late June to early July: seed usually ripe by early August
COMMENTS:	Seaside Arrow-Grass is a very common wet area species, found from salt marshes along the coast to wet peaty areas inland all along the southern Hudson Bay Lowlands. Its basal cluster of tall fleshy half-round leaves and elongated spike of inconspicuous flowers are distinctive. Perhaps its most typical site in our region is along the edges of small saline pools on the outcrop ridge from Cape Merry eastwards. It is considered a primitive flowering plant and is most closely related to the aquatic pondweeds and bur-reeds. All arrow-grasses have proven **poisonous** to cattle and sheep and should therefore be handled with care.
RANGE:	Widespread circumpolar boreal-subarctic littoral species: occurs from Churchill south around James Bay to about latitude 56°N on the eastern side of Hudson Bay.
NOTE:	A closely related species, the MARSH ARROW-GRASS (*Triglochin palustris* L.), is found occasionally in salt marshes and other saline habitats in our region. It is a **delicate plant** with slender basal leaves from a **bulb-like rootstalk** which is **not covered by old leaf bases** and which **bears slender reproductive runners.** Marsh Arrow-Grass seldom reaches 30 cm in height and has a 3-parted ovary which forms 3 long narrow fruits with sharp awl-pointed bases.

FLOWER PARTS INDISTINGUISHABLE
OR NONEXISTENT

Wildflowers with Mostly Basal Entire Grass-like Leaves; no petals and fluffy
cotton-like bristles throughout the flower spike....

832 ## Sheathed Cotton-Grass

(Eriophorum vaginatum L. ssp. *spissum* (Fern.) Hult.)

SEDGE FAMILY
Cyperaceae

OTHER NAMES: Hare's-Tail Grass; Bog or Arctic Cotton

DESCRIPTION: Perennial **densely tufted grass-like plant forming large clumps;** stems 15-60 cm tall. **Stems 3-sided,** from numerous **narrow** (1 mm wide) **basal leaves;** 2-3 stem leaves with loose surrounding sheaths and short or no blades. **Flower spike single** at the tip of the stem, **shaped like a hemisphere. Petals and sepals replaced by 2-5 cm long pure white bristles** that are **subtended by lead-coloured scales,** these with dark centres and white transparent edges, the lower ones usually turning down in fruit.

HABITAT: Marshy and peaty areas: occurs in the Meadow-Marsh community and on wet peat throughout our area.

FLOWERING: Young flower spikes in early July: 'cotton' develops in mid-July through early August

COMMENTS: Sheathed Cotton-Grass is the commonest single-headed cotton-grass in our region, growing as dense hummocks topped with white 'cotton balls' in the late summer. See the Tall Cotton-Grass account (pg. 298) for more information on these interesting plants.

RANGE: Widespread circumpolar arctic-alpine-boreal species complex: occurs all around Hudson and James bays.

NOTE: Several other single-headed species of *Eriophorum* occur occasionally at Churchill and elsewhere around the bays. They can be distinguished from the Sheathed Cotton-Grass by their darker bristles, completely dark flower scales, or solitary growth forms and are listed in the Appendix.
ALPINE COTTON-GRASS (*Scirpus hudsonianus* (Michx.) Fern.) occurs occasionally on wet shallow peaty areas at Churchill, around James Bay, and along the southern part of Hudson Bay. It can be told from the true cotton-grasses by its **crinkled rather than smooth** 1-3 cm long **white bristles.** These come only **from the tip of the narrow** 4-7 mm long **light brown flower spike.** It is also **shorter** (15-30 cm), has **no basal leaves,** and very short-bladed stem leaves.

FLOWER PARTS INDISTINGUISHABLE
OR NONEXISTENT

Wildflowers with Mostly Basal Entire Grass-like Leaves; no petals, and fluffy cotton-like bristles throughout the flower spike....

Tall Cotton-Grass

(*Eriophorum angustifolium* Honck.)

SEDGE FAMILY
Cyperaceae

OTHER NAMES: Common and Narrow-Leafed Cotton-Grass; Bog or Arctic Cotton

DESCRIPTION: **Perennial grass-like plant** from a short stout rootstalk; **stems** 20-50 cm tall, **usually solitary**, and **somewhat triangular or 4-sided in cross-section.** Leaves flat and grass-like, 3-6 mm broad, mostly basal but with several on the stem. **Flower spikes 2-10 from the tip of the stem, nodding,** subtended by 1-3 leaf-like bracts which are purple at the base. Flower spikes 1-2 cm long, **with 2-5 cm long silky white bristles when mature,** bristles replacing sepals and petals and subtended by lead grey-to black-coloured scales.

HABITAT: Wet freshwater bogs, marshes, and shores: general in the Hummocky Bog, Meadow-Marsh, Black Spruce/Larch Muskeg, and Bog communities; in shallow water and on shores of freshwater ponds, lakes, and streams throughout the region.

FLOWERING: Young flower spikes appear in late June to early July: 'cotton' not usually visible until mid-July; seed ripe and dispersing in early August

COMMENTS: Tall Cotton-Grass is the commonest multi-headed cotton-grass in our region, often forming extensive beds in wet peaty areas. Its generic name comes from two Greek words *erion* (wool) and *phoros* (bearing) which, like the common name, refer to the long flower bristles. This 'wool' or 'cotton' has been used as tinder, as wicks for Inuit oil lamps, and to stuff pillows and mattresses but is too straight and smooth to be used as a thread or fabric. The lower stems have also been eaten by the Inuit either raw or mixed with seal oil.

The long silky bristles or 'cotton' of the "Arctic Cotton" plants make them one of the most distinctive grass relatives in the North. Even people who don't know or care anything about grasses and sedges recognize this beautiful group of plants.

RANGE: Wide ranging circumpolar arctic-alpine-subarctic species complex: occurs all around Hudson and James bays with the possible exception of the far northeastern corner of Hudson Bay.

The Sedges

(Genus *Carex*)

Sedges are common grass- or rush-like plants with solid unjointed stems that are often triangular in cross-section. Their long narrow usually basal grass-like leaves are 3- rather than 2-ranked as in the grasses and often rough to the touch. Sedge flowers, like those of the grasses, are reduced in size and complexity because they rely on wind rather than insects or animals for pollination. A few technical terms specific to these reduced flowers and the modified leaves (scales or bracts) associated with them are illustrated and described below.

Sedge flowers are usually unisexual, either male with 3 stamens each, or female with a single pistil that has 2 or 3 long narrow styles and an ovary which develops into a lens-shaped or triangular achene as a fruit. No sepals or petals are present, their place being taken by a single subtending bract or scale in the male flower and two scales, one subtending and one enclosing the pistil like a sac (the **perigynium**) in the female flower. These sessile flowers are clustered into dense **spikes** which may be only male, only female, or have both sexes in different positions within the spike. The number and composition of the spikes are important characteristics in identifying sedges, as are the number of styles, shape of the achene, and color and size of the scales and perigynia. Because most keys, including the Subkey below, use flower and seed characters, you must have ripe or nearly ripe seed to identify sedges reliably.

There are about 45 species of sedges known from Churchill and this Subkey covers the 13 most common and/or easily recognizable of them. *Carex* has the largest number of species of any genus in our region and is indeed the largest genus in most places in the northern hemisphere. Sedges are eaten to some extent by wild and domestic animals, serve as valuable soil stabilizers and peat and soil formers, and are often the dominant plants in alpine and arctic regions. Although they are tiny, it is usually possible to see most features of sedge flowers and spikes with a 10 power hand lens and thus possible to key them out in this guidebook or other more technical references.

Sedges have a fascination all their own for the professional and amateur botanist – a hold perhaps akin to that of the "Times" Sunday crossword puzzle on puzzle addicts. After you have mastered most of the showy flowering plants in an area there are always lots of complicated little sedges around to defy you. I think it is this challenge, as well as the fascination with how many different ways a basically simple flower structure can be put together, that forms the basis for their attraction. A complete list of all known sedges (their classification is still highly fluid and some may have been overlooked) at Churchill is given in the Check List in the Appendix.

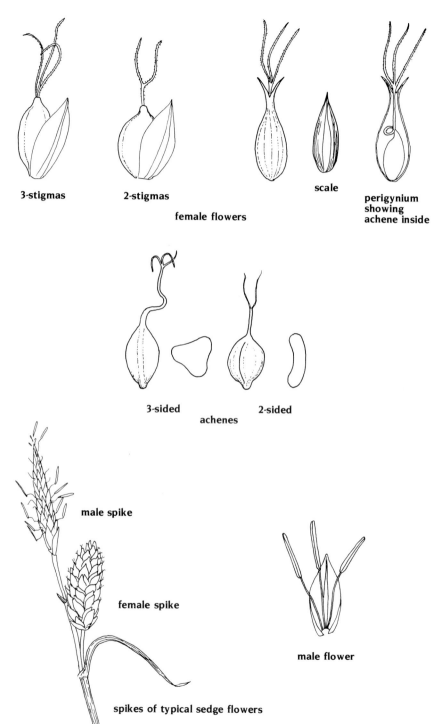

3-stigmas

2-stigmas

female flowers

scale

perigynium
showing
achene inside

3-sided

achenes

2-sided

male spike

female spike

male flower

spikes of typical sedge flowers

301

SUBKEY TO THE COMMON SEDGES (Genus *Carex*) OF THE CHURCHILL REGION

832 **Single Flower Spike Per Stem (Check for short stalked or sessile spikes at base of what appears to be single spikes)**

Stigmas 2; achenes oval or lens-shaped;

Round flower spike with male flowers
at top, female at base;
plants tufted ....CAPITATE SEDGE
(Carex capitata)

Narrowly oval flower spike either all
male or all female, sexes on separate
stems; plants single or a few from
runners ....NORTHERN BOG SEDGE
(Carex gynocrates)

Stigmas 3; achenes triangular;

Flower spikes all male or all female,
sexes on separate stems; perigynia
hairy ....RUSH-LIKE SEDGE
(Carex scirpoidea)

Flower spikes male at top, female at base; perigynia smooth;

Spike many-flowered; perigynia
3-3.5 mm long, not spreading at
maturity; scales remaining...ROCK SEDGE
(Carex rupestris)

Spike few-flowered; perigynia 5-6 mm
long, spreading horizontally at
maturity; scales shed early...........................SHORT-AWNED SEDGE
(Carex microglochin)

Several Flower Spikes Per Stem (See note at top of page)

Spikes all completely sessile and with both
sexes of flowers, male at tip, female at
base; resembling a single spike without
close inspection; stigmas 2; achenes
lens-shaped or oval...SEASIDE SEDGE
(Carex maritima)

Spikes with at least short stalks, usually all male or all female flowers, male
spikes at tip, female lower down the stem;

Stigmas 2; achenes oval or lens-shaped

Male and female spikes usually 2 or 3;
both shorter than 2 cm, perigynia
inflated at maturity ....ROCKY-GROUND SEDGE
(Carex saxatilis)

Male and female spikes more than 4;
both usually longer than 2 cm;
perigynia not inflated at maturity..............................WATER SEDGE
(Carex aquatilis)

Stigmas 3; achenes triangular;
  Tufted plants seldom over 10 cm high
    with 3-4 densely clustered short-
    stalked spikes which form a 'head'
    resembling a single spike...GLACIER SEDGE
                                                                    (*Carex glacialis*)
  Taller plants with longer distinctly-stalked and separate spikes
    Plants tussock-forming; spikes slender,
      the female drooping on delicate
      stalks ....HAIR-LIKE SEDGE
                                                                    (*Carex capillaris*)
    Plants occuring singly or in small clumps from runners; spikes larger
      and on stouter stalks;
      All spikes, even the lowest, erect;
        roots and runners smooth..............................SHEATHED SEDGE
                                                                    (*Carex vaginata*)
      At least lower female spikes
        drooping; roots covered with
        yellow or grey velvety felt-like
        hairs ....MUD/SCANT SEDGE
                                                                    (*Carex limosa/Carex rariflora*)

FLOWER PARTS INDISTINGUISHABLE
OR NONEXISTENT

Wildflowers with Basal Entire Grass-like Leaves; solid unjointed
triangular stems....

832 ## *Capitate Sedge*

(Carex capitata L.)

SEDGE FAMILY
Cyperaceae

One of the easier sedges to recognize with its **single pyramidal flower spike**
containing reduced **flowers with 2 stigmas and a lens-shaped achene**.
It forms dense tufts of erect greyish green, 5-40 cm tall, stems and leaves
that are often purplish red at their bases. The channeled 1 mm or narrower
leaves are often as long as or longer than the stems. The 6-8 mm long flower
spike is nearly as wide at its base and has a few male flowers above many
female flowers. Female flowers subtended by a short brown scale, their
sessile perigynia 2-4 mm long with a short smooth beak. This sedge prefers
calcareous dryish areas on the outcrop ridge but can also be found in damp
moss near ponds and in White Spruce communities. Flower spikes appear
in late June and remain until early August. This sedge is a widespread circumpolar boreal-alpine species which occurs from about latitude 60°N south
around both sides of Hudson and James bays.

832 ## *Northern Bog Sedge*

(Carex gynocrates Wormskj.)

SEDGE FAMILY
Cyperaceae

A common small sedge of wet, usually calcareous, habitats in the Churchill
region. Its **solitary flower spike**, each one usually **containing only male
or female flowers**, and pattern of **2 stigmas and a lens-shaped achene**
make it reasonably easy to recognize. The wiry 5-20 cm tall stems are solitary
or in small tufts from slender creeping rootstalks which also produce shorter
narrow thread-like leaves. Flower spikes 5-15 mm long, the male linear, the
female oval to cylindrical, very occasionally male above and female below.
Scales brown with a transparent edge and sharp point, somewhat shorter
than the 3-5 mm long, plump shiny many-nerved short-beaked perigynia
which become reflexed with age. This sedge seems to prefer wet peat or
gravel areas along shores, often growing with willows, but has also been
found in Black Spruce/Larch Bog and Muskeg communities on sphagnum
moss. Male spikes appear from mid- to late July, female slightly later,
maturing seed before the end of July. This species complex has a widespread
circumpolar low arctic distribution and is found from latitude 59°N south
around both sides of Hudson and James bays.

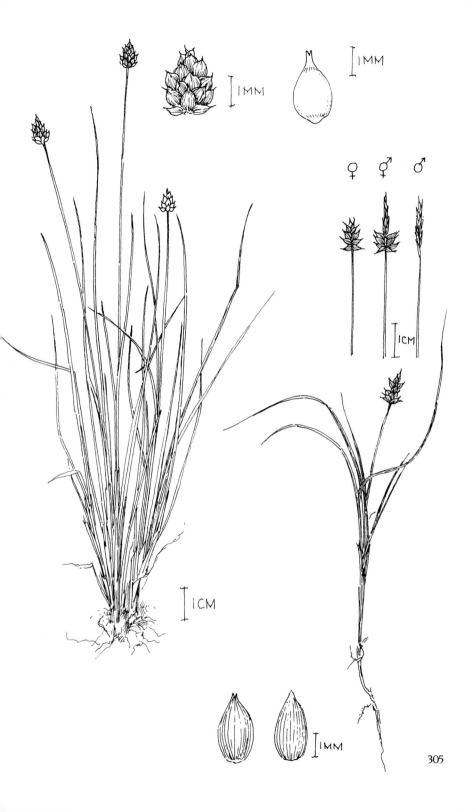

FLOWER PARTS INDISTINGUISHABLE
OR NONEXISTENT

Wildflowers with Basal Entire Grass-like Leaves; solid unjointed triangular stems....

832 ## Rush-Like Sedge

(Carex scirpoidea Michx.)

SEDGE FAMILY
Cyperaceae

One of the commonest sedges in the area, found primarily in Heath and White Spruce communities on the outcrop and gravel ridges. Its **solitary male or female flower spikes on separate stems** and female flowers with **3 stigmas, hairy perigynia and triangular achenes** are distinctive. The plants are loosely tufted or in rows from a stout dark scaly rootstalk, the stiff 15-30 cm high stems much longer than the flat 2-4 mm wide rough leaves. Male spikes oval, female narrowly cylindrical and 2-3 cm long, the blunt scales dark purple to black with a transparent edge and narrower than the 2-3 mm long hairy slightly beaked perigynia. This sedge prefers calcareous and rather dry areas but can also be found in the Hummocky Bog community and along shores. It is a wide ranging North American/Greenland/eastern Asian arctic-montane species which occurs all around Hudson and James bays. In fact the Rush-Like Sedge was originally described and named from a collection made somewhere on Hudson Bay.

832 ## Rock Sedge

(Carex rupestris Bellardi)

SEDGE FAMILY
Cyperaceae

A fairly common small sedge of dry saline or calcareous communities on the outcrop ridge. The rough wiry stems are 8-20 cm high, solitary or a few together from a slender tough scaly brown rootstalk. The flat stiff **curly tipped yellowish green leaves** are clustered at the base of the stems, equal to or slightly longer than the stems, and 1-3 mm wide. The dark 1-2 cm long flower spike has **male flowers on its upper 1/2 to 2/3 and a few female flowers (1-8) with 3 stigmas and triangular achenes below. The erect perigynia are smooth dull yellowish brown and 3-4 mm long** with a tapering base and very short slender beak. Scales are dark brown with broad transparent edges, slightly shorter but broader than the perigynia. This sedge is often associated with other calcium loving plants such as the White Mountain-Avens and is also found on gravel ridges and other dry open places elsewhere in our region. The Rock Sedge is a widespread circumpolar arctic-alpine species which occurs from Churchill north around the western side of Hudson Bay and all down the eastern sides of Hudson and James bays.

♂

♀

I 1CM

♂

I 1MM

307

FLOWER PARTS INDISTINGUISHABLE
OR NONEXISTENT

Wildflowers with Basal Entire Grass-like Leaves; solid unjointed
triangular stems....

832 ## *Seaside or Curved Sedge*

SEDGE FAMILY
Cyperaceae

(Carex maritima Gunn.)

A **dwarf species of sandy seacoasts** and calcareous sands and gravels
inland. At Churchill it is the commonest small **matted** sedge of the Sandy
Foreshore, Open and Stable Dune, and Damp Dune Hollow communities.
It is also occasionally found somewhat inland on disturbed moist gravel.
The **grey green, often curved**, 5-15 cm tall **stems** are usually **slightly overtopped by** the often **curved or curled** 1-2 mm wide **leaves** and form rows
or mats. The **3-5 sessile flower** spikes are **densely packed into** a 0.5-2 cm
long oval to pyramidal **head that without careful inspection appears to
be a single spike without careful inspection.** Each **spike** contains **male
flowers at the tip and female at the base** instead of the more common
pattern of each spike containing only one sex. Blunt oval 3-4 mm long flower
scales are brown with broad pale margins. The **smooth** slightly longer
perigynia are greenish to golden brown, nearly nerveless, **have a short
rough beak** and are somewhat spreading at maturity. They are slightly inflated around the **lens-shaped achene** which has **two long stigmas.** The
Seaside Sedge is primarily a coastal species with a circumpolar arctic-
montane distribution and it occurs all around Hudson and James bays.

832 ## *Short-Awned Sedge*

SEDGE FAMILY
Cyperaceae

(Carex microglochin Wahlenb.)

A distinctive **dwarf sedge** of moist calcareous soils. The Short-Awned Sedge
is found in the Damp Dune Hollow and Meadow-Marsh communities, around
the edges of ponds, and along moist roadsides in the Churchill area. This
loosely tufted species has slender 5-10 cm tall stems with shorter narrow
basal leaves from slender rootstalks. The 0.5-1.5 cm long **single flower spike**
has **a few erect male flowers with dark brown scales at its tip** and **3-12
female flowers below.** The female flowers make this species easy to identify
as their light brown scales are soon shed and the 4-6 mm long light brown
narrow pointed **perigynia soon become strongly reflexed.** No other
northern species has these **long narrow reflexed perigynia** with **unusual
short bristles extending out of their long beaks along with the three
stigmas.** This little sedge was originally described from Lapland and is
considered one of the most primitive members of the large genus of true
sedges (*Carex* spp.). The Short-Awned Sedge is circumpolar, with large gaps,
and low arctic in distribution and occurs all around Hudson and James bays
except for the far northern islands.

308

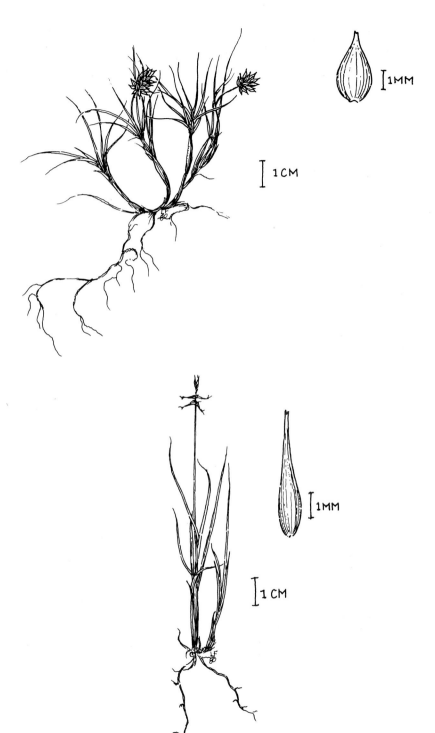

1MM

1CM

1MM

1CM

FLOWER PARTS INDISTINGUISHABLE
OR NONEXISTENT

Wildflowers with Basal Entire Grass-like Leaves; solid unjointed triangular stems....

832 ## Water Sedge

(Carex aquatilis Wahlenb.)

SEDGE FAMILY
Cyperaceae

The largest and most abundant sedge of wet areas in our region, forming extensive beds in shallow freshwater habitats. It is found along lakes, ponds, and rivers and in the Meadow-Marsh community, even on slightly saline sites. It is a tall (to 1 m), coarse, densely tufted plant from cordlike scaly yellow to brown horizontal rootstalks, each tuft composed of several sterile leafy shoots around one or more flowering stems. Flowering stems very leafy, the spikes barely longer than the 2-5 mm wide light to bluish green leaves which have distinctive **reddish brown leaf bases. Flower spikes 3-9**, the 2-4 cm long brown male spikes usually 2 or 3 (occasionally 1) at the top; female spikes 2-6, often with a few male flowers at their tips, on short stalks, 2-6 cm long and at least the lowest one subtended by a **leaf-like bract longer than the topmost spike.** Scales narrowly oval, black to brown with a midvein, shorter than the 2.5-3 mm long elliptical **pale green perigynia** which are **not inflated** or nerved and have very short beaks. The **achene is lens-shaped** and has **2 stigmas.** This very common and widespread marsh sedge was described from Lapland. It is eaten by cattle and forms part of 'slough hay' in the more southerly parts of its range. Water Sedge is a circumpolar arctic-boreal, prairie-montane species which occurs all around Hudson and James bays.

832 ## Rocky-Ground Sedge

(Carex saxatilis L.)

SEDGE FAMILY
Cyperaceae

A common medium-sized sedge of wet peat or gravel that forms distinct zones around the edges of ponds and pools and can also be found on mud in the Meadow-Marsh community. It is a coarse 15-50 cm tall somewhat tufted plant from a stout purplish creeping rootstalk. The thick stiff 2-4 mm wide keeled leaves are slightly shorter than the erect to slightly curved stems. The **2-5 dark flower spikes usually overlap slightly** but are not densely clustered and a **leaflike bract** from **below the lowest** is **nearly as long as the topmost spike.** Male spikes 1 (occasionally 2), at the top, sessile or very short-stalked, oval to club-shaped and 1-2 cm long. Female spikes below, usually 2 but occasionally 1 or 3, globe-shaped to broadly cylindrical, 0.5-2 cm long and 8-10 mm wide, the upper sessile, the lower on short stalks. The blunt oval purple to reddish black scales slightly shorter than the smooth oval nerveless **2.5-5 mm long purplish black perigynia** which have short beaks and are **inflated** around the smaller **lens-shaped achene with its two stigmas.** The shorter, broader, and less numerous flower spikes help distinguish this sedge from the somewhat similar Water Sedge (312) which is also common in wet areas in our region. The Rocky-Ground Sedge is a widespread circumpolar arctic-subarctic-alpine species complex and occurs all around Hudson and James bays.

832 *Glacier Sedge*

(Carex glacialis Mack.)

SEDGE FAMILY
Cyperaceae

A locally common usually dwarf species which **forms dense tussocks** on dry and exposed calcareous sites. The slender 5-15 cm long wiry stems are slightly longer than the clustered narrow flat strongly keeled somewhat **curved light green leaves. Flower spikes several** per stem, **crowded into** a 0.5-2 cm long **head which resembles a single spike unless you look very closely. Top spike male,** sessile and 2-7 mm long, the **lower 1-3 spikes female,** 2-10 mm long, sessile or short-stalked and with less than 5 flowers each. Scales of female flowers dark with transparent edges, often with a pale midvein, slightly shorter than the smooth oval brown 2-2.5 mm long perigynia which have short transparent beaks. **3 stigmas and a triangular achene** are present. This small sedge grows mainly in the Sandy Foreshore and Open Dune communities along the coast and the Heath and Ledge and Crevice communities on the outcrop ridge in the Churchill area but has been found on gravel ridges and eskers elsewhere around the bays. It is one of the earliest sedges to bloom, flower spikes usually appearing in early to mid-June and most seed gone by the end of July. Glacier Sedge is a circumpolar arctic-alpine species which occurs all around Hudson and James bays. It is very similar in appearance to the Rock Sedge (pg. 306) but can be distinguished from it by its several spikes and shorter perigynia.

832 *Hair-Like Sedge or Hair Sedge*

(Carex capillaris L.)

SEDGE FAMILY
Cyperaceae

A common delicate sedge of damp mossy marshes, bogs, depressions, and shores, the Hair-Like Sedge occurs in the Meadow-Marsh, Hummocky Bog, and Black Spruce/Larch Muskeg and Bog communities, along riverbanks, and around lake shores in our region. This sedge grows as **small dense tussocks** with **erect thread-like** 5-40 cm tall **stems** and **shorter light green** flat mostly basal 1-3 mm wide **leaves. Flower spikes usually 4** (from 2-8), the **topmost** always pale and **erect, male** or with male flowers at the tip and female below, 3-10 mm long and very slender, often overtopped by the upper female spike. **Female spikes** 5-15 mm **long, narrow, usually drooping on slender 1-4 cm long stalks.** Female flower scales shed early, pale with a green midrib, and shorter than the 2.5-4 mm long shining brown perigynia which have 2 strong ribs, a distinct cone-shaped beak, and are slightly inflated around the **triangular achene with** its **3 stigmas.** Leaf-like bracts present below at least the lowest spikes but seldom longer than the spike. Several varieties of this slender sedge exist, including a small one with only 3-4 spikes, the topmost always only male and the lower female on relatively short stalks, and a larger and more robust one with more spikes, the topmost always with both sexes of flowers, the lower on long drooping stalks. Both varieties exist at Churchill flowering during July and one or the other occurs all around both Hudson and James bays. The Hair-Like Sedge is a widespread circumpolar arctic-boreal-montane species.

FLOWER PARTS INDISTINGUISHABLE
OR NONEXISTENT

Wildflowers with Basal Entire Grass-like Leaves; solid unjointed
triangular stems....

832 ## *Mud Sedge and Scant Sedge*

(Carex limosa L.) *(Carex rariflora* (Wahlenb.) Sm.)

SEDGE FAMILY
Cyperaceae

These are two small closely related common sedges of wet peaty areas
and edges of ponds. They are found mainly in the Meadow Marsh, Hummocky Bog, Black Spruce/Larch Muskeg and Bog communities, and around
the edges of freshwater ponds in our region, blooming from early July
through mid-August. Both grow as **solitary or slightly clustered** 8-30 cm
tall stems from creeping **rootstalks** which produce roots **covered with** a
characteristic yellow to brown layer of velvety felt-like hairs. Leaves
narrow and much shorter than the stems, yellow green and to 1.5 mm wide
in the Mud Sedge, blue green and to 3 mm wide in the Scant Sedge. **Flower
spikes 2-3** (rarely 4), 0.5-3 cm long, **the lower all female, usually 1 in the
Mud Sedge** and **2 in the Scant Sedge, drooping on fine stalks.** Scales
purplish black with a pale mid-vein in the Scant Sedge, reddish brown in
the Mud Sedge, both broader than their smooth oval greenish grey or bluish
green 2.5 mm long perigynia which are beakless, flat on one side, and enclose
a **triangular achene with 3 stigmas.** The two sedges can easily be separated
by the darker scales, 2 female spikes and smooth upper stem of the Scant
Sedge versus the light brown scales, single female spike and roughened
upper stem of the Mud Sedge. Both sedges are widespread circumpolar
species, the Mud Sedge with a slightly more southern and montane distribution than the low arctic Scant Sedge. The Mud Sedge occurs from Churchill
south around Hudson and James bays to slightly up the eastern side of Hudson Bay while the Scant Sedge occurs all around both bays.

832 ## *Sheathed Sedge*

(Carex vaginata Tausch)

SEDGE FAMILY
Cyperaceae

A slender medium-sized sedge that occurs throughout our region in mossy
woods, bogs, and wet places, preferably calcareous. It can be found in the
Hummocky Bog, White Spruce Forest, Black Spruce/Larch Muskeg or Bog
communities and around lakeshores, blooming from early July to mid-August.
The **yellow green plants** are **solitary or a few together** from long slender
greyish brown scaly rootstalks, the stiff smooth 20-60 cm tall stems often
curved above and usually much longer than the bunched flat soft 2-5 mm
wide leaves. **Flower spikes usually 3** (from 2 to 7), the **topmost male**, light
brown club-shaped 1-2 cm long and **on a long stalk,** the **lower spikes female**
but often with a few male flowers at the tip, 1-2.5 cm long and on shorter
erect to loosely spreading stalks. The loose oval pointed scales are usually
brown with a green midrib and shorter than the thin smooth 3-5 mm long
oval yellowish brown short-beaked perigynia which tightly enclose
triangular achenes with 3 stigmas. The Sheathed Sedge can be told from
the Hair-Like Sedge by its **solitary or tufted growth form** and **erect spikes**
and from the Mud and Scant Sedges by its erect spikes and **smooth
rootstalks.** It is a circumpolar arctic-boreal-montane species which occurs
all around Hudson and James bays.

314

315

842 **Northern Bur-Reed**

(*Sparganium hyperboreum* Laest.)

BUR-REED FAMILY
Sparganiaceae

DESCRIPTION: Perennial **grass-like** rooted **aquatic plants**, the slender stems usually sticking out of the water and bearing **alternate long narrow yellow green leaves.** Leaves sessile, sheathing the stem at their bases, erect or **flexible and ribbon-like when floating;** 2-4 mm wide and 10-50 cm long; firm shiny and nerveless. **Flowers** small and inconspicuous, usually unisexual, petals and sepals lacking or reduced to small scales or bristles; **borne in distinctive green ball-shaped 5-12 mm wide heads,** the top one both male and female, the lower 2-3 only female. Fruits 3-5 mm long spindle-shaped green nutlets with very short beaks.

HABITAT: Shallow freshwater: occurs in ponds, bog pools, and quiet water along the edges of lakes and streams.

FLOWERING: Plants and young flower clusters appear from mid-July to early August: seeds ripen in late August through September

COMMENTS: Northern Bur-Reed is one of several late-season aquatic plants including the Alpine Pondweed and Spiked Water-Milfoil which appear and bloom in late July in many of the ponds around Churchill. Its long floating strap-shaped leaves and round green 'burrs' of flowers make it easy to identify. Its generic name is ancient and of an interesting derivation. It apparently comes from the Greek *sparganion*, which comes from *sparganon* or "swaddling-band", a reference to the ribbon-like leaves.

RANGE: Circumpolar low arctic-alpine species: known to occur on Hudson Bay from York Factory up the northwestern coast and along the southeastern half; also along the eastern side of James Bay.

NOTE: A closely related species, the NARROW-LEAVED BUR-REED (*Sparganium augustifolium* Michx.), is found occasionally in the ponds on the outcrop ridge and elsewhere. It can be told from the Northern Bur-Reed by its **separate male head(s) of flowers** and the **longer beaks (2 mm or more) of the female flowers** in the larger female heads.

The Grass Family is a large group of annual or perennial herbs which includes all grains (wheat, oats, rice, etc.) and most fodder plants (bluegrass, timothy, alfalfa, etc.). It therefore supplies much of the food for human beings and domestic and wild animals. Grass flowers are reduced in size and complexity from a basic flower because they rely on wind for pollination rather than insects or other animals and therefore have no need of large brightly coloured petals or nectar. There are, however, some specific technical terms referring to the specialized leaves associated with the flowers and their arrangement and these are illustrated and discussed below.

Grasses have round jointed stems which are hollow except at the nodes and alternate linear 2-ranked flat or curled leaves. The tiny flowers **(florets)** are usually perfect but have no sepals or petals, just 3 stamens, 2 feathery stigmas (to catch the abundant pollen produced), and a superior ovary which produces a **grain** as a fruit. Each floret is enclosed by 2 scale-like bracts: an outer one called the **lemma** and an inner one called the **palea** (see diagrams). The tiny enclosed florets are arranged in two-ranked **spikelets** ("small spikes") which have another pair of sterile scales or bracts, the **glumes**, at their base. A spikelet may have 1 floret or many; may have the glumes longer or shorter than the florets; may have long hair- or bristle-like **awns** from the tips or backs of lemmas and/or glumes and may be on a long slender stalk **(pedicel)** or sessile in dense spikes. All of these characters are important in identifying grasses and are used in the Subkey below. Study the diagrams and your grass specimen(s) to make sure that you understand which parts you are looking at.

Grass flowers are marvelously constructed in their own tiny way and are well worth studying with a hand lens or microscope. Grasses are some of the commonest and most abundant plants in the world and, although the arrangement of the spikelets can be complex, the flowers themselves are simple in structure. Some 35 species of grasses are known to occur at Churchill, with 9 of the most common genera and species covered in this Subkey and book. The others are listed in the Check List in the Appendix.

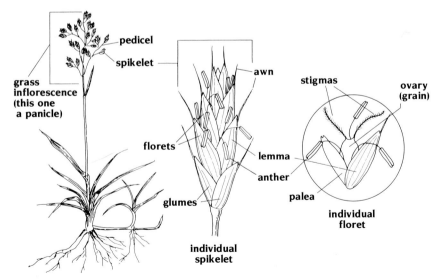

SUBKEY TO THE COMMON GRASSES OF CHURCHILL/HUDSON BAY

842 **Spikelets of Flower Heads With Visible Awns**

Awns over 2 cm long; straight; flower spike
nodding..WILD BARLEY
(*Hordeum jubatum*)

Awns under 1 cm long; flower clusters erect;
Glumes equal to or longer than lemmas
of floret; spikelets 1-flowered; lemmas
with short straight awn below middle............................REED GRASSES
(*Calamagrostis* spp.)

Glumes shorter than lemmas of florets; spikelets 2- to many-flowered;
Flower panicle under 5 mm wide; awn
straight, 2-3 mm long, from tip of
lemma; leaves very narrow and wiry......................ALPINE FESCUE
(*Festuca brachyphylla*)

Flower spike usually over 1 cm wide;
awn bent, 5-8 mm long, from back
of lemma; leaves over 1 mm wide..........................SPIKE TRISETUM
(*Trisetum spicatum*)

Spikelets of Flower Clusters Without Visible Awns

Flower spike very large and dense, 8-20 cm
long and over 1 cm wide; spikelets
sessile, 1-2 cm long...SEA LIME GRASS
(*Elymus arenarius*)

Flower panicles much smaller, dense to open; spikelets less than 1 cm long
on short to long pedicels;
Flower panicle very open; spikelets few,
3-4 mm long on long pedicels,
functionally 1-flowered, glumes
enclosing floret; yellow-brown and fragrant....................SWEET GRASS
(*Hierochloe odorata*)

Flower panicle denser; spikelets numerous and usually smaller,
not fragrant;
Flower panicle dense to open; spikelets 1-flowered;
Flower panicle dense and purple;
glumes shorter than floret;
leaves short and broad-bladed
(to 1 cm wide)...POLAR GRASS
(*Arctagrostis latifolia*)

Flower panicle dense to open;
glumes as long as or longer than
floret; leaves long and narrower..........................REED GRASSES
(*Calamagrostis* spp.)

Flower panicle dense to somewhat
open; spikelets 2- to several-
flowered glumes shorter than
lowest florets...NATIVE BLUEGRASSES
(*Poa* spp.)

FLOWER PARTS INDISTINGUISHABLE
OR NONEXISTENT

Wildflowers with Alternate Entire Grass-like Leaves; round hollow
jointed stems....

842 ## *Wild Barley*

(*Hordeum jubatum* L.)

GRASS FAMILY
Gramineae

Also known as Squirrel-Tail Grass or Foxtail Barley, Wild Barley is a common
weedy grass of disturbed gravel areas and sandy communities along the
coast. It is a distinctive **tufted perennial**, 30-60 cm high, immediately
**recognizable by its nodding flower spikes and long awns which can reach
6 cm in length.** The delicate hair-like awns do resemble the hairs of an
animal's tail or of a paint brush. The flower spikes and awns are light green
when young, turning a deep and beautiful purple when mature and pale
yellow when the seeds are ripe. It is an attractive and graceful grass although
often a troublesome weed in settlements. Native to North America and
eastern Asia, it occurs from Churchill south around James Bay and slightly
up the eastern side of Hudson Bay.

842 ## *Spike Trisetum*

(*Trisetum spicatum* (L.) Richter)

GRASS FAMILY
Gramineae

A common grass of gravel and sandy flats and dunes along the coast and
gravel ridges inland, Spike Trisetum is a **tufted perennial**, 10-50 cm high,
with a **dense erect 'fuzzy' 2.5-7 cm long flower spike** which is usually over
1 cm wide. The spike varies from silvery green to dark purple in colour,
the individual shiny spikelets on short pedicels about 6 mm long and 2-
or 3-flowered. Both glumes are shorter than the lower florets and the **lemmas
have bent 5-8 mm long awns** from their backs. **Leaves** are 1-3 mm wide,
they, **stems**, and **pedicels** all **softly hairy**. A circumpolar arctic-alpine
species, Spike Trisetum occurs all around Hudson and James bays.

FLOWER PARTS INDISTINGUISHABLE
OR NONEXISTENT

Wildflowers with Alternate Entire Grass-like Leaves; round hollow jointed stems....

842 *Alpine Fescue*

GRASS FAMILY
Gramineae

(*Festuca brachyphylla* Schultes)

Also known as the Short-Leafed Fescue, this is a common small perennial grass of dry sandy and gravelly areas often growing with Sea Lime Grass on beaches, the outcrop ridge, gravel ridges, and roadsides. **Densely tufted,** the individual clumps are usually 10-20 cm wide, their **smooth wiry stems** 10-30 cm high and **usually much longer than the stiff bristle-like leaves.** The **long narrow flower panicle** is **less than 5 mm wide,** the individual spikelets on short erect stalks. Spikelets and panicle are **dark purple to bronze in colour,** the spikelets usually **2-flowered** with **glumes shorter than the lowest floret** and **lemmas with** a **conspicuous** 2-3 mm long **straight awn from** their **tips.**

Panicles usually visible from early July to early August and the plants' small clumped growth form, short wiry leaves, and short awns are good diagnostic features. Alpine Fescue is a circumpolar wide ranging high arctic-alpine species which occurs all around Hudson and James bays.

842 *Reed Grasses*

GRASS FAMILY
Gramineae

(*Calamagrostis* spp.)

Several species of these grasses are common at Churchill and around Hudson Bay. They are difficult to identify to species, even for experts, so this account concentrates on the general characteristics of the group. Reed Grasses are slender medium to tall (to 1 m) perennials from creeping rootstalks which produce small tufts or single stems. Basal leaves are few or none and the narrow stem leaves long and flexible. Erect flower **panicle dense and spike-like or open and triangular,** made up of **many small 3-6 mm long 1-flowered spikelets** on distinct pedicels. Young spikelets often purplish, especially the tips of the glumes which are equal to, or longer than, the lemma of the floret. The **lemma has a short straight or twisted delicate awn from below its middle** and a tuft of distinctive white hairs at its base. Because the awn is delicate, it is easily broken and the floret often appears to be lacking one. Panicles are common from mid-July to the end of August.

The tallest reed grasses occur in both fresh and salt, moist to wet areas, one of the commonest, MARSH REED GRASS (*Calamagrostis canadensis* (Michx.) Beauv.), occuring mostly along freshwater streams and in Meadow-Marshes in the region. Other shorter species occur in the salt marshes and on sandy foreshores, dunes, and gravel ridges. Most are widespread arctic-alpine or boreal species and one or more of them occurs everywhere around Hudson and James bays.

FLOWER PARTS INDISTINGUISHABLE OR NONEXISTENT

Wildflowers with Alternate Entire Grass-like Leaves; round hollow jointed stems....

842 ## *Sea Lime Grass*

(*Elymus arenarius* L. ssp. *mollis* (Trin.) Hult.)

GRASS FAMILY
Gramineae

OTHER NAMES: Sea Lyme-Grass; Strand-Wheat; Dune-Grass

DESCRIPTION: **The tallest and stoutest grass of the region,** Sea Lime Grass also has the **largest flower spikes.** It averages 50 cm in height, ranging from 15 cm to more than 1 m. Growing in large colonies from stout creeping rootstalks, individual stems arise from the dead leaves of last year's stalk and bear several **firm blue green** 5-15 cm wide **leaves** with 10-30 cm long blades whose edges tend to roll under upon drying. Inflorescence **a dense spike 8-20 + cm long** and 1+ cm wide which is held stiffly erect; spikelets to 2.5 cm long, usually 2 at the upper and lower nodes and 3 at the middle nodes, each 3-flowered. **Glumes and lemmas both awnless, over 1.5 cm long, and softly hairy.**

HABITAT: Colonizer and stabilizer/binder of sand and gravel beaches, both present coastal and fossil inland ones.

FLOWERING: Flower heads appear in mid-to late June and mature in early to late July: seed usually gone by late August

COMMENTS: Sea Lime Grass is the most striking and easily identified grass of the Churchill region. Its large dense fuzzy head, tall stems, and broad leaves along with its colonial growth habit on beaches and gravel ridges make it easy to recognize. You will also find it on disturbed gravel anywhere in the region, especially on roadsides and construction sites.

The leaves of the Sea Lime Grass are used by the Inuit in some parts of the Arctic to weave baskets and whole dried plants are placed as an insulating layer between the inner and outer native boot. This latter use may have contributed to the spread of the grass when boot 'hay' was discarded at remote campsites.

RANGE: Nearly circumpolar (missing from western Europe) arctic to north temperate coastal and sand dune species: occurs all around Hudson and James bays.

325

FLOWER PARTS INDISTINGUISHABLE OR NONEXISTENT

Wildflowers with Alternate Entire Grass-like Leaves; round hollow jointed stems....

842 ## Sweet Grass

(Hierochloe odorata (L.) Beauv.)

GRASS FAMILY
Gramineae

Also known as Holy-Grass, Seneca-Grass, or Vanilla-Grass because of its **fragrant vanilla-like odour**, this grass is fairly common at Churchill and in the southern and eastern parts of both Hudson and James bays. This smooth perennial grows as single erect stems or small tufts, 30-60 cm high, from thin creeping rootstalks in moist sand and gravel. The 2-3 stem leaves are short flat and triangular, the shoot leaves much longer, 2-6 mm wide, flat and flexible. The panicle is an open pyramid up to 7 cm wide at the base, its relatively few **3-6 mm long shiny golden bronze to purple spikelets on much longer pedicels.** Spikelets are functionally 1-flowered, the glumes enclosing the **awnless floret.** Flowers appear in early to mid-July and remain visible until mid-August. Sweet Grass is a wide-ranging circumpolar low arctic-alpine species whose scientific name and common name of Holy Grass refer to its use in churches on saints' days in Europe. It has also been extensively used by native peoples in basket-making, as an incense, perfume, and natural deodorizer, for personal decoration and in many other ways. Its fragrance comes from coumarin, a potent anti-coagulent found in many grasses.

842 ## Polar Grass

(Arctagrostis latifolia (R. Br.) Griseb.)

GRASS FAMILY
Gramineae

A perennial common grass of moist peat areas on the outcrop and gravel ridges, Meadow-Marsh communities, and freshwater shores at Churchill, Polar Grass has erect 10-50 cm high stems growing singly or in small tufts from stout underground creeping rootstalks. The **short flat pointed leaves are up to 1 cm wide** and borne mainly on the stem. Its panicle is narrow and dense to somewhat open in outline, 3 to 10 cm long, with short crowded branches and **many small purplish, 1-flowered spikelets.** Spikelets are about 4 mm long, the **unequal glumes shorter than the floret** and with short sharp points; anthers usually purple. Flowers late in appearing, usually not fully developed until late July to mid-August. Polar Grass is a circumpolar high arctic species which occurs around the northern and central parts of Hudson Bay but is missing from its southern coast and James Bay.

FLOWER PARTS INDISTINGUISHABLE
OR NONEXISTENT

Wildflowers with Alternate Entire Grass-like Leaves; round hollow
jointed stems....

Bluegrasses

(*Poa* spp.)

GRASS FAMILY
Gramineae

The native bluegrasses or meadowgrasses (*Poa* spp.) are a widespread group of small-to medium-sized northern grasses which are fairly easy to determine to genus. However they can be very difficult to identify to species because of variation within, and hybridization between, the species complexes. The common lawn grass, KENTUCKY BLUEGRASS (*Poa pratensis* L.) is a typical member of this group and all bluegrasses closely resemble this species. The northern equivalent of Kentucky Bluegrass, the ALP-BORN BLUEGRASS (*Poa alpigena* (Fries) Lindm.), is common at Churchill along with 3 other widespread species. They grow mainly on the drier areas of the outcrop and gravel ridges but are also common on disturbed gravel areas such as roadsides and building sites and one species prefers the freshwater Meadow-Marsh community.

All native bluegrasses are tufted or turf-forming with rather **short narrow leaves which end in a boat-shaped tip** and usually have a double line down the midrib. The panicle is dense to somewhat open and triangular, the **spikelets 2-to-several flowered** on short to long stalks and less than 1 cm long. The **glumes are shorter than the lowest florets** and there are **no awns present.** One or more of the bluegrasses are present all around Hudson and James bays and they flower during July and early August.

FLOWER PARTS INDISTINGUISHABLE
OR NONEXISTENT

Wildflowers with Alternate Entire Submerged Leaves; aquatic plant....

842 *Alpine Pondweed*

(*Potamogeton alpinus* Balbis)

PONDWEED FAMILY
Potamogetonaceae

OTHER NAMES: Reddish Pondweed

DESCRIPTION: Soft reddish-tinged rooted perennial **aquatic plant with leafy jointed stems; submerged and floating leaves of different sizes, shapes, and textures; dense flower clusters borne above the water.** Submerged leaves narrowly oblong, to 25 cm long and 3 cm wide, **thin and translucent with rounded tips and wavy but entire edges. Floating leaves,** when present, **opposite, oval** 2-8 cm long by 1-2 cm wide, **much thicker and firmer** than the submerged leaves. Flower cluster reddish brown, of densely packed inconspicuous small flowers with greatly reduced or absent sepals and petals, cylindrical, 1.5-4 cm long, usually held above the water on a long stalk. Fruits 3 mm long achenes with curved beaks.

HABITAT: Shallow still fresh water, usually calcareous: freshwater ponds and streams throughout the region especially on the gravel ridges.

FLOWERING: Plants appear mid-July with flower clusters in late July to early August: ripe seed dispersing late August through September

COMMENTS: Alpine Pondweed is a common late season aquatic plant in the Churchill region. Its broad submerged reddish wavy-edged leaves separate it from the green strap-leaved Northern Bur-Reed and divided-leaved Spiked Water-Milfoil with which it often grows. All of the pondweeds (Genus *Potamogeton*) are important sources of food for waterfowl and muskrats.

RANGE: Circumpolar boreal-low arctic-alpine species: occurs from about latitude 60°N south around both Hudson and James bays.

NOTE: The only other common pondweed in the region is the SLENDER- or THREAD-LEAVED PONDWEED (*Potamogeton filiformis* Pers.) which grows in similar habitats around both bays. It has clusters of **very narrow thread-like** 10-15 cm long **leaves** which are **completely submerged,** and a **narrow interrupted flower cluster.** Several other species of pondweeds occur in our region, mostly along the southern part of Hudson Bay and around James Bay, but all are less common than the two mentioned above. All pondweeds can be recognized by their submerged entire leaves and clusters of small flowers/fruits at the tips of emergent stems.

Wildflowers with Alternate Entire Leaves; coarse marsh or emergent aquatic plants to 1 m high....

842 ## *Western Dock*

(*Rumex occidentalis* S. Wats.)

BUCKWHEAT FAMILY
Polygonaceae

DESCRIPTION: Stout smooth perennial plant from a thick rootstalk, its **greenish red stems 25-100 cm tall.** Alternate **long-petioled leaves mostly basal thick and somewhat fleshy,** broadly oblong to **lanceolate, up to 30 cm long** and 2-5 cm wide, entire but often wavy-edged and heart-shaped at the base. Petioles sheath the stem with their bases and **large brown stipules** completely surround the stem above the nodes **forming ochreae. Inflorescence a very large** and **much-branched panicle,** leafless, with erect branches **containing many small greenish red flowers** on slender 5-7 mm long pedicels. Flowers perfect with 6 sepals, the outer 3 small and thin, the inner 3 larger and developing into the characteristic **reddish brown 5-10 mm long net-veined wings which surround the small shining brown 3-angled achene.**

HABITAT: Marshy or wet places: general in Salt-Marsh, Meadow-Marsh, and Damp Dune Hollow communities, in pools (both saline and fresh) on the outcrop ridge and along the edges of streams and ponds.

FLOWERING: Young flower clusters appearing mid-to late July: mature seeds usually shed by the end of August

COMMENTS: This tall dock with the reddish stem, coarse leaves, and red brown flower clusters is a striking plant and common throughout the Churchill region. All of the docks or sorrels (Genus *Rumex*) have a sour juice which make their young leaves useful as salad or cooked greens. Docks have also been used medicinally as an antiseptic, to treat skin conditions such as ringworm, and for their high vitamin C content. You shouldn't eat too much of them as they contain large amounts of oxalic acid and tannins, both of which can cause kidney or other problems.

RANGE: North American boreal-subarctic species: occurs from Churchill south around James Bay to near latitude 56°N on the eastern side of Hudson Bay.

FLOWER PARTS INDISTINGUISHABLE
OR NONEXISTENT

Wildflowers with an Alternate Deeply-Lobed Leaf; round clustered sporangia at tip of the stem....

Moon Fern/Moonwort

(*Botrychium lunaria* (L.) Sw.)

ADDER'S-TONGUE FAMILY
Ophioglossaceae

DESCRIPTION: Low non-flowering perennial fern, 4-15 cm tall, from a short erect rootstalk which bears a **single smooth yellow green fleshy leaf.** This is stemlike below and **divided** above **into a leafy 'sterile blade'** and a **branched 'fertile spike'** which **bears thick round sporangia** (the spore-bearing reproductive bodies) in rows along its edges. Sterile blade attached near the middle of the 'stem', once divided into 3-9 pairs of 5-20 mm wide, often overlapping, **fan- or kidney-shaped leaflets.** Fertile blade 1-10 cm long, usually raised well above the 'leaf'. Bud of new leaf erect, not coiled into the typical fern 'fiddlehead'.

HABITAT: Open fields, meadows, ledges, and gravelly slopes and shores: Open and Stable Dune, Ledge and Crevice communities; disturbed areas and grassy places on gravel ridges.

FLOWERING: Young plants and sporangia appear as early as late June: sporangia mature in mid-August or later.

COMMENTS: This tiny fern, the only common one at Churchill, occurs in large patches on the gravel ridges and sandy dunes near the coast. It is another of those tiny plants (only 4-5 cm tall in our area) which are difficult to spot but easy to recognize with their single fleshy lobed leaves and clusters of round sporangia. The generic name comes from the Greek word meaning "a small cluster of grapes" (*botrys*), a reference to the bunches of round sporangia. The specific and common names come from the Latin for "moon", a description of the shape of the leaf segments.

RANGE: Widespread circumpolar (also in southern hemisphere) boreal-montane, subarctic-grassland species: occurs from about latitude 60°N south around both sides of Hudson and James bays.

NOTE: The only other fern you are likely to find at Churchill is the delicate FRAGILE FERN (*Cystopteris fragilis* (L.) Bernh.) which grows in sheltered crevices on the outcrop ridge. It has thin dark green several-times-divided solitary or tufted leaves which bear sporangia in circular red brown clusters on the lower sides of the leaflets.

Several other species of ferns occur around Hudson and James bays, mostly on James Bay and southeastern Hudson Bay. The majority grow in crevices in rock outcrops and cliffs and are uncommon to rare.

FLOWER PARTS INDISTINGUISHABLE
OR NONEXISTENT

Wildflowers with Alternate Toothed Leaves; striped stems....

843 *Smooth Orache*

GOOSEFOOT FAMILY
Chenopodiaceae

(*Atriplex glabriuscula* Edmon.)

OTHER NAMES: Saltbush

DESCRIPTION: **Low fleshy much-branched annual,** seldom over 10 cm tall, with **stems often red or white striped.** **Leaves** alternate, **triangular to oval** in shape, 1-5 cm long, **mealy from dot-like white hairs,** usually with at least 1-2 pairs of large basal teeth. **Tiny green flowers** clustered **in small spikes** subtended by leaves **at the tips of the branches.** Fruits 2-4 mm long dark achenes enclosed by a pair of small 4-12 mm long bracts which are fused together for about half their length.

HABITAT: Coastal sands and salt marshes: Salt-Marsh community.

FLOWERING: Mid-July onwards: seeds usually ripe in late August

COMMENTS: This small orache is locally common in the salt marshes around Churchill, often growing in large patches on mats of decaying seaweed or rich mud. As an annual, it is a late-season developer and should be looked for in areas such as Bird and Sloop's coves from mid-July onwards. The crushed pulp of this and other oraches has been used to treat insect bites and stings; leaves and the young plants can be cooked as greens, and the seeds make a useful flour.

RANGE: Apparently boreal-subarctic western North America to northwestern Europe with large gaps: known only from James Bay, Churchill, and the Seal River in our region.

NOTE: The widespread closely related ORACHE or SPEARSCALE (*Atriplex patula* L.) has been found in salt marshes at Churchill and along the western side of James Bay. Some botanists lump the Smooth Orache and other species in with the Spearscale but the two plants have a distinctly different look. **Spearscale is taller,** has **narrower and smaller leaves, a more open flower cluster** with no subtending leaves and smaller bracts and seeds than Smooth Orache.

336

FLOWER PARTS INDISTINGUISHABLE
OR NONEXISTENT

Shrubs with Alternate Entire Needle-like Evergreen Leaves; bearing aromatic blue berry-like cones....

Juniper

(Juniperus communis L.)

PINE FAMILY
Pinaceae

OTHER NAMES: Low, Common Mountain, Common, Ground, or Dwarf Juniper;

DESCRIPTION: Flat or spreading **shrub with shredding reddish bark**, seldom over 1.5 m tall in our area, commonly forming low open thickets or mats near treeline. **Leaves evergreen, crowded in whorls** of 3, 5-10 mm long, **sharp and awl-shaped**, dark green below, whitish and grooved above. **Scented berry-like cones** borne in leaf axils, green the first year, ripening to **blue black with a bloom** 2nd or 3rd year, 6-10 mm in diameter.

HABITAT: Dry sandy or rocky areas: occurs in Ledge and Crevice communities on the outcrop ridge and Lichen-Heath and White Spruce communities on both the outcrop and gravel ridges.

FLOWERING: Unrecorded for northern plants: cones probably form in July

COMMENTS: Juniper is uncommon in the Churchill region but can be found occasionally on the outcrop ridge at Cape Merry and along the coast and inland in association with White Spruce, especially at Twin Lakes.

Its prickly leaves with the white stripe on top and aromatic blue 'berries' make Juniper easy to identify. The berries are actually small fleshy cones. They smell like gin and are used to flavour this alcoholic drink in a ratio of 1 kilogram of berries to 400 litres of gin. They also flavour meats and liqueurs and have been used roasted as a coffee substitute. Stems and leaves have sometimes been brewed or soaked to make medicinal teas or poultices. Although the berries and inner bark have been eaten as an emergency food, they contain substances which can be **poisonous** when consumed in large amounts.

RANGE: Widespread circumpolar boreal-subarctic species: occurs from Churchill south around James Bay to about latitude 56°N on the eastern side of Hudson Bay.

NOTE: A small relative, the CREEPING JUNIPER (*Juniperus horizontalis* Moench), occurs on similar habitats in the southernmost parts of the bays. It can easily be told from the Common Juniper by its **long creeping stems** and blue green **triangular needles** which **overlap like shingles.**

FLOWER PARTS INDISTINGUISHABLE
OR NONEXISTENT

Shrubs with Alternate Entire or Toothed Deciduous Leaves; bearing catkins....

852
853

The Willows

(Genus *Salix*)

WILLOW FAMILY
Salicaceae

Several species of entire- and tooth-leaved willows occur at Churchill and around Hudson and James bays. All willows in our region are tall to dwarf deciduous shrubs with alternate leaves and bear their flowers in catkins (the 'pussies' of the pussy-willow) early in the spring. These dense flower clusters are either all male or all female and each sex is borne on a different plant. The tiny flowers have no sepals or petals, relying on wind for pollination and dispersal of the numerous small seeds, each with a tiny tuft of hairs. Their winter buds have only one scale covering them while the closely related poplars have several bud scales.

All willows produce aspirin-related compounds and have long been used by native peoples to treat a variety of ailments including wounds, headaches, fevers, and arthritis.

The 9 commonest and most easily recognized species of entire-leaved willows in the Churchill region are keyed below and briefly described and/or illustrated on the next pages. The 3 common toothed-leaved willows are keyed and described in the next section (pg. 358) along with one species which can have either entire or toothed leaves. All willows tend to hybridize and they can be very difficult to identify beyond the group, so don't be discouraged if your plant doesn't fit neatly into any of the descriptions given here or in the toothed-leaved section!

SUBKEY TO THE WILLOWS (Genus *Salix*)

Leaves nearly as broad to broader than long
Leaves not deeply veined, thin, pointed
at tip; catkins usually over 5 cm long ....LIME WILLOW
(*Salix lanata*)
Leaves deeply veined, leathery, round tipped; catkins less than 5 cm long
Petioles short, usually less than 5 mm
long, underside of leaf silky-hairy ....ROCK WILLOW
(*Salix vestita*)

Petioles longer than 5 mm; underside of
leaf glaucous, but nearly or completely
smooth ....SNOW WILLOW
(*Salix reticulata*)
Leaves two or more times longer than broad
Young twigs, leaves (at least underside), and catkins more-or-less hairy
Leaves 2 to 3 times longer than broad, densely grey-hairy to smooth;
female catkins grey-hairy
Leaves sessile or nearly so, to about
1.5 cm wide; catkins rarely over
2.5 cm long ....SHORT-CAPSULED WILLOW
(*Salix brachycarpa*)

Leaves with petioles over 2 mm long,
to about 3 cm wide; catkins to
7 cm long..BLUE-GREEN WILLOW
(*Salix glauca*)

Leaves more than 3 times longer than
broad, densely silvery-hairy beneath;
female catkins densely white-hairy,
more than 2 cm long......................................HOARY/SILVER WILLOW
(*Salix candida*)
Young twigs and leaves smooth; catkins smooth or hairy
Young twigs, leaves and catkins smooth
(a few hairs sometimes found on leaves
and catkins) ....BOG WILLOW
(*Salix pedicellaris*)

Young twigs and leaves smooth; catkins hairy
Dwarf, trailing shrub; catkins reddish-
hairy; twigs greenish yellow................................TRAILING WILLOW
(*Salix arctophila*)

Erect shrub, catkins white-hairy; twigs
dark red to black..FLAT-LEAVED WILLOW
(*Salix planifolia*)

Shrubs with Alternate Entire Deciduous Leaves; bearing catkins....

852
853

Snow Willow

(*Salix reticulata* L.)

WILLOW FAMILY
Salicaceae

OTHER NAMES: Net-Veined or Netted Willow

DESCRIPTION: **Tiny shrubs, never much more than 10 cm tall,** with short **greenish yellow to light brown branches from buried stems; usually growing in patches** 0.2 to 1 m across. **Leaves** borne on 1-1.5 cm slender reddish petioles; blades **round,** 0.8-5 cm wide, **edges entire to somewhat scalloped and rolled under, glossy dark green above with deeply sunken veins, pale green conspicuously net-veined** and thinly hairy to smooth **beneath. Catkins appearing with the leaves** on leafy branches, female to **3 cm long, reddish with grey hairs.**

HABITAT: Moist calcareous sandy, gravelly, or turfy places usually deeply covered by winter snow: general and common on the outcrop and gravel ridges close to the coast and in the Hummocky Bog community.

FLOWERING: Late May through early July for female catkins

COMMENTS: This tiniest of the area's willows is common nearly everywhere you look except in very wet and very dry areas. It often grows in large patches with the deciduous bearberries which it somewhat resembles. However bearberries have narrower pointed and toothed leaves and berries instead of the Snow Willow's typical small catkins. Though small, the leaves of this willow turn golden yellow in the fall and make lovely splashes of color across the tundra and cliffs along with the brilliantly red bearberry leaves.

RANGE: Circumpolar (except Greenland) widespread arctic-alpine species: occurs all around both bays except for the southern tip of James Bay.

NOTE: The very similar ROCK WILLOW (*Salix vestita* Pursh) is found occasionally at Churchill and south to around James Bay. It prefers moist rocky or gravelly areas, usually under other willow or Dwarf Birch shrubs. It can be told from the Snow Willow by its **larger size (to 1 m)** and **erect stems,** by its **shorter petioles (under 5 mm),** by its densely silvery-silky lower leaf surfaces and by its **silvery green catkins.**

FLOWER PARTS INDISTINGUISHABLE
OR NONEXISTENT

Shrubs with Alternate Entire Broad Flat Deciduous Leaves;
bearing catkins....

852 **_Lime Willow_**

WILLOW FAMILY
Salicaceae

(*Salix lanata* L. ssp. *calcicola* (Fern. & Wieg.) Hult.)

OTHER NAMES: Calcicolous, Woolly or Candelabra Willow

DESCRIPTION: **Erect ascending shrubs,** 0.2-1 m high, **with stout gnarly stems, new growth stems** and **stipules, petioles, edges, and mid-veins of young leaves covered with long woolly hairs.** Leaves 2-5 cm long, 1.5-3.5 cm broad, oval to **almost round** with a rounded to heart-shaped base and pointed tip; green above, glaucous below, subtended by large persistent stipules. **Catkins appearing before the leaves,** sessile, **very large and hairy,** the female 3-10 cm long.

HABITAT: Moist open calcareous, rocky, and gravelly places: general and common at Churchill near the coast on outcrop and gravel ridges.

FLOWERING: Late May through early July for female catkins: seeds usually dispersing in July

COMMENTS: The stoutest and woolliest of the mid-sized willows in the Churchill region, usually 20-60 cm tall. It has the largest catkins of any of our willows, these appearing before the leaves and looking like fuzzy candle flames at the ends of the branches. One of the earliest plants to bloom, usually at the edges of melting snowbanks or ponds.

RANGE: Mainly an eastern North American subarctic-low arctic species: occurs all around Hudson and James bays.

852 *Short-Capsuled Willow*

(Salix brachycarpa Nutt.)

WILLOW FAMILY
Salicaceae

OTHER NAMES: Short-Fruited Willow

DESCRIPTION: **Low erect freely branching shrub,** usually less than 2 m tall; **branches stout, greyish to reddish brown, outer layers of bark peeling, young twigs greyish hairy. Thin light green leaves have very short petioles,** are oblong to oval and usually sharply tipped, 2-3 cm long and 0.7-1 cm wide, **densely to sparsely grey hairy beneath and above. Catkins appearing with the leaves** on short leafy branches, female usually **1-2 cm long and grey-woolly.**

HABITAT: Wet calcareous or saline sandy, gravelly, or rocky places: Salt- and Meadow-Marsh communities; moist areas on sand dunes and outcrop ridge; riverbanks and open White Spruce communities.

FLOWERING: Female catkins appear late June through July: seeds usually ripe and dispersing in late July or early August

COMMENTS: This is one of the commonest medium-sized willows found in salt marshes, along riverbanks, and elsewhere along the coast. It seems to be quite tolerant of salt in both soil and air. The Short-Capsuled can be told from the Hoary Willow by its broader thinner lighter green less hairy leaves and shorter catkins.

RANGE: North American boreal-montane species (with large gaps): occurs from just north of Churchill south around James Bay to about latitude 55°N on the eastern side of Hudson Bay.

NOTE: The similar BLUE-GREEN, SMOOTH, or NORTHERN WILLOW (*Salix glauca* L.) is also common in the Churchill region and around the bays on moist, usually sheltered, sandy and rocky areas. This complex of closely related species can be told from the Short-Capsuled Willow by their **longer petioles, wider leaves, and larger catkins.**

FLOWER PARTS INDISTINGUISHABLE OR NONEXISTENT

Shrubs with Alternate Entire Deciduous Leaves; bearing catkins....

Hoary or Silver Willow

(Salix candida Flugge)

WILLOW FAMILY
Salicaceae

DESCRIPTION: Erect shrub to 2 m in our region, **young twigs 'frosted' with short white woolly hairs,** smooth and dark brown when older. **Leathery leaves** 2-10 cm long and 0.5-1.5 cm wide, narrowing to points at both ends, the **smooth edges somewhat rolled under; dull velvety silver-hairy beneath; dark to dull green above with incised veins,** usually smooth but sometimes slightly hairy. **Catkins appearing before the leaves** on short leafy branches, the **female 2-5 cm long** and **densely silvery-hairy.**

HABITAT: Wet swampy or boggy areas, often calcareous or saline: Salt- and Meadow-Marsh communities; along rivers and around lakes and ponds on moist gravel and peat; moist areas on gravel ridges and roadsides; Black Spruce/Larch Bog and Muskeg communities.

FLOWERING: Male and female catkins appear in June: seeds usually ripe and dispersing by mid- to late July

COMMENTS: Hoary Willow is common on moist to wet sites throughout the Churchill area. It is easy to recognize because of its silvery-hairy leaves and catkins which almost glow in the long northern summer days. No other willow with narrow leaves is as hairy.

RANGE: North American boreal species: occurs from slightly north of Churchill south around James Bay and up the eastern side of Hudson Bay to about latitude 56°N.

FLOWER PARTS INDISTINGUISHABLE
OR NONEXISTENT

Shrubs with Alternate Entire Deciduous Leaves; bearing catkins....

852 ## *Bog Willow*

(*Salix pedicellaris* Pursh)

WILLOW FAMILY
Salicaceae

DESCRIPTION: **Slender creeping shrub,** erect branches seldom to 1 m high in our region, with **smooth reddish brown twigs** and **dark grey bark.** Leaves **short-petioled,** firm and **leathery, elliptical to oblong** with blunt tips, 2-6 cm long, 0.5-1.5 cm wide, **green above, glaucous beneath, smooth on both sides. Catkins appearing with the leaves** on leafy twigs, the **female** about **2 cm long, smooth dark reddish purple to light brown.**

HABITAT: Wet woods, muskegs and bogs, marshy areas: moist peat around lakes and ponds; Meadow-Marsh, Hummocky Bog, Willow/Bog Birch Thicket, Black Spruce/Larch Muskeg and Bog communities.

FLOWERING: Late June through July for female catkins: seed probably ripe and dispersing by late July to early August

COMMENTS: This medium-sized willow is fairly common on moist peaty areas away from the coast. It can easily be recognized by the nearly complete lack of hairs on its leaves, twigs, and catkins.

RANGE: North American boreal-montane species: occurs from just north of Churchill south around James Bay to slightly up the eastern side of Hudson Bay.

853 *Flat-Leaved Willow*

(*Salix planifolia* Pursh)

WILLOW FAMILY
Salicaceae

DESCRIPTION: **Erect much-branched shrub, 1-3 m tall, with slender smooth very dark red to black twigs.** Leaves smooth, **dark green and shiny above, glaucous below,** 2-7 cm long, 1-2 cm wide, **elliptical to lanceolate** with pointed ends, **edges nearly entire to more commonly finely toothed. Catkins appearing before the leaves,** female 2-5 cm long, **densely white-hairy or silky.**

HABITAT: Well-drained but wet areas, usually with good snow cover: occurs along the Churchill River and other streams, around lakes and ponds, and in wet spots in the Stable Dune community and on the outcrop and gravel ridges.

FLOWERING: June (often very early) for female catkins: seed usually dispersing by mid- to late July

COMMENTS: One of the commonest taller willows in the region, usually found on wet gravel along rivers, streams, lakes, and ponds. Its shiny dark green leaves and slender smooth dark stems make it fairly easy to recognize.

RANGE: Nearly circumpolar boreal-montane-low arctic species complex (missing from eastern Asia and Greenland): occurs all around Hudson and James bays except for the far northern islands.

FLOWER PARTS INDISTINGUISHABLE
OR NONEXISTENT

Shrubs with Alternate Toothed Deciduous Leaves; bearing cone-like catkins....

853 *Scrub Birch*

(Betula glandulosa Michx.)

BIRCH FAMILY
Betulaceae

OTHER NAMES: Ground, Bog, Dwarf, or Glandular Birch

DESCRIPTION: **Low shrub** to about 1.5 m tall in our region, **young twigs densely covered with resinous wart-like glands.** Mature **leaves smooth, leathery,** 1-3 cm long, **oval to round with coarse teeth** along the edges, **green both sides or very slightly paler beneath.** Tiny flowers without sepals or petals are **borne in catkins of a single sex, both sexes** occuring **on the same plant. Female catkins** 1-1.5 cm long, looking **like small smooth light brown cones** each composed of **rows of 3-lobed bracts which bear 2 or 3 flowers** consisting of **a single ovary which develops narrow wings in the mature fruit (nutlet).**

HABITAT: Wet places, swamps, bogs, and muskeg: general in the region including Stable Dune, Meadow-Marsh, and White Spruce Forest communities; edges of ponds and streams and moist to wet areas on the outcrop and gravel ridges.

FLOWERING: Male and female catkins present in June to early July. Female catkins remain on the plant until the following winter releasing their seeds on the snow which guarantees them the moisture necessary to germinate in the spring.

COMMENTS: Scrub Birch is the only representative of the usually tree-like birches found around the bays. Its close relationship to the other birches is shown by its similar cone-like catkins and winged seeds. It is common on moist to wet sites, usually with a good winter snow cover, and most often grows with various species of willows in small to large thickets. It can be told from the willows by its coarsely-toothed round leaves, cone-like catkins and resin-dotted twigs. Scrub Birch is an important source of firewood in the treeless northern tundra.

RANGE: Widespread and variable North American arctic-alpine-boreal species: occurs all around Hudson and James bays.

FLOWER PARTS INDISTINGUISHABLE
OR NONEXISTENT

Shrubs with Alternate Toothed Deciduous Leaves; bearing cone-like catkins....

Sweet Gale

(Myrica gale L.)

BAYBERRY FAMILY
Myricaceae

OTHER NAMES: Bog-Myrtle; Meadow-Fern; Sweet Willow

DESCRIPTION: **Low shrub** usually under 1 m tall **with erect reddish brown branches, twigs short-hairy** and **with small white lenticels. Leaves grey green** 3-5 cm long 1-2 cm wide, **wedge-shaped, broadest and toothed near tips,** sparsely hairy, **strongly aromatic from abundant small golden resin dots beneath. Tiny flowers** without sepals or petals are **borne in** all male or all female **catkins,** usually on different plants. Catkins appearing before the leaves, **female cone-like** and **near the tips of twigs,** 1-1.5 cm long, mature ones consisting of clusters of small winged nutlets coated with an aromatic resinous wax.

HABITAT: Shallow water on lakeshores, in bogs, or in muskegs: Pressure-ridge, Meadow-Marsh, and Black Spruce/Larch Muskeg and Bog communities; around lakes and ponds and along rivers, usually with willows and/or Scrub Birch.

FLOWERING: Male and female catkins appearing in June to early July: ripe nutlets falling from mid-July to mid-August

COMMENTS: This attractive sweet-scented shrub is found occasionally in wet freshwater sites in our region. Good places to look for it at Churchill are along the Churchill River near the pumphouse and near the lake at Camp Nanook. Its wedge-shaped grey green leaves, cone-like catkins, and fragrance make it easy to recognize. It has been used, especially in Europe, to flavour beer, as a spice in other foods, as a tea, to repel and destroy insects such as fleas, to treat scabies, to make scented candles (it is a close relative of the Bayberry), and as a dye plant.

RANGE: North American, northern European and eastern Asian boreal-subarctic species: occurs from about latitude 61°N south around both Hudson and James bays.

FLOWER PARTS INDISTINGUISHABLE
OR NONEXISTENT

Shrubs with Alternate Toothed Deciduous Leaves; bearing catkins....

There are only three common toothed-leaved willows in the Churchill region and one which sometimes has rounded teeth and they are all relatively easy to distinguish. Please see the Entire-Leaved Willows section (pg. 340) for more information on willows.

SUBKEY TO THE TOOTHED-LEAVED WILLOWS

Catkins hairy
    Prostrate trailing shrub usually under 20 cm tall;
        Catkins silvery-hairy; leaves round
        and deeply veined, leathery ....SNOW WILLOW
                                        (*Salix reticulata*)

        Catkins reddish-hairy; leaves lanceolate,
        shiny, not deeply veined ....TRAILING WILLOW
                                        (*Salix arctophila*)

    Erect shrub usually over 1 m tall;
    catkins white-hairy; leaves lanceolate
    and shiny ....FLAT-LEAVED WILLOW
                                       (*Salix planifolia*)

Catkins smooth, low shrub under
    1 m tall...MYRTLE-LEAVED WILLOW
                                        (*Salix myrtillifolia*)

(Opposite page)
Silver Willow Community around edge of
freshwater pond with Small Yellow
Watercrowfoot, near Bird Cove.

FLOWER PARTS INDISTINGUISHABLE
OR NONEXISTENT
Shrubs with Alternate Toothed Deciduous Leaves; bearing catkins....

Trailing Willow

WILLOW FAMILY
Salicaceae

(*Salix arctophila* Cockerell)

OTHER NAMES: Arctic Marsh Willow

DESCRIPTION: **Dwarf shrubs, stems usually trailing along the ground or buried in moss, erect brownish green branches** seldom over 15 cm tall. **Leaves** 2-4 cm long, 1-2 cm wide, short-petioled, **elliptical to oblong in shape** with a pointed base and rounded to pointed tip, **edges subentire to** more commonly **finely and shallowly toothed**, blades **totally smooth dark green and shiny above, glaucous beneath. Catkins appearing with the leaves** on leafy branches, erect and large, the **female 3-10 cm tall reddish brown and thinly-hairy.**

HABITAT: Mossy tundra, lakeshores, and streambanks: general in wet but well-drained areas including Stable Dune, Ledge and Crevice, and Hummocky Bog communities, usually in moss.

FLOWERING: June to early July for female catkins: seeds usually ripe and dispersing by the end of July

COMMENTS: This is one of the two common dwarf willows in our region. It can easily be told from the equally tiny Snow Willow (pg. 342) by its longer than broad less distinctly veined leaves and by its larger reddish rather than white-hairy catkins.

RANGE: Mainly eastern and central North American (Greenland) arctic-montane species: occurs all around Hudson and James bays.

NOTE: A less common similar but erect willow, the MYRTLE-LEAVED WILLOW (*Salix myrtillifolia* Anderss.), grows in wet sites in wooded bogs and along streams and lakes. It can be told from the Trailing Willow by its smooth smaller (less than 3 cm long) **yellow green catkins** and **more obviously toothed leaves.**

862 **White Spruce**

PINE FAMILY
Pinaceae

(*Picea glauca* (Moench) Voss)

DESCRIPTION: Low to medium-sized tree reaching only about 10 m in our region. It has a slender pyramidal outline on protected areas and a ragged often one-sided outline on exposed sites. It has evergreen 4-sided 1.5-3 cm long needle-like leaves which have a green to dark green colour and pungent odour when crushed. Needles borne individually on stout smooth light grey to orange brown branchlets. Bark greyish brown, scaly in young trees becoming furrowed in older ones. The leathery hanging cones are slender, cylindrical, 5-7 cm long (always more than twice as long as wide), dark red purple when young and light brown at maturity. Cones usually drop off soon after shedding their seeds in the fall and can be found under the trees for several years.

HABITAT: Usually moist well-drained soils but sometimes on peat in bogs and muskegs at the northern limit of its range: White Spruce Scrub community on the outcrop ridge; Hummocky Bog and Muskeg communities on the plains; White Spruce Forest community on gravel ridges.

FLOWERING: New reddish cones produced in July in years when trees reproduce (they do not bear cones every year): mature brown cones present in August, usually dropping by late September

COMMENTS: The commonest evergreen tree in the coastal area around Churchill and the bays, White Spruce forms the strikingly twisted and one-sided 'krummholz' trees on the outcrop ridge and plains close to the coast. It grows as dense stands of larger more symmetrical trees on peat and gravel areas and along river valleys inland. Black Spruce does not occur until you reach 5 kilometers or more inland but you also get many small White Spruce there and need to look closely at the cones and branchlets to be sure which spruce you have. Wherever White Spruce grows it creates a boreal forest 'micro-climate' underneath its branches. This supports a variety of plants typical of forest rather than arctic regions including Northern Comandra and Labrador Tea.

RANGE: Widespread North American boreal-montane, subarctic-alpine species: occurs from the southern Northwest Territories south around James Bay to about latitude 57°N on the eastern side of Hudson Bay.

The Latin generic name *Picea* means "pitch" and pitch obtained from spruce has long been used as a medicinal and caulking agent. The tough pliable roots have been used as sewing and basket-making material by a number of native peoples.

NOTE: BLACK or BOG SPRUCE (*Picea mariana* (P. Mill.) B.S.P.) is found in inland wet acid bogs and muskegs in the Churchill area and around the southern parts of Hudson and James bays. It can be told from the White Spruce by its **narrower outline** which usually includes a distinctive '**tuft' or 'flag' of branches at the tip of the tree**, by its **slender rusty-hairy branchlets**, and by its smaller, **nearly round cones which remain on the tree for several years.**

FLOWER PARTS INDISTINGUISHABLE
OR NONEXISTENT
Trees with Whorled Entire Deciduous Needle-like Leaves; bearing cones....

Larch/Tamarack

PINE FAMILY
Pinaceae

(*Larix laricina* (Du Roi) K. Koch)

OTHER NAMES: American, Eastern, Red, or Black Larch; Hackmatack; Juniper

DESCRIPTION: **Small to medium-sized coniferous tree** with an **open pyramidal shape**, seldom reaching 15 m in height in our region. **Soft bluish green needle-like leaves borne in 2-3 cm long clusters on short lateral 'spur' shoots, turning yellow and dropping off in the fall.** The 1.2-2 cm long **oval reddish female cones** are borne on older branchlets, **turning light brown** and **releasing small winged seeds at maturity.**

HABITAT: Various moist usually calcareous sites including swamps and fens but preferring well-drained soils: Hummocky Bog, Black Spruce/Larch Bog and Muskeg communities on the plains; Pressure Ridge community around lakes and ponds.

FLOWERING: Young female cones present in early July, shedding seeds in late August to early September. Cones not produced every year but may remain on the tree for a year or more after the seeds are shed.

COMMENTS: This hardy tree is common at Churchill and southwards on moist peaty areas away from the immediate coast. Most conifers are also evergreens and keep their needle-like leaves for several years, but Larch is deciduous dropping its needles in the fall and producing new ones in the spring. Larch is easy to identify, having a beautiful leaf green colour and lacy appearance in the spring and turning pure gold in the fall. It usually starts to leaf out late in June and drops its needles in early September at Churchill.

The resinous gum produced by the Larch has been chewed for pleasure and to cure indigestion. Extracts and poultices of the bark and roots have been used as teas for enjoyment and medical purposes and to treat wounds. The inner bark is edible (in emergencies!).

RANGE: Wide ranging North American boreal-subarctic species: occurs from just north of Churchill south around James Bay and up the eastern side of Hudson Bay to about latitude 57°N.

Trees with Alternate Entire Deciduous Leaves; bearing catkins....

862 *Balsam or Black Poplar*

(Populus balsamifera L.)

WILLOW FAMILY
Salicaceae

OTHER NAMES: Hackmatack, Taccamahac, Balm-of-Gilead

DESCRIPTION: In our region a **tall shrub to small tree**, rarely reaching 10 m in height, with a **pyramidal outline** and **growing in clumps. Bark on young trees smooth and greenish brown becoming grey and deeply furrowed** on older ones. **Leaves deciduous alternate simple**, 7.5 to 12.5 cm long 4-8 cm wide, tapering to a sharp tip from a broad rounded base. Leaves **dark green above, paler** and often **bronze-coloured below from resin blotches**, borne on a thin **round petiole. Flowers** lacking sepals and petals, **produced in all male and all female catkins on separate trees**, the **female 10-13 cm long** and **producing many small 'fluffy' seeds. Winter buds long and narrow** with several **bud scales** which are **covered with a fragrant gummy balsam resin.**

HABITAT: Colonizer of open sandy or gravelly soils near water: occurs on sheltered lee slopes of the inland gravel ridges near Church-ill and tops of fossil beach ridges further south.

FLOWERING: Most northern poplars reproduce by suckering rather than by seeds. Catkins could be expected in late June through July and ripe seeds in late July through August.

COMMENTS: This small deciduous tree is uncommon at Churchill but common on fossil beach ridges from York Factory on south. Small stands of it occur on the western side of the airport ridge and off Goose Creek Road in the Churchill region. As it is the only broad-leaved tree in the area, it is easy to identify.

As a member of the willow family, Balsam Poplar produces aspirin-like compounds, and extracts of buds and bark have long been used in treating fevers, arthritis, and wounds. The aromatic resin of the buds which gives the tree its common names is used in ointments and scented articles.

RANGE: Widespread North American boreal-subarctic species: occurs from Churchill south around James Bay and up the eastern side of Hudson Bay to about latitude 58°N.

NOTE: The closely related ASPEN POPLAR or TREMBLING ASPEN (*Populus tremuloides* Michx.) is occasionally found in similar habitats around James Bay and the southernmost parts of Hudson Bay. It can be told from the Balsam Poplar by **its flattened petioles, heart-shaped leaves, and lack of resin on both the buds and lower surfaces of the leaves.**

REFERENCES

Beals, C.S., (Ed.), 1968
Science, History and Hudson Bay, Vol. I
Canada Dept. of Energy, Mines and Resources, Ottawa

Brandson, Lorraine E. and Bonnie Chartier (Comp.), 1983
Encounters on Hudson Bay, Churchill Region
Churchill Ladies Club, Churchill

Budd, A.C., 1979
Budd's Flora of the Canadian Prairie Provinces
Revised and enlarged by J. Looman and K. Best,
Research Branch, Agriculture Canada, Publication 1662
Agriculture Canada, Ottawa

Burt, Page, 1991
Barrenland Beauties, Showy Plants of the Arctic Coast
Outcrop Ltd., The Northern Publishers, Yellowknife, N.W.T.

Dredge, L.A., 1992
Field Guide to the Churchill Region, Manitoba
Geological Survey of Canada, Miscellaneous Report 53,
Minister of Supply & Services Canada, Ottawa

Gordon, Bryan H.C., 1975
Of Men and Herds in Barrenland Prehistory
National Museum of Man, Mercury Series.
Archaeological Survey of Canada, Paper No. 28,
National Museums of Canada, Ottawa

Hulten, Eric, 1968
Flora of Alaska and Neighboring Territories
Stanford University Press, Standford, California

MacIver, Angus & Bernice, 1982
Churchill on Hudson Bay
Churchill Ladies Club, Churchill

Introducing Manitoba Prehistory
Papers in Manitoba Archaeology, Popular Series No. 4
Manitoba Dept. of Cultural Affairs and Historical Resources, Winnipeg

McGhee, Robert, 1978
Canadian Arctic Prehistory
Canadian Prehistory Series
Van Nostrand Reinhold, Toronto

Meyer, David A., 1977
Pre-Dorset Settlements at the Seahorse Gully Site
National Museum of Man, Mercury Series.
Archaeological Survey of Canada, Paper No. 57
National Museums of Canada, Ottawa   pg. 368
Morton, W.L., 1997

Manitoba, A History. 2nd. ed.
University of Toronto Press, Toronto

Mulligan, Gerald A., 1987
Common Weeds of Canada
NC Press, Toronto

Newcomb, Lawrence, 1977
Newcomb's Wildflower Guide
Little, Brown, Boston

Porsild, A.E., 1979
Rocky Mountain Wild Flowers
National Museum of Natural Sciences
National Museums of Canada, Ottawa

Porsild, A.E. & Wm. J. Cody, 1980
Vascular Plants of the Continental Northwest Territories, Canada
National Museum of Natural Sciences,
National Museums of Canada, Ottawa

Ritchie, J.C., 1956
"The Native Plants of Churchill, Manitoba, Canada"
Can. J. Botany, 34:269-320

Scoggan, H.J., 1959
The Native Flora of Churchill, Manitoba
with notes on the history, geology and climate of the area.
National Museums of Canada, Ottawa (out of print)

Scoggan, H.J., 1978
Flora of Canada
National Museum of Natural Sciences Publications in Botany No. 7
National Museums of Canada, Ottawa

Scott, P.A., 1991
The Flora of Churchill, Manitoba including mosses & liverworts, native vascular plants & weeds.
Department of Zoology, University of Toronto, Toronto

Trelawney, J., 1983
Wild Flowers of the Yukon and Northwestern Canada including Adjacent Alaska
Gray's Publishing, Sidney, B.C.

Walker, M., 1984
Harvesting the Northern Wild
A Guide to Traditional and Contemporary Uses of Edible Forest   Plants of the Northwest Territories.
Outcrop Ltd., The Northern Publishers, Yellowknife, N.W.T.

A CHECK LIST OF THE VASCULAR PLANTS OF CHURCHILL, MANITOBA

by Karen L. Johnson and David White

Nomenclature based on Porsild and Cody, 1980, **Vascular Plants of the Continental Northwest Territories, Canada** (Primary name) and Scoggan, 1978, **The Flora of Canada** (Most synonyms and species not given by Porsild and Cody). Common names primarily from **Budd's Flora of the Canadian Prairie Provinces.**

EQUISETACEAE
  Equisetum arvense L.
  E. *fluviatile* L.
  E. *palustre* L.
  E. *scirpoides* Michx.
  E. *sylvaticum* L. var.
    pauciramosum Milde
  E. *variegatum* Schleich.

HORSETAIL FAMILY
  Common Horsetail
  Swamp or Water Horsetail; Pipes
  Marsh Horsetail
  Dwarf Scouring-Rush
  Woodland Horsetail

  Variegated Horsetail

LYCOPODIACEAE
  Lycopodium annotinum L. s. lat.
  L. *complanatum* L. s. lat.
  L. *selago* L.

CLUB-MOSS FAMILY
  Stiff or Bristly Club-Moss
  Ground Cedar; Trailing Club-Moss
  Mountain Club-Moss

SELAGINELLACEAE
  Selaginella selaginoides (L.) Link

SPIKE-MOSS FAMILY
  Spike-Moss; Mountain-Moss

OPHIOGLOSSACEAE
  Botrychium lunaria (L.) Sw. (incl. ssp.
    lunaria and ssp. *minganense* (Vict.)
    Calder & Taylor)

ADDER'S-TONGUE FAMILY
  Moon Fern; Moonwort

POLYPODIACEAE
  Cystopteris fragilis (L.) Bernh.
  Dryopteris disjuncta (Rupr.) Morton,
    (*Gymnocarpium dryopteris* (L.)
    Newm.)
  Polypodium vulgare L. ssp. *virginianum*
    (L.) Hult., (*P. virginianum* L.)

FERN FAMILY
  Fragile Fern
  Oakfern

  Polypody; Common Rock Tripe

PINACEAE
  Juniperus communis L.
  J. *horizontalis* Moench
  Larix laricina (Du Roi) K. Koch
  Picea glauca (Moench) Voss
  P. *mariana* (P. Mill.) B.S.P.

PINE FAMILY
  Juniper; Low or Ground Juniper
  Creeping Juniper
  Larch; Tamarack
  White Spruce
  Black Spruce

SPARGANIACEAE
  Sparganium angustifolium Michx.
  S. *hyperboreum* Laestad.
  S. *multipedunculatum* (Morong) Rydb.

BUR-REED FAMILY
  Narrow-Leaved Bur-Reed
  Northern Bur-Reed
  Many-Stalked Bur-Reed

POTAMOGETONACEAE
(ZOSTERACEAE)
Potamogeton alpinus Balbis (incl. spp.
tenuifolius (Raf.) Ogden)
P. *filiformis* Pers. (incl. var. *borealis*
(Raf.) St. John)
P. *gramineus* L.

P. *obtusifolius* Mert. & Koch
P. *richardsonii* (Benn.) Rydb., (P.
perfoliatus L. ssp. *richardsonii*
(Benn.) Hult.)
P. *vaginatus* Turcz.
Zostera marina L.

SCHEUCHZERIACEAE
Triglochin maritima L.
T. *palustris* L.

GRAMINEAE
Agropyron trachycaulum (Link) Malte
A. *violaceum* (Hornem.) Lange ssp.
violaceum, (A. *trachycaulum* (Link)
Malte var. *latiglume* (Schribn. &
Sm.) Beetle)
Agrostis borealis Hartm.
A. *stolonifera* L. var. *palustris* (Huds.)
Farw.
Alopecurus alpinus Sm.
Arctagrostis latifolia (R. Br.) Griseb.
ssp. *latifolia*
Arctophila fulva (Trin.) Rupr.
Beckmannia syzigachne (Steud.) Fern.
Bromus pumpellianus Scribn. var.
pumpellianus, (B. *inermis* Leyss.
ssp. *pumpellianus* (Scribn.) Wagnon)
Calamagrostis canadensis var. *langsdorfii*
(Link) Inman, (C. *canadensis*
(Michx.) Beauv. var. *scabra*
(Kunth) A.S. Hitchc.)
C. *deschampsioides* Trin.
C. *inexpansa* A. Gray
C. *lapponica* (Wahlenb.) Hartm. var.
nearctica Porsild
C. *neglecta* (Ehrh.) Gaertn., Mey., &
Schreb.
Catabrosa aquatica (L.) Beauv.
Deschampsia caespitosa (L.) Beauv.
Dupontia fisheri R. Br. ssp. *psilosantha*
(Rupr.) Hult.
Elymus arenarius L. ssp. *mollis* (Trin.)
Hult., (E. *mollis* Trin.)
E. *innovatus* Beal

PONDWEED FAMILY

Alpine Pondweed

Slender- or Thread-Leaved
Pondweed
Various-Leaved or Grass-Leaved
Pondweed
Blunt-Leaved Pondweed
Richardson's Pondweed

Sheathed Pondweed
Eel-Grass

ARROW-GRASS FAMILY
Seaside Arrow-Grass
Marsh Arrow-Grass

GRASS FAMILY
Slender Wheatgrass
Violet Wheatgrass

Northern Bent-Grass
Redtop

Alpine Foxtail
Polar Grass

Tawny Arctophila
Slough Grass
Arctic or Northern Awnless
Brome-Grass

Marsh Reed Grass; Bluejoint

Hairgrass-Like Reed Grass
Northern Reed Grass
Lapland Reed Grass

Narrow Reed Grass

Brook Grass
Tufted Hair Grass
Fisher's Dupontia

Sea Lime Grass

Hairy Wild Rye

Festuca brachyphylla Schult., (*F. ovina*   Alpine Fescue
L. var. *brachyphylla* (Schult.)
Piper)
F. prolifera (Piper) Fern. var.   Fertile Fescue
lasiolepis Fern., (*F. rubra* L. var.
prolifera Piper)
F. rubra L.   Red Fescue
Glyceria striata (Lam.) A.S. Hitchc.   Fowl Manna Grass
var. *stricta* (Scribn.) Fern.
Hierochloë odorata (L.) Beauv.   Sweet Grass
H. *pauciflora* R. Br.   Arctic Holy Grass
Hordeum jubatum L.   Wild Barley; Squirrel-Tail Grass
Poa alpigena (Fries) Lindm. var.   Alp-Born Blue Grass
alpigena, (P. *pratensis* L.)
P. *alpina* L.   Alpine Blue Grass
P. *arctica* R. Br. ssp. *arctica,* (P.   Arctic Blue Grass
arctica R. Br. var. *arctica*)
P. *arctica* R. Br. ssp. *caespitans*   Arctic Blue Grass
(Simm.) Nannf., (P. *arctica* R. Br.
var. *caespitans* (Nannf.) Boivin)
P. *flexuosa* Sm., (P. *laxa* Haenke ssp.   Lax Blue Grass
flexuosa (Sm.) Hyl.)
P. *glauca* Vahl   Glaucous Blue Grass
P. *palustris* L.   Marsh or Fowl Blue Grass
Puccinellia ambigua Soren.   Doubtful Salt-Meadow or Goose
    Grass
P. *langeana* (Berl.) Soren.,   Lange's or Dwarf Salt-Meadow or
    Goose Grass
P. *lucida* Fern. & Weath.   Shining Salt-Meadow or
    Goose Grass
P. *nuttalliana* (Schult.) A.S. Hitchc.,   Nuttall's Salt-Meadow or Goose
    Grass
P. *phryganodes* (Trin.) Scribn. &   Creeping Salt-Meadow or Goose
Merr.   Grass
P. *vaginata* (Lange) Fern. & Weath.   Sheathed Salt-Meadow or Goose
(incl. vars. *vaginata* and *paradoxa*   Grass
Soren.)
Trisetum spicatum (L.) Richter   Spike Tristeum

CYPERACEAE   SEDGE FAMILY
Carex amblyorhyncha Krecz., (C.   Blunt-Nosed or Sea Sedge
marina Dew.)
C. *aquatilis* Wahlenb. (inc. vars.   Water Sedge
aquatilis and *stans* (Drej.) Boott)
C. *arcta* Boott   Narrow Sedge
C. *arctogena* H. Sm., (C. *capitata* L.   Northern-Born Sedge
var. *arctogena* (H. Sm.) Hult.)
C. *atrata* L., (C. *raymondii* Calder)   Black or Black-Scaled Sedge
C. *atrofusca* Schkuhr   Dark-Brown Sedge
C. *aurea* Nutt.   Golden Sedge

C. *bicolor* Bellardi — Two-Coloured Sedge
C. *bigelowii* Torr. — Stiff or Bigelow's Sedge
C. *buxbaumii* Wahlenb. — Brown or Buxbaum's Sedge
C. *canescens* L. — Silvery or Greyish Sedge
C. *capillaris* L. (incl. ssp. *capillaris*, — Hair-Like or Hair Sedge
ssp. *chlorostachys* (Stev.) Löve, et
al. and ssp. *robustior* (Drej.)
Böch.)
C. *capitata* L. — Capitate Sedge
C. *chordorrhiza* Ehrh. — Prostrate or Creeping Sedge
C. *concinna* R. Br. — Beautiful Sedge
C. *deflexa* Hornem. — Bent or Northern Sedge
C. *diandra* Schrank — Two-Stamened Sedge
C. *disperma* Dew. — Two-Seeded Sedge
C. *garberi* Fern. — Garber's Sedge
C. *glacialis* Mack. — Glacier Sedge
C. *glareosa* Wahlenb. var. *amphigena* — Gravel Sedge
Fern.
C. *gynocrates* Wormskj. — Northern Bog Sedge
C. *heleonastes* Ehrh. — Hudson Bay Sedge
C. *lachenalii* Schkuhr — Arctic Hare's-Foot Sedge
C. *langeana* Fern. — Lange's Sedge
C. *leptalea* Wahlenb. — Bristle-Stalked Sedge
C. *limosa* L. — Mud Sedge
C. *livida* (Whalenb.) Willd. var. — Livid Sedge
grayana (Dew.) Fern., (C. *livida*
Willd. var. *radicaulis* Paine)
C. *mackenziei* Krecz., (C. *norvegica* — Norway or MacKenzie Sedge
Willd.)
C. *maritima* Gunn., (C. *dutillyi* O'Neill — Seaside or Curved Sedge
& Duman)
C. *media* R. Br. — Middle Sedge
C. *membranacea* Hook. — Fragile Sedge
C. *microglochin* Wahlenb. — Short-Awned Sedge
C. *morrisseyi* Porsild, (C. *adelostoma* — Morrissey's Sedge
Krecz.)
C. *norvegica* Retz. — Alpine Sedge
C. *oligosperma* Michx. — Few-Fruited Sedge
C. *physocarpa* Presl, (C. *saxatilis* L. — Bladder-Fruited Sedge
var. *major* Olney)
C. *rariflora* (Wahlenb.) Sm. — Scant Sedge
C. *rotundata* Wahlenb. — Round or Round-Fruited Sedge
C. *rupestris* Bellardi — Rock Sedge
C. *saxatilis* L. var. *miliaris* (Michx.) — Rocky-Ground Sedge
Bailey, (C. *miliaris* Michx.)
C. *saxatilis* L. var. *rhomalea* Fern., (C. — Rocky-Ground Sedge
miliaris Michx. var. *major* Bailey)
C. *scirpoidea* Michx. — Rush-Like or Northern Single-Spike
Sedge
C. *subspathacea* Wormskj., (C. *salina* — Salt or Salt-Marsh Sedge
Wahlenb. var. *subspathacea*
(Wormskj.) Tuck.)

CYPERACEAE, continued

C. *supina* Wahlenb. ssp. *spaniocarpa* (Steud.) Hult.	Weak or Weak Arctic Sedge
C. *ursina* Dew.	Bear Sedge
C. *vaginata* Tausch	Sheathed Sedge
C. *williamsii* Britt.	William's Sedge
Eleocharis acicularis (L.) R. & S.	Needle or Slender Spike-Rush
E. *halophila* Fern. & Brack., (E. *uniglumis* (Link) Schult. var. *halophila* Fern. & Brack.)	Salt-Loving Spike-Rush
E. *palustris* (L.) R. & S.	Creeping or Common Spike-Rush
E. *pauciflora* (Lightf.) Link var. *fernaldii* Svens., (E. *quinqueflora* (F.X. Hartm.) Schwarz)	Few-Flowered Spike-Rush
E. *smallii* Britt.	Small's Spike-Rush
E. *uniglumis* (Link) Schult.	One-Glumed Spike-Rush
Eriophorum angustifolium Honck.	Tall Cotton-Grass
E. *brachyantherum* Trautv. & Mey.	Close-Sheathed Cotton-Grass
E. *callitrix* Cham.	Beautiful or Tufted Cotton-Grass
E. *chamissonis* C.A. Mey.	Chamisso's Cotton-Grass
E. *gracile* W.D.J. Koch	Slender Cotton-Grass
E. *russeolum* Fries var. *albidum* W. Nyl.	Russet Cotton-Grass
E. *scheuchzeri* Hoppe	One-Spike or Arctic Cotton-Grass
E. *vaginatum* L. ssp. *spissum* (Fern.) Hult.	Sheathed Cotton-Grass
Kobresia myosuroides (Vill.) Fiori & Paol., (K. *bellardii* (All.) Degl.)	Bellard's Bog-Sedge or Kobresia
K. *simpliciuscula* (Wahlenb.) Mack.	Simple or Arctic Bog-Sedge or Kobresia
Scirpus caespitosus L. ssp. *austriaceus* (Pallas) Asch. & Graeb., (S. *caespitosus* L. var. *callosus*)	Tufted Bulrush
S. *hudsonianus* (Michx.) Fern., (*Eriophorum alpinum*) L. and E. *hudsonianus* Michx.)	Alpine Cotton-Grass
S. *rufus* (Huds.) Schrad.	Red Bulrush
LEMNACEAE	DUCKWEED FAMILY
Lemna minor L.	Lesser Duckweed
L. *trisulca* L.	Ivy-Leaved or Star Duckweed
JUNCACEAE	RUSH FAMILY
Juncus albescens (Lange) Fern., (J. *triglumis* L. var. *albescens* Lange)	White Rush
J. *alpinus* Vill. ssp. *nodulosus* (Wahlenb.) Lindm., (J. *alpinus* var. *rariflorus* Hartm.)	Alpine Rush
J. *arcticus* Willd.	Arctic Rush
J. *balticus* Willd. var. *littoralis* Engelm.	Baltic Rush

374

JUNCACEAE, continued

J. *biglumis* L. — Two-Glumed or Two-Flowered Rush

J. *bufonius* L. s. lat. — Toad Rush
J. *castaneus* Sm. (incl. ssp. *castaneus* vars. *castaneus* and *pallidus* Hook.) — Chestnut Rush
Luzula confusa Lindeb. — Northern Wood-Rush
L. *groenlandica* Böch. — Greenland Wood-Rush
L. *multiflora* (Retz.) Lej. ssp. *frigida* (Buch.) Krecz. var. *contracta* Sam. — Many-Flowered Wood-Rush
L. *parviflora* (Ehrh.) Desv. — Small-Flowered Wood-Rush

LILIACEAE — LILY FAMILY
Smilicina trifolia (L.) Desf. — Three-Leaved Solomon's-Seal
Tofieldia pusilla (Michx.) Pers. — Bog or Scottish Asphodel

ORCHIDACEAE — ORCHID FAMILY
Calypso bulbosa (L.) Oakes — Venus-Slipper
Corallorhiza trifida (L.) Chat. — Early Coralroot
Cypripedium passerinum Richards. — Northern or Franklin's Lady's-Slipper
Habenaria hyperborea (L.) R. Br., (*Platanthera hyperborea* (L.) Lindl. — Green-Flowered Bog Orchid
H. *obtusata* (Pursh) Richards., (*Platanthera obtusata* (Pursh) Lindl.) — Small Northern Bog Orchid
Listera borealis Morong — Northern Twayblade
L. *cordata* (L.) R. Br. — Heart-Leaved Twayblade
Orchis rotundifolia Banks — Round-Leaved Orchid
Spiranthes romanzoffiana Cham. — Hooded Lady's-Tresses

SALICACEAE — WILLOW FAMILY
Populus balsamifera L. — Balsam or Black Poplar
P. *tremuloides* Michx. (small vegetatively-reproducing colony growing next to railway track) — Aspen Poplar; Trembling Aspen
Salix alaxensis (Anderss.) Cov. — Alaska or Feltleaf Willow
S. *arbusculoides* Anderss. — Shrubby or Small Tree-Like Willow
S. *arctophila* Cockerell — Trailing Willow
S. *athabascensis* Raup, (S. *glauca* L., in part) — Athabasca Willow
S. *bebbiana* Sarg. — Beaked Willow
S. *brachycarpa* Nutt. — Short-Capsuled Willow
S. *candida* Flügge — Hoary or Silver Willow
S. *cordifolia* Pursh var. *callicarpea* (Trautv.) Fern., (S. *glauca* L., in part, including ssp. *callicarpaea* (Trautv.) Böch.) — Broad-Leaved or Blue-Green Willow
S. *lanata* L. ssp. *calciola* (Fern. and Wieg.) Hult., (S. *calciola* Fern. and Wieg.) — Lime or Woolly Willow

375

SALICACEAE, continued

S. *myrtillifolia* Anderss.   Myrtle-Leaved Willow
S. *pedicellaris* Pursh   Bog Willow
S. *planifolia* Pursh, (S. *phylicifolia* L.)   Flat-Leaved Willow
S. *reticulata* L.   Snow or Net-Veined Willow
S. *vestita* Pursh   Rock or Hairy Willow

MYRICACEAE   BAYBERRY FAMILY
Myrica gale L.   Sweet Gale; Bog-Myrtle

BETULACEAE   BIRCH FAMILY
Alnus crispa (Ait.) Pursh   Green Alder
Betula glandulosa Michx.   Scrub or Dwarf Birch
B. *pumila* L. var. *glandulifera* Regel   Swamp or Dwarf Birch

URTICACEAE   NETTLE FAMILY
Urtica gracilis Ait., (U. *dioica* L. ssp.   Stinging Nettle
gracilis (Ait.) Seland.)

SANTALACEAE   SANDALWOOD FAMILY
Geocaulon lividum (Richards.) Fern.   Northern Comandra

POLYGONACEAE   BUCKWHEAT FAMILY
Koenigia islandica L.   Common or Iceland Koenigia
Polygonum amphibium L. var.   Swamp Persicaria; Water
stipulaceum (Coleman) Fern.   Smartweed
P. *boreale* (Lange) Sm.   Northern or Boreal Knotweed;
    Doorweed
P. *lapathifolium* L.   Pale Persicaria; Dock-Leaved
    Knotweed
P. *viviparum* L.   Alpine Bistort or Viviparous
    Knotweed
Rumex arcticus Trautv.   Arctic Dock
R. *maritimus* L. var. *fueginus* (Phil.)   Golden Dock
    Dusen
R. *occidentalis* S. Wats.   Western Dock
R. *triangulivalvis* (Danser) Rech. f.,   Western Dock
(R. *salicifolius* Weinm. ssp.
triangulivalvis Danser var.
mexicanus (Meisn.) C.L. Hitchc.)

CHENOPODIACEAE   GOOSEFOOT FAMILY
Atriplex glabriuscula Edmon.   Smooth Orache
A. *patula* L. (incl. vars. *patula* and   Orache; Spearscale
hastata (L.) Gray)
Chenopodium capitatum (L.) Aschers.   Strawberry Blite
C. *gigantospermum* Aellen, (C.   Maple-Leaved Goosefoot
hybridum L.)
C. *glaucum* L. ssp. *salinum* (Standl.)   Saline Goosefoot
Aellen
Salicornia borealis Wolff & Jeffries   Northern Samphire
Suaeda maritima (L.) Dumort.   Western Sea-Blite

PORTULACACEAE
Montia lamprosperma Cham., (M. fontana L.)

CARYOPHYLLACEAE
Arenaria humifusa Wahlenb.
Cerastium alpinum L. s. lat.
C. beeringianum Cham. & Schlecht.
Honckenya peploides (L.) Ehrh., (Arenaria peploides L.)
Melandrium affine J. Vahl, (Lychnis furcata (Raf.) Fern.)
M. apetalum (L.) Fenzl ssp. arcticum (Fries) Hult., (Lychnis apetala L.)

Minuarta dawsonensis (Britt.) Mattf., (Arenaria stricta Michx. var. dawsonensis (Britt.) Scoggan)
M. rossii (R. Br.) Graebn., (Arenaria rossii R. Br.)
M. rubella (Wahlenb.) Hiern., (Arenaria rubella (Wahlenb.) Sm. & A. verna L. var. pubescens (Cham. & Schlecht.) Fern.)
M. stricta (Sw.) Hiern., (Arenaria stricta Michx. var. uliginosa (Schleich.) Boivin)
Moehringia lateriflora (L.) Fenzl, (Arenaria lateriflora L.)
Sagina nodosa (L.) Fenzl
Spergularia marina (L.) Griseb.
Stellaria calycantha (Ledeb.) Bong. s. lat.
S. crassifolia Ehrh.
S. edwardsii R. Br., (S. longipes Goldie var. edwardsii (R. Br.) Gray and S. ciliatosepala Trautv.)
S. humifusa Rottb.

S. longifolia Muhl.

S. longipes Goldie s. str.

S. monantha Hult., (S. longipes Goldie pro parte)
S. stricta Richards., (S. longipes Goldie pro parte)
S. subvestita Greene, (S. longipes var. subvestita (Greene) Polunin)

RANUNCULACEAE

Anemone multifida Poir.

PURSLANE FAMILY
Blinks; Boreal Blinking-Chickweed

PINK FAMILY
Spreading or Low Sandwort
Alpine Chickweed
Beringian Chickweed
Sea-Purslane; Sea-Beach Sandwort

Arctic Bladder-Campion; Mountain Cockle
Nodding Lychnis; Cockle

Dawson's Sandwort

Ross's Sandwort

Early or Reddish Sandwort

Marsh or Upright Sandwort

Blunt-Leaved Sandwort

Pearlwort; Knotted Pearlwort
Salt-Marsh Sand Spurry
Northern Stitchwort or Starwort

Fleshy Stitchwort or Starwort
Edward's Stitchwort

Low Chickweed, Stitchwort or Starwort
Long-Leaved Stitchwort or Chickweed
Long-Stalked Stitchwort or Chickweed
One-Flowered Stitchwort or Chickweed
Straight Stitchwort or Chickweed
Slightly-Hairy Chickweed

CROWFOOT OR BUTTERCUP FAMILY
Cut-Leaved Anemone

RANUNCULACEAE, continued

A. *parviflora* Michx.	Small Wood or Northern Anemone
A. *richardsonii* Hook.	Yellow Anemone
Caltha palustris L. var. *palustris*	Marsh-Marigold
Ranunculus aquatilis L. (incl. vars. *eradicatus* Laestad. and *capillaceus* (Thuill.) DC.)	Large-Leaved Watercrowfoot White Water Buttercup
R. *aquatilis* L. var. *subrigidus* (W. Drew) Breit., (R. *circinatus* Sibth.)	Large-Leaved Watercrowfoot White Water Buttercup
R. *cymbalaria* Pursh	Seaside Buttercup
R. *hyperboreus* Rottb.	Boreal or Arctic Buttercup
R. *lapponicus* L.	Lapland Buttercup
R. *pallasii* Schlecht.	Pallas's Buttercup
R. *pedatifidus* Sm. var. *leiocarpus* (Trautv.) Fern.	Northern Buttercup
R. *purshii* Richards., (R. *gmelini* DC. var. *hookeri* (D. Don) L. Benson)	Small Yellow Watercrowfoot
R. *sceleratus* L. ssp. *multifidus* (Nutt.) Hult., (R. *sceleratus* var. *multifidus* Nutt.)	Celery-Leaved Buttercup
Thalictrum venulosum Trel. (First record 1987)	Veiny Meadow-Rue

FUMARIACEAE	FUMITORY FAMILY
Corydalis aurea Willd.	Golden Corydalis
C. *sempervirens* (L.) Pers.	Pink Corydalis

CRUCIFERAE	MUSTARD FAMILY
Arabis alpina L.	Alpine Rock Cress
A. *arenicola* (Richards.) Gelert	Sand-Dwelling or Arctic Rock Cress
Barbarea orthoceras Ledeb.	American Winter Cress
Braya humilis (C.A. Mey.) B.L. Robins. s. lat. (incl. var. *interior* (Böch.) Boivin)	Low Northern Rock Cress or Braya
Cardamine pratensis L. var. *angustifolia* Hook.	Meadow Bitter Cress
Cochlearia officinalis L.	Scurvy-Grass
Descurainia richardsonii (Sweet) O.E. Schulz	Gray Tansy Mustard
D. *sophioides* (Fisch.) O.E. Schulz	Northern Flixweed
Draba alpina L.	Alpine Whitlow-Grass or Draba
D. *aurea* M. Vahl	Golden Whitlow-Grass or Draba
D. *cana* Rydb., (D. *lanceolata* auctt. non Royle)	Gray Whitlow-Grass or Draba
D. *glabella* Pursh (inc. vars. *glabella* and *orthocarpa* (Fern. & Knowl.) Fern.), (D. *hirta* auctt. non L.)	Smoothing Whitlow-Grass or Draba
D. *incana* L. var. *confusa* (Ehrl.) Lilj.	Hoary Whitlow-Grass or Draba
D. *lactea* M.P. Adams, (D. *fladnizensis* Wulf. var. *heterotricha* (Lindbl.) J. Ball)	White Arctic Whitlow-Grass or Draba

378

CRUCIFERAE, continued

D. *nemorosa* L. var. *leiocarpa* Lindbl.   Yellow Whitlow-Grass or Draba
D. *nivalis* Lilj.   Snow Whitlow-Grass or Draba
Erysimum cheiranthoides L. (incl. ssp.   Wormseed Mustard
    altum Ahti)
Eutrema edwardsii R. Br.   Edward's Eutrema
Hutchinsia procumbens (L.) Desv.,   Prostrate Hutchinsia
    (*Hymenolobus procumbens* (L.)
    Nutt.)
Lepidium bourgeauanum Thell.   Common Pepper-Grass
L. *densiflorum* Schrad.   Common Pepper-Grass
L. *ramosissimum* A. Nels.   Branched Pepper-Grass
Lesquerella arctica (Wormskj.) S.   Northern Bladderpod
    Wats.
Rorippa islandica (Oeder) Borbas   Marsh or Iceland Yellow Cress
    (incl. vars. *hispida* (Desv.) Butt. &
    Abbe and *fernaldiana* Butt. &
    Abbe)

SAXIFRAGACEAE   SAXIFRAGE FAMILY
Chrysosplenium tetrandrum (Lund) Th.   Golden Saxifrage
    Fries, (C. *alternifolium* L.)
Mitella nuda L.   Bishop's-Cap; Miterwort
Parnassia kotzebuei Cham. and   Small or Kotzebue's
    Schlecht.   Grass-of-Parnassus
P. *palustris* L. var. *neogaea* Fern., (P.   Northern or Large
    multiseta (Ledeb.) Fern.)   Grass-of-Parnassus
Ribes hudsonianum Richards.   Northern Black Currant
R. *lacustre* (Pers.) Poir.   Swamp Gooseberry; Bristly Black
    Currant
R. *oxyacanthoides* L.   Northern Gooseberry
R. *triste* Pallas   Swamp Red Currant
Saxifraga aizoides L.   Yellow Mountain Saxifrage
S. *caespitosa* L. s. lat. (incl. ssp.   Tufted Saxifrage
    caespitosa and ssp. *exaratoides*
    (Simm.) Engl. & Irmsch.)
S. *hirculus* L. s. lat.   Yellow Marsh Saxifrage
S. *oppositifolia* L.   Purple or Red-Flowered Saxifrage
S. *rivularis* L.   Alpine Brook Saxifrage
S. *tricuspidata* Rottb.   Three-Toothed Saxifrage

ROSACEAE   ROSE FAMILY
Dryas integrifolia M. Vahl (incl. ssp.   White Mountain-Avens
    chamissonis (Spreng.) Scoggan)
Fragaria virginiana Dcne. ssp. *glauca*   Smooth Wild Strawberry
    (S. Wats.) Staudt, (F. *virginiana*
    Dcne. var. *glauca* S. Wats.)
Geum aleppicum Jacq.   Yellow Avens
G. *macrophyllum* Willd. var.   Large-Leaved Avens
    perincisum (Rydb.) Raup, (G.
    perincisum Rydb.)
Potentilla anserina L.   Silverweed
P. *egedii* Wormskj. (incl. var.   Egede's Cinquefoil
    groenlandica (Tratt.) Polunin)

ROSACEAE, continued

P. *fruticosa* L.	Shrubby Cinquefoil
P. *hyparctica* Malte (incl. var. *elatior* (Abrom.) Fern.)	Arctic Cinquefoil
P. *multifida* L.	Branched Cinquefoil
P. *nivea* L. (incl. ssp. *chamissonis* (Hult.) Hiit.)	Snow Cinquefoil
P. *norvegica* L.	Rough Cinquefoil
P. *palustris* (L.) Scop. (incl. var. *parvifolia* (Raf.) Fern. & Long)	Marsh Cinquefoil
P. *pensylvanica* L. (incl. vars. *glabrata* (Hook.) Wats. and *pectinata* (Raf.) Lepage)	Prairie Cinquefoil
P. *pulchella* R. Br. s. lat.	Beautiful Cinquefoil
P. *tridentata* (Sol.) Ait.	Three-Toothed Cinquefoil
Rosa acicularis Lindl.	Prickly Rose
Rubus acaulis Michx., (R. *arcticus* L. ssp. *acaulis* (Michx.) Focke)	Stemless Raspberry
R. *chamaemorus* L.	Cloudberry; Baked-Apple Berry
R. *paracaulis* Bailey	Dwarf Raspberry

LEGUMINOSAE   PEA FAMILY

Astragalus alpinus L.	Alpine Milk-Vetch
A. *eucosmus* B.L. Robins.	Elegant Milk-Vetch
Hedysarum mackenzii Richards., (H. *boreale* Nutt. var. *mackenzii* (Richards.) C.L. Hitchc.)	Northern Hedysarum; Sweet Vetch
Lathyrus japonicus Willd. (inc. vars. *japonicus* and *aleuticus* (Greene) Fern.)	Beach-Pea
L. *palustris* L.	Marsh Vetchling
Oxytropis bellii (Britt.) Palibine, (O. *arctica* R. Br. var. *bellii* (Britt.) Boivin)	Bell's or Arctic Locoweed
O. *campestris* (L.) DC. var. *johannensis* Fern.	Late Yellow Locoweed
O. *varians* (Rydb.) K. Schum., (O. *campestris* (L.) DC. var. *gracilis* (A. Nels.) Barneby)	Varying Locoweed
Vicia americana Muhl.	American Vetch

GERANIACEAE   GERANIUM FAMILY

| *Geranium bicknellii* Britt. | Bicknell's Geranium |

LINACEAE   FLAX FAMILY

| *Linum lewisii* Pursh, (L. *perenne* L. var. *lewisii* (Pursh) Eat. & Wright f. *lepagei* (Boivin) Lepage) | Lewis' Wild Flax; White Flax |

CALLITRICHACEAE   WATER-STARWORT FAMILY

| *Callitriche hermaphroditica* L. | Northern Water-Starwort |

EMPETRACEAE   CROWBERRY FAMILY

| *Empetrum nigrum* L. ssp. *hermaphroditum* (Lange) Böch. | Black Crowberry |

380

VIOLACEAE
V. *pallens* (Banks) Brain., (V.
macloskeyi Lloyd var. *pallens*
(Banks) C.L. Hitchc.)
V. *palustris* L. (may include V.
epipsila Ledeb.)
V. *renifolia* Gray var. *brainerdii*
(Greene) Fern.

VIOLET FAMILY
American Sweet White Violet

Marsh Violet

Kidney-Shaped Violet

ELAEAGNACEAE
Shepherdia canadensis (L.) Nutt.

OLEASTER FAMILY
Canada Buffaloberry;
Soapberry

OÑAGRACEAE
Epilobium angustifolium L.
E. *davuricum* Fisch., (E. *palustre* L. s.
lat.)
E. *glandulosum* Lehm. var.
adenocaulon (Haussk.) Fern., (E.
watsonii Barbey)
E. *latifolium* L.

E. *palustre* L. var. *palustre* (perhaps
incl. other varieties)

EVENING-PRIMROSE FAMILY
Fireweed
Dahurian Willowherb

Northern Willowherb

Broad-Leaved Fireweed or
Willowherb
Marsh Willowherb

HALORAGACEAE (HIPPURIDACEAE,
in part)
Hippuris tetraphylla L. f.
H. *vulgaris* L.
Myriophyllum exalbescens Fern., (M.
spicatum L. var. *exalbescens*
(Fern.) Jeps.)

WATER-MILFOIL FAMILY

Four-Leaved Mare's-Tail
Common Mare's-Tail
Spiked Water-Milfoil

UMBELLIFERAE
Cicuta bulbifera L.
C. *mackenzieana* Raup
Heracleum lanatum Michx.
Sium suave Walt.

PARSLEY FAMILY
Bulb-Bearing Water-Hemlock
Water-Hemlock
Cow-Parsnip
Water-Parsnip

CORNACEAE
Cornus canadensis L.

DOGWOOD FAMILY
Bunchberry

PYROLACEAE
Moneses uniflora (L.) Gray
Pyrola asarifolia Michx. (incl. var.
purpurea (Bunge) Fern.)
P. *grandiflora* Radius
P. *minor* L.
P. *secunda* L. s. lat. (incl. var.
obtusata Turcz.)

WINTERGREEN FAMILY
One-Flowered Wintergreen
Pink Wintergreen

Large-Flowered Wintergreen
Lesser Wintergreen
One-Sided Wintergreen

ERICACEAE
Andromeda polifolia L.
Arctostaphylos alpina (L.) Spreng.

HEATH OR HEATHER FAMILY
Bog-Rosemary
Alpine Bearberry

ERICACEAE, continued

A. *rubra* (Rehd. & Wils.) Fern., (A.   Red Bearberry
   alpina (L.) Spreng. ssp. *rubra*
   (Rehd. & Wils.) Hult.)
A. *uva-ursi* (L.) Spreng.   Bearberry; Kinnikinick
Chamaedaphne calyculata (L.) Moench   Leatherleaf
Kalmia polifolia Wang. (incl. vars.   Bog Laurel
   polifolia and *microphylla* (Hook.)
   Rehd.)
Ledum decumbens (Ait.) Lodd., (L.   Dwarf Labrador Tea
   palustre L.)
L. *groenlandicum* Oeder   Labrador Tea
Loiseleuria procumbens (L.) Desv.   Alpine Azalea
Oxycoccus microcarpus Turcz.   Swamp Cranberry
Rhododendron lapponicum (L.)   Lapland Rose-Bay
   Wahlenb.
Vaccinium uliginosum L. s. lat. (incl.   Alpine Bilberry or Blueberry
   ssp. *pubescens* (Wormskj.) S.
   Young)
V. *vitis-idaea* L. var. *minus* Lodd.   Dry-Ground Cranberry; Mossberry

PRIMULACEAE   PRIMROSE FAMILY
Androsace septentrionalis L.   Pygmyflower
Lysimachia thrysiflora L., (Naumbergia   Tufted Loosestrife
   thrysiflora (L.) Duby)
Primula egaliksensis Wormskj.   Greenland Primrose
P. *stricta* Hornem.   Erect Primrose

GENTIANACEAE   GENTIAN FAMILY
Gentiana acuta Michx., (Gentianella   Northern Gentian
   amarella (L.) Börner ssp. *acuta*
   (Michx.) J. Gillett)
G. *propinqua* Richards., (Gentianella   Arctic Gentian or Felwort
   propinqua (Richards.) J. Gillett)
Lomatogonium rotatum (L.) Fries   Star Gentian; Marsh Felwort

MENYANTHACEAE (GENTIANACEAE)   BUCK-BEAN FAMILY
Menyanthes trifoliata L.   Buck-Bean; Bog-Bean

HYDROPHYLLACEAE   WATERLEAF FAMILY
Phacelia franklinii (R. Br.) Gray   Franklin's Scorpionweed

BORAGINACEAE   BORAGE FAMILY
Mertensia maritima (L.) S.F. Gray   Seaside Lungwort
M. *paniculata* (Ait.) G. Don   Tall Lungwort

LABIATAE   MINT FAMILY
Dracocephalum parviflorum Nutt.,   American Dragonhead
   (Moldavica parviflora (Nutt.) Britt.)
Mentha arvensis L. var. *villosa*   Field or Wild Mint
   (Benth.) S.R. Stewart
Scutellaria galericulata L. var. *pubescens*   Marsh Scullcap
   Benth., (S. epilobiifolia A. Ham.)

SCROPHULARIACEAE
Bartsia alpina L.
Castilleja raupii Pennell
Euphrasia arctica Lange
E. hudsoniana Fern. & Wieg.
E. vinacea Sell & Yeo
Limosella aquatica L.
Pedicularis flammea L.
P. groenlandica Retz.
P. labradorica Wirsing
P. lapponica L.
P. sudetica Willd.
Rhinanthus borealis (Stern.) Chab.

LENTIBULARIACEAE
Pinguicula villosa L.
P. vulgaris L.
Utricularia intermedia Hayne
U. minor L.
U. vulgaris L.

PLANTAGINACEAE
Plantago juncoides Lam. var. glauca
    (Hornem.) Fern., (P. maritima L.)

RUBIACEAE
Galium boreale L., (G. septentrionale R.
    & S.)
G. brandegei Gray, (G. trifidum L. var.
    pusillum Gray)
G. trifidum L.

CAPRIFOLIACEAE
Linnaea borealis L. var. americana
    (Forbes) Rehd., (L. borealis L.
    var. longiflora Torr.)

VALERIANACEAE
Valeriana septentrionalis Rydb., (V.
    dioica L. var. sylvatica (Sol.) Gray)

CAMPANULACEAE
Campanula uliginosa Rydb., (C.
    aparinoides Pursh var. uliginosa
    (Rydb.) Gl.)
C. uniflora L.

COMPOSITAE
Achillea lanulosa Nutt., (A. millefolium
    L. var. lanulosa (Nutt.) Piper)
A. nigrescens (E. Mey.) Rydb., (A.
    millefolium L. var. borealis (Bong.)
    Farw.)
Antennaria pulcherrima (Hook.)
    Greene

FIGWORT OR SNAPDRAGON
    FAMILY
Velvet Bells
Purple Paintbrush
Northern or Arctic Eyebright
Hudsonian Eyebright
Hudsonian Eyebright
Mudwort
Flame-Coloured Lousewort
Elephant's-Head
Labrador Lousewort
Lapland Lousewort or Rattle
Purple Rattle
Yellowrattle

BLADDERWORT FAMILY
Small or Hairy Butterwort
Common Butterwort
Flat-Leaved Bladderwort
Lesser Bladderwort
Greater Bladderwort

PLANTAIN FAMILY
Seaside Plantain

MADDER FAMILY
Northern Bedstraw

Brandegee's Bedstraw

Small Bedstraw

HONEYSUCKLE FAMILY
Twinflower

VALERIAN FAMILY
Northern Valerian

BLUEBELL FAMILY
Marsh Bellflower

Alpine Bluebell

SUNFLOWER OR ASTER FAMILY
Yarrow; Milfoil

Yarrow

Showy Everlasting

383

A. *rosea* (Eat.) Greene	Rosy Everlasting
Arnica alpina (L.) Olin (incl. ssp. *angustifolia* (J. Vahl) Maguire and ssp. *attenuata* (Greene) Maguire)	Alpine Arnica
Artemisia tilesii Ledeb. (incl. var. *elatior* T. & G.)	Herriot's Sage
Aster junciformis Rydb., (A. *borealis* (T. & G.) Prov.)	Rush Aster
A. *puniceus* L.	Purple-Stemmed Aster
Chrysanthemum arcticum L.	Arctic Daisy or Chrysanthemum
Erigeron acris L. var. *asteroides* (Andrz.) DC.	Northern Daisy Fleabane
E. *elatus* (Hook.) Greene, (E. *acris* L. var. *elatus* (Hook.) Cronq.)	Tall Fleabane
E. *humilis* Graham, (E. *unifloris* L. var. *unalaschkensis* (DC.) Boivin)	Lowly Fleabane; Purple Daisy
E. *hyssopifolius* Michx.	Wild Daisy
E. *lonchophyllus* Hook.	Hirsute Fleabane
Matricaria ambigua (Ledeb.) Kryl., (*Tripleurospermum phaeocephalum* (Rupr.) Pobed.)	Sea-Shore Chamomile
Petasites palmatus (Ait.) Gray	Palmate-Leaved Colt's-Foot
P. *sagittatus* (Banks) A. Gray	Arrow-Leaved Colt's-Foot
Senecio congestus (R. Br.) DC. (incl. vars. *congestus* and *tonsus* Fern.)	Marsh Ragwort
S. *indecorus* Greene	Rayless Ragwort
S. *pauperculus* Michx.	Balsam Groundsel
Solidago multiradiata Ait. (incl. vars. *multiradiata* and *scopulorum* Gray)	Alpine Goldenrod
Tanacetum huronense Nutt. var. *bifarium* Fern. (first record 1984)	Indian Tansy
Taraxacum dumetorum Greene	Horned Dandelion
T. *lacerum* Greene	Lacerate Dandelion
T. *lapponicum* Kihlm., (T. *croceum* Dahlst.)	Lapland Dandelion

INDEX

392

NOTES

NOTES

NOTES

NOTES

Watercolours by Linda Fairfield; black and white drawings by Linda Fairfield except pg. 251 by Betsy Thorsteinson. Photographs by Robert R. Taylor except: pgs. 117 & 291, Richard Staniforth; pg. 163, Joyce Holmes; pg. 197, Andrea Iwanowsky; pg. 209, Janina W. Swietlik; pgs. 18 & 19, 56, 79, 99, 111, 125, 139, 145, 151, 153, 169, 175, 177, 181, 219, 233, 237, 255, 265, 275, 279, 285, 299, 331, 337, 345, 347, 349, 353, 359, Karen Johnson

Design: David Hopper/Teri McIntyre
Typesetting: Linda Nelson
Separations: Image Color
Negative Stripping: Image Graphics
Printing, 2nd: Friesens

Printed in Canada

LEAF SHAPES

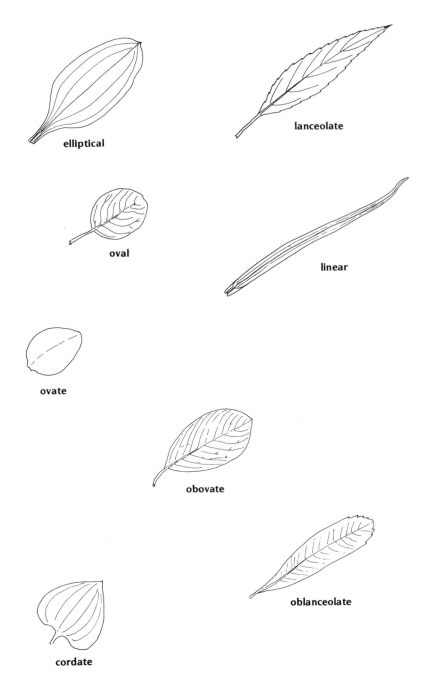

elliptical

lanceolate

oval

linear

ovate

obovate

oblanceolate

cordate